FORESTS
OF BRITAIN

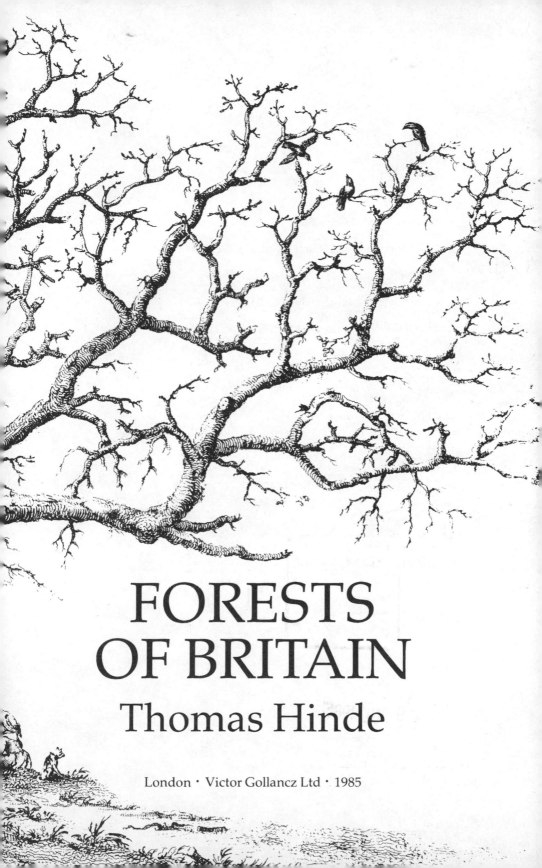

FORESTS
OF BRITAIN
Thomas Hinde

London · Victor Gollancz Ltd · 1985

First published in Great Britain 1985
by Victor Gollancz Ltd,
14 Henrietta Street, London WC2E 8QJ

Published in association with Tigerlily Ltd

British Library Cataloguing in Publication Data
Hinde, Thomas
    Forests of Britain.
    1. Forests and forestry—Great Britain
    I. Title
    333.75'0941   SD179
ISBN 0-575-03506-4

Typeset by Centracet
and printed in Great Britain by
R. J. Acford, Chichester

CONTENTS

FORESTS, WOODS AND PLANTATIONS

By a forest most people mean a large area of growing trees.

Some, on the other hand, mean an area of land, not necessarily tree-growing, where special laws once applied and which was reserved by the king for his hunting. Forests of this second kind were widely established in England by William I, and extended and maintained by his Norman and Plantagenet successors. As well as woodland, they included cultivated land, commons, farms, villages and even towns. No forest in this legal sense survives today, but some one-time royal forests are still forests in the tree-growing sense, some remain unenclosed land but are treeless, and some survive as the names of pieces of countryside.

This book aims to describe our major forests in both senses of the word, but gives most attention to those which exist today as forests in the first sense: at one extreme the royal forest of Dean on the English-Welsh border, at the other the twentieth-century Forestry Commission's forest of Kielder on the English-Scottish border. But it also describes those royal forests which survive as unenclosed but mainly treeless countryside—Exmoor and Dartmoor, for example, and the slightly less deforested Ashdown Forest; and it mentions more briefly those which have largely disappeared except in name—the Lancashire forest of Bowland, for example.

Because the word forest can mean several things it is a word which ecological historians avoid. They made a different and more useful distinction between *woods* and *plantations*.

A plantation, as the name implies, is a piece of woodland which has been planted. It usually consists of trees of a single species (but sometimes of several species) all of the same age. A twentieth-century Forestry-Commission conifer forest is a typical plantation or group of plantations—though some plantations are much older. Plantations become of interest to ecological historians only if they are infiltrated by other species, or if they survive beyond the age at which they reach

7

maturity.

A wood, on the other hand, consists of a number of different species of trees and underwood, all of various ages. The 'Ancient and Ornamental' oak, ash and beech woods of the New Forest are typical woods.

So today a forest, in the tree-growing sense, can consist solely of woods, or solely of plantations, or can contain some of each. The same is true of a one-time royal forest, but this may also be treeless and contain neither or have entirely disappeared as a physical feature.

The Wildwood

The history of today's forests in Britain begins with the retreat of the last Ice Age in 8300-8200 BC. England was then still connected to mainland Europe and the retreating ice was followed by advancing trees. The evidence for most statements of this sort about British vegetation in any period before Roman times comes from the study of tree pollens. These pollens have a long life when trapped in layers of peat, lake mud or acid soil. By dating the layers the trees which were growing at that time can be identified.

First to follow the ice north came juniper, then birch, then about 7500 BC pine, which pushed the birch into highland areas. Hazel, elm, oak, alder and (rather later) small-leaved lime followed. For the next 2,000 years till around 5500 BC when Britain became separated from the continent these and a number of other species—50 to 70 in total, known as native trees—went through a process of establishing themselves in different proportions in different parts of Britain. The megalithic hunters who lived among them interfered little with this process. The whole country was then covered by a single great forest which Oliver Rackham, the authority on woodland history, has conveniently called the wildwood.

In most of the Scottish Highlands the commonest trees of the wildwood were birch and pine. In an area reaching from these to just south of the Humber, and another area which included most of Wales except the south-west corner, oak and hazel were commonest. In south-west Wales and Cornwall, hazel and elm predominated. In the rest of the country, a central area including most of the Midlands and the Home Counties, small-leaved lime was probably commonest, but this has only been established with certainty on its periphery.

So the common idea that a great oak forest covered

England and Wales in prehistoric times is not correct. Pollen evidence seemed to support the traditional picture till it was realized that oak pollen, which is wind-distributed, suggested that oaks were more numerous than they in fact were. Limes, on the other hand, are insect pollinated, and as a result the distribution of their pollen suggested fewer than we now believe existed.

Between about 3100 and 2900 BC there was a marked and rapid decline of elm trees in the wildwood. This elm decline coincided with the arrival of neolithic man, and was probably connected with his farming practices. Young elm shoots make good browsing for animals and he may have systematically collected them for winter fodder. But it is also possible that elms were attacked by some equivalent to Dutch elm disease.

From this time onwards, during the neolithic period and the Bronze Age—1700 to 500 BC—large areas of the wildwood were converted to fields for the growing of crops, or to grazing land. This caused important changes in the British tree population. Pines entirely disappeared from England and Wales, probably because they were easily cleared by burning and do not coppice (sprout from stumps) or sucker (grow again from roots). The Scots pines of England today were re-introduced and are naturalized but not native.

And limes were much reduced in number. They were probably grubbed out before other trees because they commonly grew on fertile soil. All over Britain woodland survived, but a pattern of settlements with farm land around them was imposed on the wildwood. Woodland close to settlements was affected by the cutting of wood for fuel and by the grazing of animals which destroyed undergrowth and left only standard trees.

When the Celts arrived in Britain around 400 BC they brought with them heavy iron ploughs, enabling them to cultivate the clay soils of valleys which had till then been left wooded. This caused further destruction of the wildwood which was still continuing at the time of the Roman occupation during the first century AD.

It is easier to be definite about what trees were growing in Britain up to this time, than about the nature of the woods in which they grew. Was the wildwood densely or thinly forested? Were the trees chiefly well-grown specimens or scrub? What effect did the death of a particular tree have on the wood around it? Did many die together in a particular area or was the process of death and replacement a gradual one? The answer to most of these questions is that we cannot be sure.

In the peat bogs of the Fens large oaks and pines with few low side branches have been found, suggesting that in this area tall trees stood close together. But the Fens may not have been typical, and elsewhere grass pollen suggests that woodland rides were common. So does frequent evidence of hazel, which will not flower successfully in shade.

Before written records, one way to discover the nature of woodland is to examine surviving wooden artefacts. In Britain by far the oldest of these, and the only ones to survive from pre-Roman times, are the so-called corduroy roads, built across peat bogs, in particular across the Somerset Levels. The earliest has been dated 3174 BC, around the time of the arrival of neolithic man. The straight poles used in such tracks are remarkably similar to those which would have been produced by a coppiced mediaeval wood. This suggests that some woods were already being managed to provide a regular supply of modest-sized wood.

If this is so, the woods themselves would in the main have been coppiced as they were in mediaeval times. This method of getting a continuous supply of wood (brushwood, poles, branches and trunks of less than two feet in girth) as opposed to timber (large trunks or branches suitable for beams, planks and gateposts) from an area of woodland depends on the fact that many native British trees—ash, lime, oak, hazel, maple, wych elm—and some naturalized ones—sweet chestnut and sycamore—when cut down shoot again from the base or 'stool'. Some make shoots as much as eleven feet in length in the first year.

All may be harvested at intervals of from four to 60 years. In England during mediaeval times, these intervals tended to get longer, probably because larger poles were needed, or poles like those of sweet chestnut which could be split for fencing posts, but coppicing remained an essential, some would say the most essential, part of a wood's value. Stools of coppiced trees spread as they grow older and some today

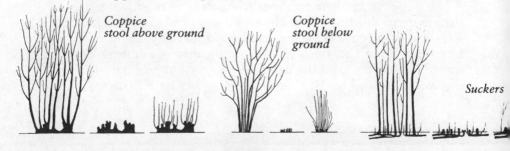

Coppice
stool above ground

Coppice
stool below
ground

Suckers

have reached fifteen feet in diameter. They appear to live and give crops indefinitely and one ash stool in East Anglia is over 1,000 years old.

Certain trees, in particular elm and aspen, when felled do not coppice but sucker (grow again from their surviving root systems), forming clusters of shoots known as clones. Like coppice shoots, suckers can be regularly cropped at intervals of from four to 60 years. Though it was also possible to obtain successive crops of wood by pollarding trees—cutting their shoots at between six to fifteen feet above the ground —pollarding with an axe was hard work and less common than coppicing.

Roman and Saxon Times

The Romans continued the process of extending the cultivated land of Britain at the expense of its trees. During the 350 years of their occupation England became an important grain-growing and exporting country and many new areas were cleared for this purpose. In Wales and on the Scottish borders they also systematically cleared woodland for military reasons.

They brought industry to Britain, for example iron smelting and forging in the Weald and in the Forest of Dean, lead smelting in Derbyshire and pottery making at Castor (Petersfield) in Cambridgeshire. And every Roman city and settlement needed fuel for heating and cooking, and on a smaller scale every country villa needed fuel for heating its baths. All needed a continuing supply of wood from a source which would not become exhausted. It seems most likely that managed and regularly cropped coppice woods provided

Stub

Shredded Tree

Pollard

bolling

such a supply, and an analysis of Roman charcoal suggests that they were burning the same sizes of wood from the same sorts of trees that would have been grown by a coppiced wood of many centuries later.

When the Romans left, some land reverted to woodland, but it is no longer thought that, during the dark age which followed, large proportions of the countryside went back to secondary woodland. Whatever happened at first, the Saxons subsequently reclaimed most of the land which the Romans had cultivated, and cleared more. They built with timber, and so needed not only supplies of wood for posts, studs and panels of wattle infilling but also great timbers from fully-grown trees for cruck-built and timber-framed houses. A wood of coppice stools with standard trees could have provided both sorts of material, but it seems more likely that at this time coppices provided wood and large timber could still be cut from wilder unmanaged areas of woodland.

In Saxon times there is the first written evidence of British woodland in the form of charters which contain 'perambulations'. These, as the name suggests, define a piece of land by describing a walk round its boundaries. Some perambulations can be used to identify woods which still survive. Hardly surprisingly, the Saxon perambulations as a whole confirm that the country remained more wooded than it is today.

Domesday Book

The first written evidence to cover most of England is provided by the Domesday Book. This great survey, compiled in 1086, is enormously important, but it has its limitations. In some counties it describes woods by their area, in others by their dimensions, but in others only by their worth when rented out to fatten pigs (pannage), or by the number of pigs which could be grazed or fattened in a particular wood. It is not easy to calculate from such information how much woodland in total survived. For what it is worth, it has been estimated that in Lincolnshire 3.4 per cent of the country was still wooded, or about half again as much as today, but Lincolnshire may not have been typical.

This does not mean, of course, that that amount of the wildwood survived. By this time virtually all woodland had been exploited or managed in one way or another. Only an area of the Forest of Dean, shown blank in Domesday Book, may still have been undisturbed, and the sale of 71 giant oaks from here by Henry III for the building of the Dominican Friary at Gloucester between 1241 and 1265 may mark the destruction of the last piece of English wildwood.

In Scotland, where there was stone to build with and peat to burn, areas of wildwood survived longer, and the Highland pine woods were little interfered with till 1600. In Glenmore, Inverness-shire, giant decayed trees were found in about 1830 which probably formed part of an undisturbed piece of woodland. Today no wildwood survives in Britain. The tradition that Wistman's Wood on Dartmoor is prehistoric woodland has been proved false.

Mediaeval Woodland

In mediaeval times there is a great deal more evidence about British woodland, in particular from detailed surveys by bishops and abbots of the lands up and down the country which their diocese and abbeys owned. Over the country as a whole the amount of woodland continued to decline, though at a slower rate than in earlier times.

The *annual* value of a coppiced wood was greatest if it contained no standard trees. Standards create below them an area in which coppiced trees make less growth. Nevertheless, the mediaeval practice was to grow a number of standards in a coppice and periodically to fell some of them. These were especially needed for the frames of timber-framed houses, for which oak was almost always used, but occasionally elm. Timber-framed houses which survive today are the grander ones which used large timbers, and as a result they give a false picture of the age at which standard trees were normally felled. Most were cut at less than 70 years old, long before they would be considered mature today.

Thus a mediaeval wood might contain a mixture of coppiced underwood, of small standard trees often growing from coppice stools and of taller standards. Because oak was such an important building timber it would seem likely that most of the standards would have been oak. Pollen evidence

13

supports this idea, but it may exaggerate the proportion of oaks among all the trees of a wood. Standards give pollen year after year, but many species do not flower for several years after they have been coppiced so would be under-represented by their pollen. Hazel is an exception and flowers from its second year, with the result that pollen counts also exaggerate the amount of hazel in mediaeval woods. Probably there was a large mixture of species. In one Suffolk wood which has a continuous history of growing standards with coppice trees, 43 species have been identified.

The woods around a mediaeval village were an essential part of its economy. Apart from providing pannage for pigs and herbage for other animals, and material for building houses, they gave wood for house repair, for burning and for many farm purposes. The right to take wood for these purposes went under different names in different parts of the country but was typically called *firebote* for firewood, *haybote* for hedging wood and *housebote* for house repairing wood.

But, as in Roman and Saxon times, wood was also used for industrial purposes, in particular for the smelting and forging of iron. There is no doubt that the iron industry used large amounts of wood and in some parts of the country probably used timber too, especially from the sixteenth century onwards when blast furnaces were introduced. But whether or not it *destroyed* woodland is much less certain. On balance it seems likely that it relied on renewable supplies of wood for charcoal making from coppices and pollards and that iron-masters valued and preserved rather than destroyed woodland. It was agricultural counties like Norfolk with no industry which lost their woods, whereas these survived in the Forest of Dean where iron had been worked since Roman times. Those who complained at the time, as many did, probably resented industry taking wood which had previously been used for hearth and home, or, in Tudor times, were anxious about a shortage of timber for the navy.

The old iron industry of England, based on charcoal made

in English forests, first went into sharp decline in the mid-seventeenth century because it could not compete with Swedish iron made from better ore by cheaper labour, then finally collapsed at the end of the eighteenth century when a method of using coke instead of charcoal had been invented.

Alongside mediaeval woods which were systematically harvested for wood and timber there existed all over England at the time of the Domesday Book large areas of wood pasture. By the thirteenth century much of this had gone. Partly it disappeared because grazing prevented trees from regenerating, partly because it was the most obvious land for enclosure, and once enclosed was transformed into fields for stock or for the growing of crops.

Later Woodland History

During the last five centuries the area of ancient woods in Britain has continued to decline. Other industries as well as iron have been blamed, in particular the glass industry. Certainly between 1550 and 1700 this consumed large amounts of wood. So, in the early nineteenth century, did the tanning industry, which used mainly oak bark. In 1810, at its height, 500,000 tons of oak were being cut or felled a year. But again coppices provided most of the wood for these industries.

In parts of the country where there was no stone, timber — mostly oak—was needed for house building until building in brick became common in the eighteenth century. There were periods of great rebuilding, some the result of economic or social change, some of particular disasters like the Great Fire of London. Ship building also took timber. One thousand oaks were needed for a ship the size of Nelson's *Victory*. From the sixteenth century onwards there were regular alarms that we might run out of oak trees. But in fact the navy never required more than a fraction of the oak taken by the tanning industry, and even the merchant navy, a far larger consumer of oak than the navy, probably took less than did tanning.

The felling of mature oaks for these purposes altered the character of woods by temporarily reducing the proportion of standard trees in relation to underwood, but felling, even of standards, does not necessarily destroy a wood. It is a common misconception that the great fellings of the two World Wars destroyed the forests of Britain, but it can equally well be argued that these put them to their proper use for the first time for hundreds of years.

The underlying cause of the destruction of ancient woods is that over the centuries they have come to be less important to the economy of the country. Coal, and more recently oil, gas and electricity have replaced wood as a fuel. In the seventeenth century hop growing created a new market for poles, for which ash was found to be particularly suitable, but in general farming and house repairing have come to depend less and less on wood and industries which used wood as a raw material have declined, till they are now almost but not quite reduced to the chestnut post and paling industry of the south of England. There has therefore been steady economic pressure towards the grubbing out of woods producing mainly wood, so that the land can be used for other crops.

Woods which have survived have done so sometimes because the land they occupy is too steep or infertile for other use, sometimes because those with rights in them have fought successfully to defend their rights, sometimes because public bodies have saved them for their recreational value or as features in the landscape, sometimes because private owners have preserved them for hunting or shooting. None of these is a very sound economic reason, and it is interesting to wonder whether high-priced oil and coal, and the consequent boom in wood-burning stoves, far from endangering our surviving woods, may make them valuable again and redress the balance between wood and timber.

Carpenter   Joiner

Forest owners have recognized this possibility. Coppicing has again become economic—only a few years ago contractors had to be paid to do such work, now they will willingly buy the right. And the Forestry Commission is carrying out experiments on the economics of what they unattractively call 'biomass'. It remains to be seen whether the sort of wood they find economical for growing biomass will have much resemblance to the coppiced woods of mediaeval England.

It is timber rather than wood which has remained an economic crop. The history of this change of attitude goes back to the fifteenth century. Though the 1482 statute which allowed owners of woods in forests to fence them for seven instead of three years after they had been coppiced was nominally concerned with the protection of coppice woods as a whole, it was probably inspired by interest in the standard trees for which coppices were a nursery. Sixty years later, in 1543, a statute of Henry VIII ordered that *all* woods *must* be enclosed for four years after coppicing and that at least twelve standard trees must be left per acre. Numerous other Tudor and Stuart statutes were aimed at protecting timber trees in forests.

Tree-planting for timber began in England in the late sixteenth century (rather earlier in Scotland), continued in the eighteenth and nineteenth centuries and increased dramatically after 1919. This was at the end of the First World War, which Lloyd George said we came closer to losing for lack of timber than for lack of food. As a result the Forestry

Wheelwright   *Cooper*

Commission was established and since then has created huge plantations, largely of conifer, all over the country. In one sense these have reforested the country, and during the last 20 years they have been managed in a less ruthlessly commercial manner, to encourage wild life and make them less alien in the landscape. All the same, conifers have destroyed even more of the country's ancient woods than the farmers who have grubbed them up or the villages and towns which have sprawled over them. Below conifers, once they are well grown, no underwood survives, and the complex biological systems of many centuries are finally destroyed.

ROYAL FORESTS

On to the English countryside as it existed in 1066 with its villages, manors, fields, commons and woods, William I imposed his royal forests. It was once thought that the Saxon kings had hunting forests, and they do seem to have had customary hunting rights beyond the royal demesne. Swaincotes (courts for trying minor forest cases) were held in Saxon times and Canute's *Constitutiones de Foresta* suggests that there was a written Saxon law of the forest. But this document is now believed to be a Norman forgery, designed to show that forests were not a foreign introduction. It was William I who first defined the bounds of the royal forests, including in them far larger areas than the Saxon kings had claimed. His forests and their law closely resembled the ducal forests of Normandy.

Twenty years after William's arrival, Domesday Book records some English forests, but not all of them. They were largely in the wilder more hilly or wooded parts of the country, especially in Hampshire and along the Welsh borders, but also in such counties as Oxfordshire, Wiltshire, Buckinghamshire, Surrey, Sussex, Northampton and Essex. His successors, William Rufus and Henry I extended their forests, and, after the civil war of Stephen's reign, so did Henry II. At one time or another the entire counties of Cornwall, Devon, Surrey and Essex came under forest law, and by the thirteenth century a quarter of the country was royal forest.

The actual land of forests was often 'held of the king by someone else'. Typically this 'someone else' was either a noble or a religious institution. In theory all other forest land was royal demesne, but in practice there were specific royal manors within forests which were administered separately. These apart, however, the rest of the forest *was* the king's, just as the country's highways were.

When forests were finally disafforested those who held forest land might enclose it and exclude Commoners. The

king, in compensation for giving up his hunting rights, was often allowed to enclose part of the remainder. The Commoners were also sometimes allowed land, either individually as on Exmoor, or together as in Brecknock. The rest was sold.

Though forests were often in the wilder parts of the country, few consisted solely of woodland or even of empty countryside. It was their law, not their physical features which united them. The nineteenth-century historian, G. J. Turner, describes a forest as 'a definite tract of land within which a particular body of law was enforced, having for its object the preservation of certain animals . . . Other persons might possess lands within the bounds of a forest, but were not allowed the right of hunting or of cutting trees in them'.

Forest law was first defined by a statute of 1184 known as the Assize of Woodstock, but was almost certainly functioning as a separate system with its own courts 50 years before in Henry I's reign, and had probably been established soon after the conquest. It was complex and varied over the centuries. Broadly speaking, it not only forbade hunting in royal forests, but, as Turner says, limited what those who possessed land in a forest could do with their own property. In particular it forbade them to build on their land, to cut timber or wood except for their own use and to assart their land—turn it from woodland into agricultural land.

The deer and wild boar of the forest were invariably the king's, as was his right to hunt them. On forest land which was not private he also owned the timber, wood, grazing rights and mineral rights, but each of these he might grant to individuals or to such institutions as monasteries. He might grant them directly, or grant his foresters the right to dispose of them.

Around the country there were also private hunting reserves, some of them acquired from the king in areas which had once been royal forest. These were known in England as chases. Here the owner might keep and hunt his own deer.

Parks were different again, and consisted of fenced areas for deer. In a royal forest the king had his own deer parks. With his permission other people might also have parks. In Elizabeth's reign one estimate was that there were still 69 forests, thirteen chases and 700 parks.

Purpose of a Forest

The traditional view was that the Norman and Plantagenet kings established and enlarged their forests to provide them with hunting grounds, a sport to which they were addicted. Forest law certainly forbade poaching of the king's deer and boar. Those which forbade the cutting of trees or the assarting of woodland were partly intended to preserve the deer's environment. And the forest warden and his foresters had the duty of arresting poachers and caring for the deer.

Certainly, English kings from William I to Henry VIII hunted enthusiastically. About Henry II it was said, 'He was addicted to the chase beyond measure; at crack of dawn he was off on horseback, traversing waste lands, penetrating forests and climbing the mountain-tops, and so he passed restless days.'

But from Henry II's time onwards the king valued his forests as much for economic reasons as for the hunting they provided. Punishments for forest offences less and less often took the form of death, mutilation or imprisonment and more often of fines which were in the nature of taxes rather than deterrents. Typically, when woodland was assarted the offender would not be compelled to return the land to woodland provided he paid an agreed rent.

Penalties of this sort were at one time the most important way in which the king raised money from his forests. But from the thirteenth century he began to exploit their products more systematically. He would either sell their timber or wood directly, or raise money by granting licences to fell or cut trees.

Forest grazing and pannage were also valuable, as the institution of agisters to manage them proves. Particular woods provided pannage for a certain number of pigs and were sold at a price per pig. Strict rules limited pannage to a few weeks in the autumn, and grazing was not allowed during the month around midsummer, known as the fence month, when the deer dropped their calves.

Where the king held the mineral rights in his forests, as he usually did, he raised money by selling them, or through complicated arrangements which gave the miners permission to mine. Other rights which were generally his, but which individuals often acquired or held by tradition going back to before the land was afforested, were those of cutting peat to burn, of cutting heather and bracken for animal bedding or thatching and of taking building stone. The king might also charge for 'cheminage', or way-leave—the right to carry goods through a forest.

Finally the king was interested in his beasts of the forest not only for sport but for food, especially in winter when there was no other fresh meat. The mediaeval court was in the habit of moving from place to place, feeding on the venison as it went. When, at the end of King John's reign, the court ceased to be itinerant, the king would regularly send his huntsmen to distant forests to obtain venison. In 1251 alone Henry III ordered 100 bucks from the forest of Galtres, 100 from other forests for delivery as presents to various places, 100 more from the Forest of Dean to be sent to Westminster and 60 does from Chute Forest for Christmas.

Forest Officials

In charge of all royal forests until 1229 was the king's chief forester. He was a man of at least as much importance as the king's other three senior civil servants—one mediaeval historian, Sidney Painter, suggests that 'a strong argument could be advanced for the thesis that the royal official who wielded the most actual power during John's reign was the chief forester, Hugh de Neville'.

The chief forester travelled the country holding forest eyres, or courts, in the different counties, much as judges of assize do today. Most notorious of the chief foresters, remembered 50 years later for his severity, was Alan de Neville, uncle of Hugh, who carried out the 1175 eyre for Henry II.

...This Alan so long as he lived enriched the royal treasury, and to please an earthly king did not fear to offend the king of heaven. But how much gratitude he earned from the king whom he strove to please, the sequel showed. For when he was brought to his last, the brethren of a certain monastery, hoping, it seems, to secure something of his substance for their house, besought the king to allow them to carry away his body to their burial place. Whereupon, the king revealed his sentiments towards him in these terms. 'I,' he said, 'will have his wealth, you shall have the corpse, and the demons of hell his soul.'

From 1239 the chief forester's job was divided and two justices were appointed, one for forests north of the Trent, one for those south.

In charge of a particular forest was its warden—in some

forests he had such other names as keeper, steward or master forester. He was normally appointed by the king, but in certain forests, Savernake for example, the position became hereditary. The warden's deputy was commonly called lieutenant of the forest.

Below the warden and lieutenant came verderers, chosen by election among local freeholders, usually for life. Each forest would have between two and six verderers, who were usually knights. Their chief duty was to keep records of those accused of forest offences and bring them to court. They sat as judges at swainmotes where cases were first heard, before all but the most minor ones were passed on to the forest eyre.

Not so important as verderers were foresters, who were responsible for the vert (trees) and venison (deer and wild boar) in their own parts of the forest which were often called their bailiwicks, or sometimes their walks. They had the power to arrest people found hunting in the forest. They managed the deer, protecting them in the fence month and providing them with feed in winter. They were paid salaries by the day, and also had the right to a certain number of trees a year, and to pannage and pasturage for a certain number of animals. Foresters sometimes claimed the right to be fed or housed by other forest dwellers or institutions. In Edward III's reign a forester of Inglewood claimed from the abbot of St Mary's, York, the right to eat and drink with the abbot's servants every Friday and to take away with him whenever he wanted 'a flagon of the best ale, two tallow candles, a bushel of oats for his horse, and a loaf of black bread for his dog'. Some were walking and some riding foresters. The riding foresters had larger bailiwicks, were better paid and might carry bows.

Foresters-of-fee had similar duties to foresters, but their posts were usually hereditary and most were gentlemen. Often the service they gave in return for their position was simply the guarding of the forest, though they sometimes made the king a payment as well. They had a right to the income of their bailiwicks.

The woodwards of a forest were in a different position. Some, as the name suggests, were responsible for the forest timber and wood. Others were privately employed by owners of woodland in the forest. These had the dual responsibility of acting for the owner in protecting his rights in his woodland, and acting for the king in ensuring that the king's rights were also respected. So they would have to allow the

Of the place where and howe an assembly should be made, in the presence of a Prince, or some honorable person.

king's deer to enter, and see that no felling or clearing was carried out without the king's permission.

Forest agisters regulated the grazing of cattle in forests and collected rent for this and payments for pannage for pigs. Other officials were rangers, not heard of till the mid-fourteenth century, who had duties similar to those of mounted foresters, but were usually responsible for the purlieus or disafforested parts of a forest. They would have to drive deer back from these into the forest itself. Forest deer parks were managed by parkers who might have under them palers for constructing the park's pale.

Finally there were regarders, whose duty it was to carry out regular surveys of all aspects of the forest from its woods, grazing, buildings and boundaries to the behaviour of the warden and his foresters, and to present this survey which was called the regard to the forest eyre every third year. They were people of standing, normally knights, and each forest had at least twelve.

Forest Courts

Clearly forest regards were presented far less often as forest eyres rarely met so regularly. For Pickering Forest, for example, there was no eyre for 54 years from 1280 to 1334. As a result those who had been accused had often died before their cases came to court.

The warden, the verderers, foresters, agisters and regarders were all summoned to the eyre. So were all free tenants who held land inside the forest, representatives of all townships in the forest and all who had been accused of serious forest offences since the last eyre.

Venison offences included not only straightforward poaching, but also receiving illegally killed deer or giving refuge to offenders. Though penalties eventually became so light that a poacher was likely to be less severely punished by a forest court than by a court of common law or a manor court, offenders had been severely punished in the reigns of William I and II, sometimes with death or mutilation, and were often tried by ordeal.

Vert offences were the cutting, felling or damaging of trees or the assarting of woodland. In theory punishment was more severe if the trees were those of the king's land, but in practice little distinction was made between those and the trees of private woodland. When private woods were wasted the courts could permit the king to seize them.

Below the forest eyre came the swainmote, which administered justice during the intervals between eyres. It usually met two or three times a year and gradually began to handle and punish all minor vert offenders, but all serious cases had to be retried by the eyre and punishments confirmed. Below the swainmote came an even less important court often called the woodmote, which commonly met every two months but merely took note of offences and passed them on to the swainmote for trial.

This system, as W. R. Fisher points out in his book, *The Forest of Essex,* was leisurely in the extreme: first presentation, then conviction and lastly, often many years later, punishment. But it was well suited to harassing offenders who would have to come repeatedly to court and be punished if they failed to appear. Similarly, there is no evidence that the very severe punishments of mutilation and death which could be handed out by the forest courts until the reign of Richard I, were often awarded and they may have been important chiefly as threats.

History of Royal Forests

The first three Norman kings maintained and increased the royal forests, but during the civil war of Stephen's reign forest administration collapsed. When Henry II came to the throne in 1254 he not only re-established forest law and claimed back all the land which had made up Henry I's forests, but afforested more. During his reign and the reigns of his two sons, Richard and John, resentment increased against these new afforestations, and in general against the way in which forest law restricted the liberties of those who held land in forests. Though John never succeeded in raising anything like the sum of money from his forests which Henry II had raised in the eyre of 1175 (£12,305), he did raise £4,486 in 1212, and everywhere he strictly enforced forest law so that he could sell exemptions or disafforestations. It was for this reason that royal forests contracted during his reign. Typically, in an attempt to raise money from the Cistercians, he withheld their grazing rights in royal forests, so that twelve abbots 'threw themselves at his feet' to beg for these to be restored, or the monks would suffer intolerable hardship.

Finally in 1215, by clauses in Magna Carta, John agreed to abandon all that he had afforested in his own reign. Two years later the young King Henry III was forced to issue a Charter of the Forest, by which all Henry II's afforestations were to be 'viewed by good and lawful men' and all which were not royal property were to be disafforested.

The Forest Charter of Henry III confirmed other concessions, in particular prohibiting the punishment of anyone taking venison with loss of life or limb. In future he was to be fined, imprisoned if he could not pay, and if after a year and a day he still could not pay, exiled.

Five years later, towards the end of 1222, there occurred a devastating storm which brought down many thousands of trees all over the country, making it possible as a result to get a good idea of royal forests at that time. The king sent orders to 43 forests, telling the wardens not to let the fallen timber be touched till it had been valued. They included 'Dene', 'Nova Foresta', 'Rockingham', 'Savernac', 'Pickering', 'Witchwud', and 'Selwud'. Elsewhere, in Patent and Close rolls of the time, 27 further forests are named.

For about 100 years the Forest Charter was the basis on which royal forests were administered. During this time they remained an important institution, both to the king and to all who lived in them or owned rights in them. Thereafter they declined both in size and importance. A first step in this decline were the disafforestations agreed by Edward I in 1300 and confirmed by Edward III in 1327. In practice they were accepting what Henry III had agreed but failed to carry out.

More significant was the inefficient way in which forests began to be administered. Visiting justices came less and less regularly to hold eyres, and in the south of England there is no record of a mediaeval forest regard after 1360. The underlying reason for this was that forests were growing less valuable to the king. Edward I had established a system of national taxation which made his forest revenues seem unimportant.

In this decline there were interruptions. The Tudors tried to revive forest administration, and Charles I, when in financial need, tried desperately to exploit rights in the forests which he claimed were still his. He was the last king to stock the royal larder with venison from his forests, and for Christmas 1640 ordered 104 does and five hinds from 21 forests, Rockingham to supply 24 of the does.

After the Restoration Charles II took an interest in the trees and deer of the royal forests, restocking some of them, but they continued to shrink in size as large parts were enclosed or granted to aristocratic landowners. From this time onwards the crown only showed concern with its forests when politicians, civil servants or seamen spread alarm about a shortage of oak trees for building warships. Commissioners made fifteen reports on this subject between 1786 and 1793, reporting separately on the New Forest, Alice Holt and Woolmer, Rockingham and Sherwood. Despite these reports, the years of land enclosure between 1770 and 1850 were those when most royal forests were finally disafforested.

During the following 30 years there was a reaction. In famous law suits the Commoners of Ashdown and Epping Forests fought for and saved many of their rights and as a consequence saved their forests. But only here, in the New Forest and in the Forest of Dean, does any semblance of mediaeval forest administration remain.

Other forests survive in the tree-growing sense and some keep their ancient names. Wychwood, Macclesfield, Rockingham and many more can still be found on the map. But they are either privately owned or owned or managed by private forestry companies, water boards or the Forestry Commission.

FORESTS YESTERDAY AND TODAY

It would be possible to describe the history of British forests in another way. At first, indeed for most of the Middle Ages, they were places to fear. The wildness of the pre-Norman forest is vividly suggested by a tenth-century description of Saxons hunting for the head of their murdered King Edmund:

Then they all went together into the woods, looking everywhere among bushes and brambles to see if they could find the head. And, wonder of wonders, God in his wisdom sent a wolf to watch over the head, and protect it against other wild beasts day and night. The men went about searching, and constantly calling out to one another, as is the custom of woodsmen, 'Where art thou now, my companion?' And the head answered them, saying 'Here, here, here.' Every time they called the head spoke back to them. There lay the grey wolf watching over the head, with it clasped between his two forepaws. He was greedy and hungry, yet for the sake of God he dared not eat the head but preserved it from other creatures. Then were the men amazed at the wolf's guardianship, and took the holy head away with them, thanking the Almighty for the miracle. And the wolf followed them as they bore away the head, until they came to the town, just as if he were tame, and then returned to the forest.

The forest was feared in particular because it harboured robbers and their bands. Robin Hood is only the best known of many outlaws who may today seem romantic figures but were little loved in their time. In the west, the Forest of Clun was the hideout of Eadric the Wild. As the king crossed Windsor Forest in the early thirteenth century he came close to being ambushed by Richard Siward and his band. Siward was considered such a menace that the sheriffs of ten counties were warned about him and urged to arrest him. When the Black Prince visited Chester around the same time, the citizens asked him to have the nearby Forest of Wirral disafforested because of the shelter it gave to robbers. Chester was a particularly unruly county. Where it bordered with the

Peak District of Derbyshire, Sir John de Davenport, supreme forester of the Forests of Leek and Macclesfield, claimed in 1316 his dues of two shillings and a salmon for every master robber taken and one shilling for each member of his band.

It was another five centuries before the country's forests, by then thoroughly tamed, began to be seen as havens for wild life and places where city dwellers could discover nature. The work of saving them, begun in the 1860s by the Commons Preservation Society, is now being continued by the National Trust, the Nature Conservancy Council, local conservation societies and conscientious county councils. Among these the Forestry Commission must be included. For too long this body has kept the reputation which it gained and indeed earned during its first 40 years as a destroyer of Britain's ancient woodlands, not to mention its wild life and traditional landscape.

For the last 20 years it has followed policies which are having the opposite effect, preserving wherever possible ancient woods, planting a proportion of broadleaf species, providing habitats for all forms of wild life and encouraging visitors, in ways which no private owners would or could. The fastest-growing trees in the best conditions take at least 40 years to mature, and, as Oliver Rackham has written, some of the more complex woodland organisms take 300 years to develop. To vary forestry policy at the whims of doctrinaire governments which last only five years is clearly absurd, but all too often this is what has happened.

Forest Animals

Bear and lion lived in the prehistoric forests of Britain, but by the Norman Conquest they were probably extinct. Of the surviving animals, William I made red deer, roe deer and wild boar, together with fallow deer which he imported, 'beasts of the forest', or the king's game. The meat of all four was called venison.

Wolves, badgers, foxes, martens, wild cats, otters, hares, rabbits and squirrels were also hunted, but were not beasts of the forest and were not protected. Outside royal forests in unenclosed land anyone could hunt them except in areas where the right had been exclusively granted to an individual or an institution. The word 'warren' was used for this right, and those who obtained it were granted 'free-warren'.

Red deer are the largest British deer, the stag standing four feet high at the shoulders, and were at one time found in most of the country's forests. Today they survive in large numbers in Scotland, though they have grown smaller, probably because they have been driven from the valleys to the mountains where food is sparser. In England the best-known herds live on Exmoor, but there are a surprising number of smaller herds, including ones in Windsor Great Park, Sherwood Forest and the New Forest.

Fallow deer were the deer which the Normans hunted in the ducal forests of Normandy and they almost certainly brought them to England soon after the Conquest. They were well adapted to living off poor forest land. They are on average about a foot shorter at the shoulder than red deer. The expanded points of their antlers make them easy to distinguish. Often they have spotted coats, but certain herds, Epping's for example, are a uniform dark-brown or black on their backs, and other herds may contain animals of very different colours including occasional albinos. Fallow deer remain common in England but rare in Wales or Scotland.

Roe deer are the smallest native species, a full-grown buck standing only 26 inches high at the shoulders. They existed in many forests up and down the country, and there are specific references to them in the records of the Peak Forest, Sherwood Forest, Pickering Forest and the Forest of Dean. They ceased to be a beast of the forest by a judicial decree of 1339. For a time they were driven out of the south of England but were re-introduced to Dorset to be hunted in the early nineteenth century and today have spread as far west as the edges of Exmoor and as far east as the borders of Kent. They are pretty animals but not easily seen because they live in thick undergrowth and are nocturnal.

Wild boar were also widely distributed. Henry I was a keen hunter of boar, and John and Henry III both sent for boar from the Forest of Pickering where they were numerous. The constable of the castle, who was also keeper of the forest, was ordered to help the king's huntsmen and to see that the meat was well salted and the heads soaked in wine. James V of Scotland had wild boar stock brought from France for Falkland Forest. In the sixteenth century they survived in Lancashire, Staffordshire and County Durham; in Elizabeth's reign they were reported in Cranborne Chase; James I hunted boar in Windsor Forest as late as 1617, but although cross-bred or feral pigs survived in the New Forest in the

nineteenth century, genuine wild boar are last recorded in England in Charles II's reign.

Wolves were common in British forests up to and during the thirteenth century and were hunted as pests rather than for sport or meat. Peasants would be granted land tenures in return for wolf hunting. In Sherwood and Rockingham Forests these tenancies were still being renewed in the fifteenth century. In England wolves survived longest in the Peak Forest, in Blackburnshire and Bowland Forests in Lancashire and in the Wolds of Yorkshire. They probably died out during the reign of Henry VII, but in Scotland a wolf, believed to be the last, was killed in 1743.

Foxes were also considered to be pests, and could be freely killed except in royal forests where a special licence was needed. Owners of land near forests would be given such licences, which allowed them to hunt at all times of the year except the fence month. Traps were used and so were terriers to dig out foxes from their earths, and greyhounds to pursue them when above ground. Unlike today's foxhounds, these followed by sight rather than scent.

Hares were usually included in licences to hunt foxes in royal forests, though there was an exception in the warren of Somerton in Somerset where the hare was considered a beast of the forest and therefore the king's game. As with fox hunting, it seems that the hunting of hares was only allowed by licence so that the deer would not be disturbed. In one forest those who had hunted illegally were said to have done so 'to the terror of the deer'.

Licences were also issued for the hunting of badger with

hounds, a practice which continued till the nineteenth century, when at least one West Country clergyman had his pack of badger hounds.

Otters are rarely mentioned in the records of royal forests, but there are occasional reports of their being killed, and a similar licence was probably needed. Fox, hare, otter and to a lesser extent badger may have been hunted because they were pests, but hunting with hounds, whatever its original purpose, is sport and likely to acquire the rituals and status of a sport. The king may have had his reserved beasts of the forest, but not have been above pursuing other quarry. Edward IV is known to have had a pack of otter hounds and James II eventually made fox hunting a respectable sport for the aristocracy.

The wild cat and the marten (once called the martin, now sometimes called the pine marten or the marten cat) were hunted under similar licences in royal forests. The wild cat, a fierce, yellow-grey creature with a broad head, larger body than a domestic cat's but a relatively short tail, became extinct in England in the mid-nineteenth century, but survives in remote parts of northern Scotland. The marten is still fairly common in the north of England as well as in Wales and Scotland.

Rabbits were introduced to England by the Normans, not the Romans as commonly thought, and the right to hunt them in royal forests or warrens became a valuable one. Licences for hunting occasionally included squirrels. These were, of course, the native red squirrel, not the grey squirrel, an import from North America which exists in England only because it was released by the London Zoo and others who had imported it. In the south-east of England it has now replaced the red squirrel, which it used to be thought to have driven out. In fact it more probably filled a gap left by the red squirrel which in this part of the country was already decimated by disease.

Grey squirrels are considered a pest. The Forestry Commission shoots, traps and poisons them and the Ministry of Agriculture has launched unsuccessful campaigns for their elimination. They can destroy quite large trees by ring-barking them, and permanently spoil young ones as timber by attacking their top branches. Trees native to North America seem to suffer less. On the other hand, grey squirrels particularly favour sycamore, which they kill by stripping its bark, and so, in the view of some foresters, usefully reduce the proportion of sycamore in woods which this species would otherwise swamp.

It is not too difficult to guess why these last four animals never became hunted in the way the previous four did. Wild cats, martens and squirrels live in trees and take refuge here, where dogs can't pursue them. As for rabbits, they are still hunted in a wider sense of the word, but never provide the cross-country pursuits which stir the huntsman's blood.

This list by no means includes all the wild life of the forest. Stoats and weasels are still common throughout the country, and polecats, the smaller, darker, more destructive and smellier relation of the marten, survive in Wales and northern Scotland. And two species of deer (escapes, like the grey squirrel) are now often seen. The muntjak from Asia, about the size of a small sheep with a dog-like bark, may in fact today be the commonest deer in the country. Sika deer, from Japan, are less common but important because in many areas they have hybridized with the red deer and perhaps contributed to reducing its size.

Rats, water rats (correctly water voles), moles, dormice, field mice, harvest mice, bank voles, shrews, hedgehogs and twelve varieties of bat are all found in forests. So are toads, frogs and newts, lizards including the slow worm, and snakes. Most coarse fish occur in forest ponds or streams and trout too where the water is suitable. As for birds, they are a subject in themselves and beyond the scope of any brief summary. Today such game birds as pheasants, grouse and woodcock are found in forests, as are pests like pigeon and rook, but only swans were ever considered 'birds of the forest' in the sense that they were reserved to the king.

It is in woods which form part of forests, as opposed to plantations, that most of these species thrive. Here they form an integral part of a complex biological system, parallel to and interlocking with the wood's flora. But adjoining plantations of different ages, even of conifers, provide useful habitats for some species, and interfaces between conifer and broadleaf plantations are often favoured by more species than plantations of one or the other. The Forestry Commission's new policy of planting streambeds with a variety of broadleaf species creates just such interfaces.

Other animals besides grey squirrels can damage trees, in particular deer and rabbits. So can such birds as blackcock and capercaillie, by defoliating them or uprooting them when young. The most expensive item in establishing a plantation is often the fence to exclude deer. During the last few years a simple device for protecting young trees has been developed which is proving so effective that it looks set to become the zip fastener of modern forestry. It is commonly called a 'Tuley tube', after its inventor, Graham Tuley, a Forestry Commission research worker at Alice Holt Forest.

The Tuley tube comes in various forms but essentially consists of a cylinder of semi-transparent plastic about four feet in height which is set around each tree seedling. This not only protects the tree from all but the tallest animals and much reduces the amount of weeding needed but acts as a miniature greenhouse. Most species grow between twice and three times as fast as they do without protection. The tubes last up to five years, then disintegrate.

Hunting Dogs

The greyhound was the commonest mediaeval hunting dog. It was larger than today's greyhound, sometimes with a longer and sometimes a curled coat. It hunted by sight, not scent.

A dog which hunted by scent was called a 'branche', if large or a 'bercelet' if small. The one resembled today's foxhound, the other today's beagle. Bercelet were sometimes called 'limehounds' or 'lymers' from the cord of lime fibre by which they were held.

The mastiff was more often used for house protection but could also hunt. It was a large fierce dog, like today's mastiff.

These divisions apart, the dogs of particular packs were sometimes described by the quarry they pursued, as foxhounds are today. They occur in records as the latin equivalents of harthound, buckhound, boar hound, otter hound and hare hound.

Mastiff

Unless permission had been granted, only dogs which had been 'lawed' were allowed in the forest. The lawing of a dog was the cutting off of the three claws of its forefeet to prevent it from chasing game. The operation was performed by a single blow with a wide chisel, after the dog had been persuaded to place its foot on a wooden chopping block. By Henry III's Charter of the Forest of 1217 anyone who let his unlawed dog roam in a royal forest was to be fined three shillings.

Forest Trees

There are between 50 and 70 native British trees—trees which arrived naturally in this country after the retreat of the ice in about 8300-8200 BC—and a small number of naturalized ones. Almost all occur in British forests. So do a number of exotic trees, for example Corsican pine and Norway spruce, which have been extensively planted by the Forestry Commission. Where parts of forests have been landscaped for their appearance rather than the production of timber, individual specimens of many other exotic species will be found, from the North American conifers imported in such variety in the nineteenth century, to Lebanon cedars, to ornamental Japanese maples.

Most British woods, if left to themselves for a sufficient time, might in theory become oak woods. But, apart from begging the question of what *is* an oak wood (a wood in which oak is the commonest standard tree should not necessarily be called an oak wood if trees of some other species form the underwood), in practice this does not seem to have happened. Even in the wildwood, Britain's prehistoric forest, oak did not everywhere predominate and during the last 5,000 years, either for natural reasons or because of man's interference, woods consisting mainly of other species have continued to exist.

Certainly oak could be described as the most typical large English forest tree, but even this needs qualifying. There are two common varieties of oak in this country: *Quercus robur* (also called English or pedunculate oak) and *Quercus petraea* (also called durmast or sessile oak). English oak is more common in the heavier soil of southern England, but found as well in highland valleys. Durmast is more common in the north and west. One way to distinguish them is that English oaks have long acorns growing on stalks while durmast have short ones growing close to the twigs. For 50 years from about 1790 durmast oak was discouraged by foresters. In the Forest of Dean and the New Forest, areas were systematically planted with English oak. And except in Scotland durmast was anyway always rarer, but not so rare as might be thought since it prefers woodlands and is less likely to be seen by the casual observer than English oak, the typical oak of parkland and hedgerow.

Oak has commonly been used for timber. It was the material most often used for timber-framed houses and for wooden ships. It had many farm uses—it will survive for long periods in the open without paint or preservative—and in parts of the country was used for roofing shingles or weatherboarding. Large areas of oak woods were coppiced in England, Wales and Scotland, first for the iron industry, then until the middle of the nineteenth century for bark for tanning. It is one of the best burning woods. Particularly fine oaks can be seen in the Forest of Dean, and remarkable ancient ones in the New Forest and Sherwood Forest.

Twelve other large or largish native or naturalized trees form substantial proportions of the standard trees of certain English forests: elm, ash, beech, lime, hornbeam, yew, maple, birch, holly, sycamore, Scots pine and sweet chestnut. Alder, and some varieties of willow and poplar, are widely found but rarely predominate.

Elm was once common in English forests but is less so today since so many were killed by Dutch elm disease in the 1970s. One variety which suffered severely was the English elm, *Ulmus procera,* the large tree which used to be such a hedgerow feature all over southern England and the Midlands. Cornish elm—*Ulmus stricta*—also suffered. Varieties collectively known as *Ulmus carpinifolia* which were common in East Anglia and parts of the West Country were attacked too, but so far elms in the north of England and Scotland have suffered less severely than those in the south. Wych elm, *Ulmus glabra,* is less vulnerable but has also been affected. It is often thought of as a small tree but can reach a height of 120 feet. Unlike other elms which sucker, it was commonly coppiced.

Like oak, elm was used for building, but less extensively, and for such other outdoor purposes as farm troughs because it does not split when exposed to weather. In earlier centuries elm shoots were gathered for winter cattle food.

Common lime, *Tilia vulgaris*, is the most generally seen lime today, much planted in parks and gardens. It is a hybrid between two native limes, the small-leaved *Tilia cordata*, common in English prehistoric woodland, and the rarer large leaved *Tilia platyphyllos*. Small-leaved lime, however, never spread north of Cumberland, and large-leaved is a rare tree, only found wild in Herefordshire, Radnorshire and the West Riding of Yorkshire, all limestone areas. Lime wood is fine grained and used for making musical instruments. The inner bark was valued in mediaeval times for cord making and it is still used for bast mats.

Lime is less common than it once was in English forests, but still predominates in some ancient woods, for example Welland Park in the Forestry Commission's Sherwood Forest complex.

Ash, *Fraxinus excelsior,* occurs in many British forests, and occasionally predominates. It prefers north or east-facing hillsides, where it can find deep moist soil. Ash was at one time a much valued wood for its strength and elasticity, and was used for tool handles and for oars. It is said to be able to bear more strain than any other European native timber. It makes good hop poles, a use particularly recommended by William Cobbett who, in his book *Woodlands*, published in 1825, passionately recommends the growing of ash as a crop. For many uses ash was coppiced, and in general it was cut young, its timber considered to be at its best between the ages

Hornbeam

Wild Service

of 30 and 60 years, though it will live to 200 and even longer if pollarded.

Beech, *Fagus sylvatica*, arrived comparatively late in Britain but had reached southern England before 3000 BC. It spread rapidly north after the arrival of neolithic man, but is only a true native south of a line from Carmarthen to King's Lynn. North of this it is widely planted and has become naturalized.

Beech is generally thought to prefer chalky soil, but is found on many other types. When grown close together for timber its light-excluding horizontal foliage suppresses all underwood. Old woods as well as plantations can be managed to give them this monotonous quality, and such beech-woods are seen typically on the Chilterns. In the New Forest, the Forest of Dean, the Ashdown Forest and many others beech grows in more interesting mixed woods. Beech timber was much valued for furniture making, and was used, for example, in the traditional craft of bodging—the making of spokes and legs for upright chairs.

As a native tree the hornbeam, *Carpinus betulus*, never spread north of a line from Worcester to Norfolk, but to the south of this line it grew extensively. It is often mistaken for beech and found in similar places, but can be distinguished by its double-toothed leaf, winged seeds, often fluted barley-sugar-like trunk and, in their season, by its catkins. Its wood is extremely hard and disliked by carpenters because it blunts

ple

Birch

tools. It was once used to make cogwheels for wind and water mills. It is a good firewood, said to burn like a candle. Many once-pollarded hornbeams can be seen in Epping Forest, and newly-pollarded ones in Hatfield Forest.

Yew, *Taxus baccata,* is one of only three native British conifers—juniper and Scots pine are the others. It is believed to be the longest lived of all British native trees and its trunk grows to massive size because of its habit of making new shoots from the lower part of its bole which become united with the old wood. It grows fast when young but rarely exceeds 50 feet when full grown. Its leaves are poisonous to cattle and the seeds of its berries to humans.

Its very hard wood was at one time much valued for furniture. A fencing post of yew is said to outlast one of iron. Its branches were used for bows, and being poisonous it is said to have been planted in churchyards for this purpose. It is also found in almost all British forests, and occasionally outnumbers other trees to form complete woods.

Birch, *Betula pendula,* or silver birch as this species is often called, is the hardiest native tree. It is widespread throughout England, Wales and southern Scotland, though in the Scottish Highlands it is often replaced by the similar downy or white birch, *Betulus pubescens.* Birch can endure great heat as well as cold, and can take the form of scrub in hostile conditions or grow to 100 feet in favourable positions. As a standard tree it rarely lives for more than 100 years and is mature at 50. It will burn, its bark was once used for tanning leather and it is still much used in plywood. Birch can be found in every British forest.

The native English maple, *Acer campestre,* is a comparatively small tree, commonly between 20 and 50 feet high when full grown. It occurs in English forests from Durham south, but is more often seen as underwood than as a standard tree. Maples were commonly coppiced.

Sweet chestnut, *Castanea sativa,* is a naturalized tree, probably brought to this country by the Romans. It is a larger and can be an even longer-lived tree than the oak, surviving for 500 years if allowed. Its timber is valued for furniture and many other purposes, and on the continent commonly used as a building material. In England it is still coppiced for its poles which can be split into fence posts or palings. In such continental countries as Italy it regularly produces a crop of nuts, once much valued as substitutes for flour, but in Britain the nuts are often small and empty. Sweet chestnut can be seen in many forests and there are particularly fine ones in Windsor Great Park.

Sycamore, *Acer pseudoplatanus,* was probably introduced into England in the fifteenth century though some while earlier into Scotland. It has spread all over the country and survives in the most exposed places, where gales and a salty atmosphere would destroy other trees. It grows fast to a height of 80 feet, reaching maturity in 50 or 60 years, and lives for up to 250. Sycamores will be found in most British forests.

Alder, *Alnus glutinosa,* was among the early trees to reach Britain, following after juniper, birch, pine, hazel, oak and elm. It is a small tree (though it can occasionally grow to 100 feet), widespread from Caithness south, but chiefly found near streams and rivers or on wet land. The wood is used for turning and also for piles, since it has a long life under water. Its charcoal was once valued for gunpowder making, for which it was said to be the best and it was encouraged in such forests as the Dean for this purpose.

There are many willow species, most of which will be found here and there in British forests. Willows include sallows, one of which, the sallow or goat willow, is the earliest to flower, known for its gold and silver catkins; the other, the grey sallow, *Salix cinerea,* is the most widespread willow in Britain. Some willows, the ossier and the purple ossier, for example, commonly remain shrubs, but others, like the crack willow and the white willow, grow to 70 feet. Willows grow fast and only the cricket bat willow has much value as timber. Willow was often pollarded and produces a quick crop of poles, but the pollard usually lets in water and rots at the centre. Most species prefer river banks or wet places and this is where they will be found in forests.

Aspen, *Populus tremula,* black poplar, *Populus nigra,* and white poplar, *Populus alba,* are native species. Grey poplar, *Populus canescens,* once thought a native, is now considered a hybrid between aspen and white poplar. Like willows, poplars grow fast and produce a light timber of little value except for box making. Of these four species, aspen is shortest, 50 to 60 feet when full grown; grey will reach 90 feet and black as much as 100 feet. Black poplar is easily recognized by the grotesque swellings on its trunk. It does not grow in woods, but will be found here and there, like the others, in moist places in forests.

Holly, *Ilex aquifolium,* can grow to 50 feet, but rarely

does. It is widely found in forests and at one time was planted to protect other young trees from grazing cattle. In royal forests it was regularly cut to provide deer with winter feed. Though its lower leaves are spiky, its higher often are not; perhaps it developed in this way because it only needed to protect itself up to a certain height. Its hard white wood burns well and is valued for carving.

Three sorbuses, rowan or mountain ash, *Sorbus aucupavia*, wild service, *Sorbus torminalis*, and whitebeam, *Sorbus aria*, are commonly found as small forest trees. Rowan, now so common in suburban gardens, is found throughout the country, especially in Scotland. Despite its name and similar leaves it is unrelated to ash. Its berries are orange or scarlet and used for jellies or wine. Whitebeam often remains shrub-like but can grow to 40 feet. It is an English, not a Scottish tree, with bright scarlet berries. Wild service resembles whitebeam but is smaller and its berries are greenish-brown. These sorbuses are too small to produce timber of value, though their wood can be burned.

Gean cherry, *Prunus avium*, wild or dwarf cherry, *Prunus cerasus*, and bird cherry, *Prunus padus*, are all native British trees, found occasionally in forests. Gean cherry is commonest, found throughout the country. It can grow to 100 feet. Wild cherry is small and bushlike, and not found north of Cumberland. Bird cherry, on the other hand, is a northern species not found south of Leicestershire and south Wales. It is a small tree, ten to 30 feet in height. All have white blossom in April or May.

Most crab apple trees now found in woodland or hedgerow are hybrids with cultivated species. They are fairly common in British forests and the true crab, *Malus sylvestris*, is also occasionally found. Crab apples can grow to 50 feet, but commonly remain bushlike to old age. They can be coppiced or pollarded and their wood burns well. Their timber is fine-grained and valued for carpentry.

Many of the above species can form the underwood of a forest, either in the form of scrub or coppice, as well as forming its standard trees. There are also a few trees which are found as underwood but rarely as standards: hazel, hawthorn, blackthorn and elder are the commonest of these. Hazel produces a nut crop and coppices well. Hawthorn is best known as a hedge plant, but also found extensively in forests where, like holly, it was used to protect other young trees. Blackthorn is also common, but almost never grows to be a tree. It is well known for its bitter fruit, the sloe. Elder has useless pithy wood when young, but its mature branches burn well, and its fruit and flowers are used for wine.

Scots pine, *Pinus sylvestris,* was the third British tree to follow the ice north in prehistoric times. It spread rapidly into Highland regions and is now native only in Scotland. Here Caledonian pines of true genetic stock can still be seen in such forests as Affric and Rannoch. Elsewhere, and all over England and Wales, it was re-introduced and has now become naturalized. It does particularly well on sandy soils and can be found in all British forests.

Exotic Trees Scots pine was used in many early conifer plantations, but from the mid-sixteenth century at latest Norway spruce, *Picea abies,* the well-known Christmas tree, was imported from Europe where it is native from France to Russia. It is still extensively planted but in wet exposed sites on thin acid soil does less well than sitka spruce. It can grow to 110 feet and live 200 years.

Sitka spruce, *Picea sitchensis,* one of the numerous exotic trees sent to Britain by the plant collectors of the early nineteenth century, first arrived from its native western America in 1831. It is now planted more widely than any other tree in Britain. Typically, Coed y Brenin Forest in Wales is over 50 per cent sitka spruce. Its foliage is deep blue-green above and silver below. Its soft white cones are about half the length (three inches) of the Norway spruce's. It grows taller and in 42 years can reach 125 feet.

European larch, *Larix decidua,* was the second exotic conifer to be imported, arriving from Europe where it is native from Poland to the French Alps, in 1620. Though less productive than some other conifers, it grows well at intermediate heights, has many uses and is particularly valued today because it is deciduous and helps vary the appearance of conifer forests. When in leaf larches can be distinguished from other conifers by their tufts of leaves.

Japanese larch, *Larix kaempferi,* came much later, in 1861. It grows more vigorously and is now generally preferred. It can be distinguished by its orange twigs in winter. Still more vigorous is hybrid larch. This cross between the other two species occurred by accident in Perthshire where two neighbouring plantations were noticed in 1904 to have produced hybrid seedlings.

Though Scots pine has one great advantage over most

45

other conifers—when well grown its rough bark is least damaged by red deer—and for this reason is still widely planted, Corsican pine, *Pinus nigra,* first imported in 1759, does better in polluted atmospheres and is often today preferred—for example in Sherwood Forest. It has larger cones and its upper trunk does not have the orange-tinted bark of the Scots pine. It grows especially well on sandy soils.

Lodgepole pine, *Pinus contorta,* introduced from North America in 1832, does better on high, poor ground, but is particularly susceptible to damage by red deer.

Western hemlock, *Tsuga heterophylla,* came also from the western part of North America but about 20 years later. It succeeds in shade and is often planted below broadleaf trees. It can grow to a great height—one tree in Argyll reached 140 feet—and is commonest in Scottish and Welsh forests.

Douglas fir, *Pseudotsuga menziesii,* sent from the same area still earlier (1827) by the collector David Douglas, prefers sheltered sites but will grow to even greater heights. A Douglas fir was the tallest tree in Britain (170 feet) till 1971.

Now it has been passed by a grand fir, *Abies grandis.* Plantations of this species and of the related noble fir, *Abies procera,* are becoming increasingly common in British forests. Both arrived from the same part of the world in the 1830s, both make slow growth for five years then grow fast to great heights. The cones are carried only on the crown and disintegrate when ripe, so are seldom seen.

Southern beech, *Nothofagus,* became an increasingly fashionable forestry tree during the last ten years and there are many, though relatively small, plantations of *Nothofagus procera* and *Nothofagus obliqua.* It grows as fast as most conifers, is less damaged by grey squirrels than native broadleaf species and looks less alien than conifer in the landscape. But the hard winters of the last few years have shown that it is somewhat tender and foresters have become more cautious about its prospects.

FORESTS OF SUSSEX

Ashdown

The most villainously ugly spot I ever saw in England [William Cobbett wrote from Lewes on 8 January 1822, after crossing Ashdown Forest], a heath, with here and there a few birch scrubs upon it . . . This lasts you for five miles, getting, if possible, uglier and uglier all the way, till, at last, as if barren soil, nasty spewy gravel, heath and even that stunted, were not enough, you see some rising spots, which instead of trees, present you with black, ragged, hideous rocks. There may be Englishmen who wish to see the coast of *Nova Scotia*. They need not go to sea; for here it is to the life. If I had been in a long trance (as our nobility seem to have been), and had been waked up here, I should have begun to look about for the Indians and the squaws, and to have heaved a sigh at the thought of being so far from England.

Unproductive or ill-managed land infuriated Cobbett. Three years later, when visiting Romney Marsh, he paid the forests of Sussex a back-handed compliment.

The cattle appear to be all of the *Sussex* breed. Red, loose-limbed, and, they say, a great deal better than the Devonshire. How curious is the *natural economy* of a country! The forests of Sussex; those miserable tracts of heath and fern and bushes and sand called Ashdown Forest and Saint Leonard's Forest . . . those wretched tracts and not much less wretched farms in their neighbourhood, *breed the cattle* which we see *fatting* in Romney Marsh.

The two forests which Cobbett names were among six which existed in the county in the Middle Ages. In the south was **Arundel**; strung out across the centre from west to east were **St Leonard's**, **Worth**, **Ashdown** and **Waterdown**. In the south-east was **Dallington**. With the exception of Arundel they had all once formed part of a single great forest which measured, according to the Anglo Saxon Chronicle, 120 miles across and 30 in width, and reached at one end into Hampshire and at the other into Kent. In 731 Bede described it as almost inaccessible, inhabited by deer and wild swine. It

was known to the Saxons as Andredeswald, hence the name
Weald which still describes this long stretch of uplands lying
roughly midway between the North and South Downs with
Ashdown Forest near its centre.

From the Norman Conquest Sussex also had deer parks.
By the early 1600s there were around 100, some carved out
from the six forests, others standing on their own. Just how
densely much of it remained wooded in the Middle Ages is
shown by the fact that Edward I, when he travelled from
London to Chichester in 1276, employed fifteen guides. Parks
and forests together have kept Sussex the most wooded
county in England, though ironically Ashdown Forest, the
only forest of which a large part survives as a single entity, is
almost as bare now as it was in Cobbett's time.

One reason for its survival is simple. Mostly it stands on
the sort of infertile sandy soil which Cobbett described so
accurately. And though this has never prevented vegetation,
including a proportion of trees, it has discouraged covetous
agriculturalists. Its Commoners may also have played a part
by defending their rights with unusual obstinacy—rights
which were described by the eighteenth-century agricultural
reformer, the Rev. Arthur Young, as 'unexceptionally the
most perfect nuisance that ever blasted the improvement of a
country'.

Today, when the farmer-businessman is the chief enemy of
the country-side and its wild life, travellers across Ashdown
Forest are more likely to be delighted by this expanse of
unproductive country only 35 miles from the centre of
London. At the same time they will probably be sorry to find
so much heath when the word forest makes them believe that
the area should be woodland. This belief is probably false
—there was always much open country on the high Weald. It
is certainly false to think that today's forest of heath,
bracken, gorse and birch scrub is the result of modern
mismanagement, neglect or arson. The Ashdown Forest
could be wooded or allowed to wood itself without too much
difficulty, but it is managed with the opposite purpose. Now
that there is so little heath in the south of England, this is
what the Conservators believe they should preserve.

Whether or not Bede's description of the forest of the
Weald as inaccessible was accurate in the mid-eighth century,
there is now ample evidence that before this it had been
extensively occupied. C. F. Tebbutt, today's forest historian,
by collecting flints over a number of years, has identified sites

which made up an extensive network of Stone Age settlements, some mesolithic, some neolithic. Today, according to J. K. Irons, author of a thesis on the forest, 30 per cent of all known rock and cave settlements of mesolithic man in England and Wales are in the Ashdown Forest area.

The Roman occupation of Ashdown Forest has been known for much longer, from the remains of their iron industry. These can be found in many parts of the forest, particularly in the Maresfield and Broadstone Warren areas. Until recently the Saxons were thought to have abandoned the forest, but in 1980 a Saxon bloomery furnace for smelting was found, one of only a very few in the country, showing that by about AD 800 they also were exploiting it.

From the Norman Conquest till 1371 the forest was more in the nature of a chase than a royal forest, and though it occasionally reverted to the king, or sometimes to the queen, it was usually in the possession of the lords of Pevensey Castle. Each of the six rapes into which Sussex was divided had its forest, and Ashdown was part of the forest of Pevensey rape—surprisingly, considering how far it lies from the coast, but the rape of Pevensey extended to the Surrey border.

As for its size at this time, Domesday Book does not mention it, and Sussex is anyway one of the counties where woods are described not by their acreage but by the number of pigs for which they could provide pannage. At a rough estimate, it was probably 18,000 acres, certainly the largest of Sussex's forests.

The origin of its name is even more uncertain. It was referred to in Henry I's reign as 'Essessdon', around 1245 as 'Asshedoune', around 1300 as both 'Essesdoun' and 'Assesdon', and in 1371 as 'Ashdon'. If ash trees had ever been common on the forest they would provide a simple explanation, but ash was always a rare tree, as it is today; all the ancient buried trees identified by the Rev. Edward Turner, mid-Victorian rector of Maresfield, were either oak or fir (Scots pine). No alternative explanation of the name is known.

In 1371 Edward III gave the forest to his third son, John of Gaunt, Duke of Lancaster. From this time it was known as the Great Park of Lancaster. Despite its size it was probably now, like other parks, enclosed by a pale to contain the deer; a survey of the end of the sixteenth century says that the park measured 35 miles by the pale. The hunting lodge which

Edward II built on the forest near Nutley was used by John of Gaunt. This lodge, together with its associated chapel are one of the forest's mysteries for both have so completely disappeared that their sites are unknown.

Soon after John of Gaunt's death in 1399 the Duchy of Lancaster was vested in the crown, and Ashdown again became a royal forest, but the duke had been a sufficiently memorable figure still to be referred to in the nineteenth century by locals of Nutley as King John, and the name, Lancaster Great Park, continued to be used for many years.

Throughout the Middle Ages the history of the forest consists mainly either of reports of gifts of forest land or forest rights to various religious establishments or landowners, or of tantalizingly brief reports of poaching, theft of wood and timber and other forest offences. Only occasionally do real people emerge from the records of the courts which dealt with these cases.

Despite royal grants the area of the forest seems not to have diminished significantly during this time. But by the end of the period such woodland as it had had was much reduced. At the time of the Conquest woods which became part of the forest could provide pannage for around 7,000 pigs. Two hundred years later in 1272 there was only pannage for 2,784 pigs. And during the next century records show that Ashdown frequently had no acorn pannage, and the pig feed was entirely beech mast, known as 'evesfold'. At the beginning of the seventeenth century the same survey which gives the length of the pale reports of the forest that 'it is a barren ground and hathe no covert of any underwood saving great Trees and in some of the Covers birchen Trees . . . there is no faire launde in it but only hethes and they are not playne but all holtes'.

By Tudor times poaching had become a sufficiently serious problem for there to be fuller details of several cases. In Mary's reign the Master of Game of Ashdown charged 20 persons including keepers that in 'the great waste ground called the Forest of Ashdowne' they had gathered one night at Hartfield 'having with them divers and many grey hounds, crossbows and arrows, longbows and arrows, pikes, forks, bills and clubs and arrayed with coats of fenses and skulls of iron' and that they 'in the most riotous manner did chase her Majesty's deer and did kill one Red deer and four fallow deer and carried them away, and wounded and ill-treated the keepers of the said deer.' Six weeks later, 26 others, who were charged that they had committed similar offences, defended themselves by claiming that they had gathered for a wood-court and were not poaching but walking through the forest to survey the waste.

Towards the end of Henry VIII's reign the waste of the woodland in the forest was so serious that various commissions were appointed to make investigations. Acts were passed in 1558, 1581 and 1585 to control the cutting of wood for charcoal making and forbid the use of timber for this purpose, and James I ordered wood not to be used for glassmaking. The cause of much of this royal concern was fear of a shortage of oak for building warships. Well separated standard oaks with spreading upper branches of the sort which grew in Sussex forests had precisely the elbow joints which ship builders needed. But the destruction of timber continued and, as in so many English forests, reached a climax during the Civil War.

The Sussex iron industry was blamed at the time and has been blamed since for the destruction of the forests of Sussex. It is easy to see why. Most of the evidence comes from the cries of distress of those who saw wood which they had been accustomed to use for fuel, house repairs, fence making and other domestic purposes gobbled up by the charcoal burners to make fuel for furnace and forge. In 1612 Drayton made this point in verse:

> Jove's oak, the warlike ash, vein'd elm, the softer beech,
> Short hazel, maple plain, light asp, the bending wych,
> Tough holly, and smooth birch, must altogether burn,
> What should the builder serve, supplies the forger's turn.

At about the same time, one surveyor wrote, 'I have heard there are or lately were in Sussex 140 hammers and furnaces for iron . . . [which] spend each of them in every 24 hours two, three, or foure loades of charcoale, which in a yeare amounteth to an infinit quantity.'

But the truth is that in Sussex underwood or coppice wood was used for making charcoal and there was no necessary connection between the harvesting of this and the destruction of woodland, provided it was given the chance to grow again. The *Victoria County History* misunderstands this point. Writing about the later using of wood for hop poles, it says that the wide demand for these in the eighteenth century led 'to the consumption of a quantity of young timber, particularly chestnut and ash in the coppices, without any commensurate planting to replenish the supply for the future'. It is the essence of a coppice wood that it is self-replacing and does not need replanting.

Even at the time some people realized that using coppice wood for charcoal, far from destroying woodland and timber, had the opposite effect. A grand jury at Lewes in 1661 investigating the decline in the iron industry wrote, 'As woods maintain iron workes soe doe iron workes mutually maintain them . . . Nor can any timber be destroyed by Iron workes being about four times in value more than the price of cordwood commonly used for that purpose . . . If the English iron works cease the coppices will be grubbed up, which are the great nurseries of timber.'

It is still true that the iron industry consumed huge quantities of wood. The plant itself was of astonishing size. The first part, the furnace, could measure as much as 24 × 24 feet in area and be 26–28 feet high. It might be kept working for 40 weeks and during each working week of six days burn 24 loads of charcoal, each weighing eleven quarters (2¾

cwt). The sandstone on which the furnace was built would be gradually eaten away so that at first it would produce 'pigs' of iron of 600–700 lbs, and later 'sows' of 2,000 lbs.

These huge blocks of cast iron were next treated in the forge (also called the iron mill or hammer) where parts were melted off and first beaten with sledge hammers then with a water-powered hammer weighing seven to eight hundredweight. At first the Sussex iron industry seems to have produced specific iron items, but by the sixteenth century it was producing mainly iron bars. From the middle of that century it also cast large numbers of cannon.

The industry in Sussex had a long history and one invariably connected with Sussex woodlands which supplied its fuel. Near Maresfield on the southern edge of Ashdown Forest Roman coins were found in cinder beds from iron workings which show that these operated over several centuries. The Roman industry was based on bloomeries, small furnaces without water-powered bellows which never melted the iron and instead of pigs or sows of cast iron, produced soft iron containing less carbon, in the form of 'blooms' —sponge-like lumps weighing five to ten lbs. Roman bloomeries are found all over the forest.

The Saxons never revived the industry on the Roman scale, though Domesday records an iron works of some kind in the East Grinstead area and the Saxon bloomery furnace mentioned earlier has recently been found near Nutley. Nor is

Charcoal burners

there much evidence of iron production for the first 150 years after the Norman Conquest. Then there are steadily increasing records of orders for large quantities of such things as horse shoes, nails and iron heads for arrows.

The industry was at its peak from the reign of Henry VIII to around the middle of the Commonwealth. During this period there were furnaces in many parts of Sussex, in particular on the forests of St Leonard's, Worth and Ashdown. In his definitive work on the subject C. F. Tebbutt has described nearly 200, reaching from one in Hampshire to one in Kent. On or near the Ashdown Forest itself, Newbridge became in 1493 the first in the country to use bellows powered by water. There are two other forges and furnaces nearby at Pippingford. Near Buxted at the other end of the forest an equally important event for the iron industry occurred when in 1543, for the first time in England, a cannon was cast in one piece. Earlier cannon had been made up of separate pieces of wrought iron which were held together with bands then welded. Now the solid barrel was bored out with a steel-tipped drill. Large numbers of these cannon were soon being made. In Worth Forest, for example, one manufacturer in two years produced 56 tons of cannon and 52 tons of shot. In Elizabethan and Jacobean times many fortunes were made by the iron masters of Sussex, some aristocratic, some nouveau riche, and their fine houses survive.

The Sussex iron industry declined and ultimately disappeared in two stages, for two reasons, neither of them a shortage of wood for the furnaces and forges. The first decline occurred between the years 1653 and 1664, and was the result of a trade war with Sweden. The same grand jury at Lewes in 1661 reported that 'It will be proven upon oath that some Swedes who brought over iron this yeare, being demanded why they imported soe great quantities at such low rates, plainly affirmed that they hoped thereby to destroy the makeing of Englishe iron'.

A period of revival followed. As late as 1762 large numbers of guns from 3-pounders to 32-pounders were sent to Woolwich from Gravetye and Warren forest—Gravetye (now a well-known hotel) lies close to Ashdown and was later the home of the gardener, William Robinson, who left it to the Forestry Commission. But now the discovery of how to use coke for iron smelting produced a rapid decline, since coke was a cheaper fuel than charcoal. Twenty-six years later, in 1788, there were only two furnaces in the county, and the final one, at Ashburnham, blew out in 1811, after a drunken workman had failed to add lime to the ore to enable it to flux.

A hundred and fifty years before the extinction of the last Sussex iron furnace, there had been important developments for Ashdown Forest of a different sort. During the Commonwealth, when the forest as a royal manor was in Parliament's hands, a number of committees visited it to restore administrative order and collect overdue rents. They made detailed suggestions for developing its various parts, but as soon as Charles II returned to the throne he set these aside and agreed to its total disafforestation. In this way he set in motion events leading to the first of the great law suits which ultimately saved a large part of the forest.

Richard, Earl of Dorset, and George, Earl of Bristol, both benefited from Charles's permission to disafforest Ashdown, but after complex financial and legal dealings it was the Earl of Dorset who obtained control of the forest. Neither he nor his tenants were able to profit as they hoped because of 'the crossness of the neighbourhood'. Corn which they sowed was trampled down, fences destroyed, and ditches filled. When they re-sowed, the same things occurred. Those who committed these nuisances were the Commoners of the forest who believed that they had been deprived of their rights in the land now being enclosed and cultivated.

These rights had probably varied over the years, but a charter of 1273 gives a clear idea of what they had been at that date. Then 208 customary tenants dwelling around the forest had the right to all windfall wood (unless torn up by the roots), and also to take brushwood, furze and broom for fuel. They might graze as many cattle on the forest as they could maintain in their own buildings throughout the winter, but not graze them on the forest during the autumn six weeks of pannage (Michaelmas to Martinmas). They might also

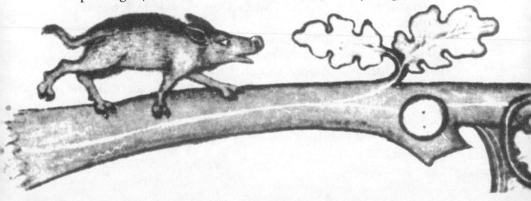

have as many swine on the forest as they could maintain on their own land, except for the month around the nativity of John the Baptist, the so-called fence month when the deer had their fawns. Finally they had the right to burn brushwood, furze and broom *on* the forest to improve the pasture. Interestingly, the right to collect and carry away litter for animal feed or bedding is not mentioned.

In return for the rights to pannage they paid either various sums per pig according to its age, or one pig in ten. For their other rights they paid in total that year 39s 0½d in cash, one hen each at Christmas and two eggs at Easter.

The inquisition of 1546 gives a vivid account of how the Commoners in practice collected their 'wind fallen wood and rot fallen wood'. At sunrise of Hok Monday (the second Monday after Easter) the head forester blew his horn 'in the high of the south ward', at which all the foresters blew horns in their own wards, as a signal that collecting could begin. The Commoners could pile and mark their wood, but had to remove it by Michaelmas.

When, in 1689, after 28 years of provocation, the Earl of Dorset and others took the Commoners to court, asking to be 'quieted in the enjoyment of their lands', they claimed that the Commoners had their various rights only in return for services rendered or in compensation for damage done by deer. Since they now gave no service and the deer had been destroyed, the rights should have ceased. The Commoners —John Newnham with 50 acres of land at Nutley Inn, and 140 others—claimed that the rights had belonged to their lands, independent of conditions, from 'time out of mind'.

Four years later a compromise was reached which defined Ashdown Forest as it has survived until today. A commission set aside 6,400 acres of forest on which the Commoners had the sole right to pasture their stock and to cut birch, willow and alder. They were excluded from the remainder of the 13,991 acres, and the Lord of the Manor's rights here, and his rights to trees of other species on the whole forest were confirmed.

Satisfactory as this compromise seems to have been found for over 100 years, it meant that Ashdown Forest in its modern form—the area reserved to the Commoners—is a highly irregular shape, made up of a circle of pieces of land, many themselves intricately shaped, surrounding the large disafforested islands of Hindleap Warren, Broadstone Warren and Pippingford Park. If the forest today seems an extensive area of wild country, this is in part because these islands and many of the other pieces of land interwoven with the areas reserved for the Commoners have also largely remained uncultivated.

Throughout the nineteenth century the Commoners and the Lord of the Manor disagreed increasingly about what each might do on the Commoners' parts of the forest, and in 1878 Earl De La Warr, descendant of the Earl of Dorset who had brought the law suit of 1689, challenged the right of two Commoners to cut and take away litter. He claimed that it could only be taken from the forest in the stomachs of their animals. When Bernard Hale, one of the defendants, was asked why he thought the earl had brought the case he replied, 'I merely regarded it as another instance of Lord De La Warr's, or his solicitor's, wish to create trouble in the neighbourhood.'

The underlying cause of the problem, in Tebbutt's opinion, was the high price of straw at the time, because of the huge quantities needed to stable horses in London. The Commoners wished to cut bracken to sell it to farmers of the neighbourhood, who would use it for bedding their own animals so that they could sell their straw in London. The Commoners were mostly poor farmers, who could not live off their farms and needed periodic employment of this sort.

The earl won his case, the judgement saying that the Commoners had only the right to 'take away by the mouth or bite of their cattle, and not to cut or carry away any part of the natural produce of the soil'. But the Court of Appeal reversed the previous judgement, agreeing with Hale that for 60 years he and his predecessors had taken as of right, brakes, fern, heather and litter from the forest.

While this case was proceeding, other Commoners were advised that whatever its result their own rights would not be established. They therefore brought a cross action against the earl, employing the solicitors who had successfully defended Epping Forest against enclosure, asking that the earl be restrained from quarrying on the forest, planting larches and Scots pines and encouraging squatters.

Again a compromise was reached by which the forest was brought under the Commons Act of 1876. A board of Conservators was to manage it, and among other things to allow public access to Crows Nest, Camp Hill, King's Standing, Gill's Lap and other places of interest. So for the first time the Commoners and the Lord of the Manor were not the only parties to have rights in the forest, but the general public was also given its share.

Since then the law governing the management of Ashdown Forest has been revised; firstly in 1937, and more recently, by the Act of 1974. 'I think the new act is a very good one,' says the forest's recently returned Superintendent, holder of the job for the past thirteen years. 'Others think it's a very bad act. "It's our forest and we wish those horrid people would go away," that's the attitude of certain locals.'

The clause of the act which sets out the purposes for which the forest shall be managed reads, 'It shall be the duty of the conservators at all times as far as possible to regulate and manage the forest as an amenity and place of resort subject to the existing rights of common upon the forest and to protect such rights of common, to protect the forest from encroachments and to conserve it as a quiet and natural area of outstanding beauty.'

The problem, in the Superintendent's opinion, is that these aims are not compatible. Conserving the forest as an area of outstanding natural beauty may conflict with the public's right of access and with the rights of the Commoners, not to mention those retained by the Lord of the Manor. The present question of whether or not orienteering should be allowed is typical. He and the Conservators maintain that it is a suitable countryside pursuit, but he admits that it may marginally impinge on the Commoners' sheep and could certainly be said to affect the forest's naturalness and quiet.

In a few months orienteering will be forgotten, but horse riding is a perennial problem. Every horse that rides on the forest does a certain amount of damage to the paths, making them less suitable for the public to walk. But in a smaller way so does every walker do damage. Continually he would ask himself whether he had got the balance right and the recreational benefits were in proportion to the damage.

Motor cycling is forbidden. The flying of model aeroplanes is not. It is the only permitted activity which the Superintendent believes is against the spirit of the act. 'All we can do is confine those buzzing things to an area where they cause least annoyance. We couldn't ban them if we wanted. We had more trouble with that clause of our by-laws than any other. Model aeroplanes have a very powerful lobby.'

The Conservators who employ the Superintendent number sixteen. Eight are appointed by the East Sussex County Council, two by Wealden District Council; five are elected by the Commoners and the sixteenth is the Lord of the Manor or his representative. In theory the local authorities control the forest, but in practice the control they exercise is remote. At present only three of the Conservators are councillors, and as a result their loyalty is to the forest and the Act rather than to the two councils.

The justification for the local authorities' large share of power is that they pay 75 per cent of the £90,000 which it now costs annually. The balance is raised by the forest itself, from such things as the sale of riding permits, charges for wayleaves and fees for the right to sell ice creams. It would charge for car parking if the cost of collection would not exceed the amount collected. The forest also sells Christmas trees, but these are only cut when they would anyway need to be removed. Scots pine and birch both spread like weeds, to the disadvantage of the heather.

All these activities are limited by the Act, which forbids the runnings of the forest as a commercial enterprise. No more than ten acres can be planted with trees in one year and no single planting can be of more than one acre. No part of the forest is managed by the Forestry Commission. To carry out all work on the forest, as well as its administration, the Superintendent has one 'grossly overworked' secretary, book-keeper, radio operator, four rangers and two workmen.

Today's Commoners may mostly live on housing estates at Nutley and commute to Crawley New Town, but they still present problems. When their rights were confirmed in 1887 there were less than 100 of them, but because their rights are connected to holdings of land and these holdings were frequently divided over the next 80 years, by 1965 there were over 1,300 Commoners. In that year all who held rights of this kind throughout the country were obliged to register them, and because many failed to do so the Commoners of Ashdown Forest were reduced to 576. Already since then they have increased again to 660.

Half today's Commoners have holdings of under an acre, and many much smaller. 'You can't honestly claim to be able to overwinter animals in a garden of under an eighth of an acre,' the Superintendent says. 'And most of them aren't the sort of people who want their estovers [wood for burning and repairing their houses]. They've got oil-fired central heating. The one real right left to them is to vote for their five conservators. And to talk.'

In practice they are each allowed a nominal sheep. If they have two acres or more they get ten sheep and two cattle per acre plus one mill horse, but only up to 150 sheep and 30 cattle. 'We have to have a limit. Our biggest Commoner has 530 acres of commonable land and the forest couldn't possibly support 5,300 sheep.'

Cattle are what he would like to see on the forest. They are much better at controlling the vegetation, will tread down bracken and take the tops out of young birch trees which sheep would nibble round. But today there are no cattle, and only one farmer puts out a sizeable number of sheep. Even he may not be able to afford to do so for long. Last year cars killed 40 of them.

The only way to protect them would be to fence the forest, but its complicated shape would make this hopelessly expensive (one cattle grid costs £5,000, and there would have to be many) and the open character of the forest would be spoiled. The real problem, the Superintendent considers, is that farming has changed. 'We don't have the dog and stick farmer any more—not in Sussex.' He doubts whether serious grazing will ever return to the forest.

Though some of the physical evidence of the forest's past has disappeared, much can still be seen. An observant rambler might even now pick up a mesolithic arrow head. More obviously, a section of the great Roman road which began at Lewes and took the products of the Wealden iron industry to London has been exposed near Duddleswell crossroads. It was metalled with bloomery slag and can be traced for some distance as it crosses open country to the north.

Of the Roman industry itself, most evidence today is to be found four miles to the north-west around Garden Hill, which Tebbutt has tentatively identified as its administrative centre in this part of the Weald. There are remains of a villa with a bath house, as well as many other buildings, and the area is littered with bloomeries. In woodland nearby the Wealden Iron Research Group has built its own bloomery, and, using charcoal made in a covered trench, has produced blooms, then hammered them into recognizable lumps of metal.

The road itself, however, ran closer to Fairwarp where the industry was so concentrated that it left seven acres of slag. Much of this was removed for road making in the nineteenth century, and it was during this work that coins were found of the emperors Vespasian (d. AD 69) and Diocletian (AD 286). Slag is a neutral element in which coins survive, while none have been found in the acid soil of the rest of the forest. Traditionally it was possible to walk from Fairwarp across the forest to Nutley without ever leaving the shade of trees, and it was these oak coppices which certainly provided charcoal for the mediaeval furnaces of the area and probably for the Roman bloomeries too.

The slag around Fairwarp gave the nearby entrance to the forest its name: 'Sinderhatch'. All around the forest names ending in 'hatch' or 'gate' indicate its one-time boundaries, from Plawhatch to the west, to Coleman's Hatch to the north to Lampool Gate to the south. The ending 'leap' suggests the position of the Great Park's pale. At a leap the deer could jump into the park but, because of an internal ditch, not jump out. Today's forest boundary still sometimes corresponds with the mediaeval pale, and one of the clearest examples of this can be found near the Goat crossroads—where the Goat public house once stood.

A steep path descends to two typical squatters' enclosures, the first picturesquely called Lavender Platt. A little way to the north, ditch and bank are still clear. At one point the bank is topped with a garden fence which, even if made of different material, gives a good idea of what the park's boundary would have looked like. At another point a sunken way through bank and ditch marks an entrance.

Of evidence of the Saxons use of the forest nothing can now be seen. The one known bloomery was discovered by chance in the path of a waterline being laid across the forest in the upper Millbrook area. During a five-day emergency dig before the bulldozers arrived all was recorded and photographed, and the furnace dated at AD 800-835.

Nor has anything yet been discovered for certain of John of Gaunt's hunting lodge. At one time Chelwood Vatchery was thought the most likely site. Writing in 1902, the Rev. C. N. Sutton, Rector of Withyham, says that its ruins are still to be seen in the woods here. But the Vatchery, as the name implies, was an area for raising cattle, granted to the monks of Michelham Priory in early mediaeval times and Tebbutt believes that a hunting lodge would hardly have been built on a piece of land granted to a religious foundation for agricultural purposes, and that these were ruins of the monks' grange. The site of the associated chapel, where Wycliffe is said to have preached, also remains a mystery. Chapel Wood lies to the south of the Chelwood Gate to Nutley road, but Dr Martin of Chelwood Gate has recently published a suggestion that the chapel is now incorporated into one of the old stone houses on the opposite side.

Names like the Vatchery are reminders that Ashdown Forest, like all mediaeval forests, was never solely reserved for hunting but that all manner of agricultural activities went on within its bounds. Two miles to the east, at the Beeches, there are marlpits on an outlier of the Wadhurst clay where Commoners at one time dug and baked the clay for spreading on their land. Nearby stands Nutley Windmill, now put back into working order by enthusiasts of the Uckfield Preservation Society, and the oldest working mill in Sussex. This post mill is a good example of its type, the vast post on which the whole mill turns exposed to its base and not, as so often, enclosed by the miller's grain store. In 1983 all the teeth of one wheel were renewed. Hornbeam is used for such gear wheel teeth, partly because it is hard, partly because it is

straight-grained and does not chip at the corners. The track to the mill provides fine views to the north-west over countryside which seems to be forest but is in fact largely the disafforested areas of Pippingford Park and Broadstone Warren.

But the forest was certainly much hunted and one of its hilltops, King's Standing, today crowned with a clump of Scots pines planted by the nineteenth century sporting Lord of the Manor, is said to have got its name because Edward II hunted here. Whatever the truth of this legend, there was certainly a Tudor hunting lodge here, similar to Queen Elizabeth's Hunting Lodge at Chingford which still survives in Epping Forest.

In 1972 when forest rangers were making a car park here they unfortunately demolished a bank which contained quantities of Tudor brick and tile. Tebbutt believes that this discovery, together with evidence provided by aerial photographs taken in 1929 showing a number of rectangular enclosures around King's Standing, prove that the lodge existed, though nothing now survives above ground. There is supporting evidence in an account of how the forest was managed, given in 1691 by the son of a forest ranger during the law suits of that period. This old man remembered that the foresters of the different wards of the forest each had enclosures round their lodges for their horses and for feeding their 'call deer'. These were probably semi-domesticated decoys, used to collect others into the enclosures. All would then be driven past the royal hunting party, a form of sport preferred by the Tudors who were less keen on the literal chase than their energetic predecessors.

Several other hilltops are connected by their names or by nearby ruins to the forest's past. The highest, Gill's Lap (671 feet), is a corruption of Gill's leap. It is at its most picturesque in winter when the Old Surrey and Burstow hunt meets here, and has views towards Hartfield of 500 Acre Wood, a conifer plantation edged with birch which now lies outside the forest. Close by, another hilltop is Christopher Robin's 'Enchanted Place'. This part of the forest is Pooh country (A. A. Milne lived near Hartfield) and the bridge where Pooh and Piglet played pooh sticks is a mile to the north over the lower Millbrook.

Another, Castle Camp, acquired its name in the late eighteenth century when a number of regiments camped here. A few years ago when the snow had flattened the bracken it was easy to make out a long line of tumulus-like mounds which in fact were the remains of a standard army kitchen layout. Parallel mounds of earth were built, fires lit between and kettles slung from crossbars.

As for evidence of the forest's fifteenth- and sixteenth-century iron industry, this is most abundant near Newbridge, to the south-west of Hartfield. Here was the furnace which was the first in England to use water-powered bellows. Higher up the stream are extensive remains of the two furnaces in Pippingford Park, one including a gun casting pit. The old hammer pond which powered these forges is clearly defined but now dry.

Place names and archaeological remains apart, the forest is romantically connected with its past by its deer. They have a long history. Red deer were an essential part of mesolithic culture. Mesolithic settlements are usually found below the crests of ridges, at points where the whole valley first comes into view, from which the deer could be observed. This is just one discovery which suggests that they managed as well as hunted their deer.

Fallow deer were introduced to Ashdown Forest by the Normans, as they were to other English forests, and both red and fallow deer were hunted here throughout mediaeval, Tudor and Jacobean times. But it is probably a mistake to think of them as wild forest animals when they were treated more like the roaming stock of a ranch. To quote just one example, in 1539 a survey estimated that there were 300 red deer on the forest of which 50 were male, and 700-800 fallow deer of which 100 were male. These unnatural proportions suggest systematic culling.

In 1641 the forest was still said to be well stocked with red and fallow deer. By 1650 there were only 120 survivors and seven years later all deer were said to have been destroyed and the forest to have been almost entirely dispaled. Certainly at the time of the 1689 law suit the Lord of the Manor could claim that there were no longer any deer to damage the Commoners' farms.

Red deer never returned, and fallow deer for 100 years were rarely seen. Only one witness in the case which began in 1878 claimed to have seen deer. He was then 87 and remembered meeting a pair when he was eleven. One tradition is that the last deer was killed in 1808 by the Hartfield Harriers near Gill's Lap, after a chase of two hours, but a final doe may have been killed 12 years later near Kid's Hill.

Fallow deer

The fallow deer which returned in the early part of this century probably escaped from Buxted Park. Today there are between 300 and 400, though rarely that number on the forest at one time. By habit they spend the day in nearby disafforested (but more wooded) parts and come into the forest to feed at night. They give only modest help in controlling the forest's vegetation. In the Superintendent's experience 'the confounded things eat what you don't want them to', ignoring the ubiquitous birch and taking the tops out of young regenerating beech.

Four hundred are as many as the forest can support. The numbers are kept down by passing cars. Each year the rangers find about 25 dead deer on the roads and calculate that as many again die from injury or leave the forest in car boots. With a million and a half visitors a year it would be unsafe to allow any shooting in the forest, but some are occasionally culled on neighbouring farms.

So far there are no roe deer on the forest, but they are spreading steadily east in their re-colonization of the southern counties of England, and have already reached the woods around Sheffield Park, close to the south.

Beyond the broad principles laid down by the Act of 1974, conservation of the forest is now the central concern of those who manage it, and conserving the fallow deer, its most picturesque wild life, is an important part of this policy. But the deer are not its most interesting creatures. The blackcock, once common, has gone, but the rare Dartford warbler is sometimes seen, and hen harriers are winter visitors. Migrating stonechats, normally seen on coastal heaths, are commoner on Ashdown Forest than on any other inland site in the country.

Among unusual plants, the hairy greenweed (*Genista pilosa*) appears from time to time in various parts of the forest. More important than the forest's rarities is its total heathland ecology, in which a large number of animals, birds, plants and insects, as well as numerous lichens and fungi, together form a self-complementing pattern of wild life.

The first necessity in conserving this ecological pattern is to know more exactly of what species it consists. Left to itself with no interference from man or beast, young oak would be nursed up by the pine and birch so that Ashdown would in the end become an oak forest. In practice this does not happen for several reasons, of which the removal of young pines is only one. Some young trees are destroyed by the Commoners' sheep, others by forest fires. A balance is achieved, and at present no planting is being done, but it has been a haphazard balance.

Recently the forest has been lucky to have a naturalist at work compiling a full description of its wild life. From this the Superintendent will be able to decide that certain areas demand instant attention if they are to be preserved as heathland, others must be left a few years, others, for lack of money and labour, must be abandoned to nature.

So today the forest is being exposed to another systematic influence, alongside and to some extent in competition with Commoner, Lord of the Manor and general public, not to mention iron master of the past and potential oil extractor of the future. The bleak forest as Cobbett saw it may yet be preserved in a country where there are now all too few natural but villainously ugly spots left.

Dartford Warbler

Lime Avenue near Brambridge

FORESTS OF HAMPSHIRE

The New Forest

For 900 years the New Forest has been among the largest and most splendid in England. At its greatest it was bounded to the east and south by Southampton Water and the Solent, and to the west and north by Dorset and Wiltshire. It was some 21 miles in width and nineteen in depth. Gradually, as other forests have diminished or disappeared it has come to seem more remarkable, both as a wild piece of countryside in an increasingly suburban country, and as a reserve for all manner of animals, plants and insects which need its special evironments. But during most of its long history it was also the forest which aroused most anger because of the arbitrary and ruthless way in which William I was said to have created it.

Typically, Henry of Huntingdon wrote in 1135 that 'to form the hunting-ground of the New Forest he caused churches and villages to be destroyed, and, driving out the people, made it a habitation for deer'.

It was not till 650 years later that the historian Richard Warner questioned this sort of suggestion, writing that 'William of Malmesbury, H. Huntingdon, Walter Mapes, and some other prejudiced monkish writers [had] vilified the Norman'. He argued that 'lands comprised in this tract appear, from their low valuation in the time of the Confessor, to have always been unproductive in comparison with other parts of the kingdom'.

In William Cobbett's time the same accusations were still being repeated and the specific suggestion that William destroyed 36 churches gave Cobbett the opportunity for five pages of more than usually fine invective: 'Supposing them to have been so rich in the produce of the soil as to want a priest to be stationed every mile and 200 yards in order to help them eat it; supposing, in a word, these historians not to be the most farcical liars that ever put pen upon paper, this country must at the time of the Norman Conquest, have literally *swarmed* with people.'

Warner and Cobbett were certainly right: much of the land which became the New Forest was so poor that it had never been cultivated. It lies in a shallow basin, surrounded by a ring of low chalk hills. Cranborne Chase and the Wiltshire downs to the west, the Hampshire downs to the north and east, and the hills of the Isle of Wight to the south are surviving parts of this ring. When the basin at their centre was submerged, deposits of clay and sand were washed into it. These were exposed as it rose above the sea, and subsequently covered with gravels created from weathered flint associated with the chalk.

These gravels make up the first of the three distinct surfaces of the forest. Typically they form the splendid moor-like countryside which can be seen along the Cadnam to Downton road, where the forest is at its highest (419 ft), and support birch, gorse, heath, certain hardy grasses and a few self-sown Scots pines. Most botanists agree that 1,000 years ago there would have been no pines, but otherwise the vegetation would have been similar.

Where streams have washed away the gravels they have exposed slopes of well-drained clay and loam. Even this is not ideal agricultural land, but today it supports the oak, beech, yew, holly and thorn of the forest's ancient woods. It also provided the greenish clay used by the Romans for pottery and for bricks at Beaulieu.

Bogs and marshes are the forest's third type of surface. They occur where water penetrates the sands and gravels but cannot escape through the impermeable clay below, and support alder thickets, willow, heath, bracken, sedge, bog-moss and cotton grass.

If William chose for the New Forest land that was on the whole infertile, forest law was here as elsewhere much resented; the whole history of royal forests describes how this resentment gradually forced the king to reduce the size of his forests, modify forest law and substitute fines for imprisonment and mutilation. At first, however, the opposite happened, and William's son Rufus, a man whose face was as red as his hair, extended the royal forests and added to the penalties its courts could impose. It seems a fair guess that his unpopularity was connected with the forest's best-known historical incident.

On 2 August 1100, when Rufus was hunting in the forest, one of his party, Walter Tyrrell, accidentally shot and killed him. That at least was the story accepted at the time and is the story still told by the Rufus Stone which was erected in 1745 and stands where the accident was supposed to have happened.

Here stood the Oak Tree on which an arrow shot by Sir Walter Tyrrell at a stag glanced and struck King William II surnamed Rufus on the breast, of which stroke he instantly died on the second day of August *anno* 1100.

King William II being thus slain was laid on a cart belonging to one Purkess and drawn from hence to Winchester, and buried in the Cathedral Church of that City. That the spot where an event so memorable happened might not hereafter be unknown this Stone was set up by John, Lord Delaware, who has seen the tree growing in this place.

Surrounding events make this none too plausible story seem even less so. There were said, for example, to have been numerous sinister portents. William Rufus himself dreamed the previous night of blood spouting from his chest to hide the sun, and hesitated to hunt next day. Elsewhere in the forest, the Earl of Cornwall met a black goat carrying a naked wounded man who warned him that he was a malevolent spirit, about to procure William's death for his ill treatment of the Church. Tales of this sort can, of course, be explained as inspired hindsight, but they could also have been spread later to suggest that William was the victim of supernatural forces rather than human conspiracy. And though the fact that William's body lay abandoned for a day can be explained by a general panic at what had happened, it could also suggest the flight of conspirators. More significantly, Walter Tyrrell, who fled the country, was never pursued and his English estates never confiscated.

But by far the most suspicious circumstance was that Henry, Rufus's younger brother, became king instead of his older brother, Robert, Duke of Normandy. As Rufus had no children he had agreed that Robert should succeed him, but Robert was conveniently away on a crusade and Henry, who had been one of the hunting party, took the opportunity to ride to Winchester, demanded the keys of the king's treasury, ride on to London, and have himself crowned king just three days after his brother's death. This was quick work, even when coronations were not necessarily ceremonial occasions.

As the truth is never likely to be known, the incident has produced much inspired speculation. Marjorie Triggs suggests that Rufus had been preventing Henry from marrying a young nun named Matilda. Three months after he became king, Matilda was declared by Archbishop Anselm to be no nun and Henry did indeed marry her. A more far-fetched theory suggests that Rufus was a voluntary sacrifice of an ancient fertility cult. Duncan Grinnell-Milne, in *The Killing of William Rufus*, claims to prove that the king's 'chief hunter' was employed by Walter Tyrrell's brother-in-law to fire the shot.

His carefully argued book, complete with diagrams showing the positions of each member of the hunting party, assumes that the killing took place where the Rufus Stone now stands, in Canterton Glen near the northern edge of the forest. It was erected here because tradition named the place of the king's death as Thorougham, which had been identified with Fritham. Unfortunately it has been discovered that Parks Farm on the Beaulieu estate in the south-east corner of the forest was originally called Thorougham.

Here at Beaulieu stood the forest's best-known building, Beaulieu Abbey. It dated from 100 years later, and, since the Reformation, has been only a picturesque ruin, but for 300 years it was the forest's most important religious house. In 1204 King John gave the Cistercian order 10,000 acres of forest land for founding the abbey, because, according to tradition, his ill treatment of some Cistercian abbots had given him terrifying dreams of punishment. By 1538 it had acquired far more extensive property including Beaulieu parish and parts of the Brockenhurst estate, as well as rights of grazing, pannage, turbary and fuel on the forest. Cistercian abbeys specialized in sheep farming and wool processing and at Beaulieu the abbey based its wool production on its forest herds of sheep.

Pope Innocent III gave the abbey right of sanctuary over the whole original estate, and two well-known historical characters took sanctuary at Beaulieu: the Countess of Warwick, after her husband, Warwick 'the King-Maker', had been killed at the battle of Barnet, and the imposter, Perkin Warbeck, after his troops had deserted him at Taunton.

Throughout the Middle Ages the New Forest resembled other royal forests: similar forest officers administered forest law which interfered in similar ways with the rights of forest dwellers. Though the forest remained, and remains today, a huge area, certain outlying parts were gradually disafforested. At first kings came regularly to hunt here, but, as elsewhere, their interest in hunting gradually declined to an interest in the forest's venison and the other financial returns it brought them.

But from the sixteenth century the New Forest's history becomes less typical, and concerned more closely than that of most other forests with its timber. Although only its clay soils ever grew fine hardwood trees, its oaks were much valued because, like those of the Sussex Weald, they grew with spreading tops, so producing types of timber which ship builders needed. They were also valued from the second half of the seventeenth century because they lay close to the revived royal dockyards at Portsmouth, and in the eighteenth century by the forest's own shipyard at Buckler's Hard.

Between 1745 and 1818, 54 warships were built here, including *Agamemnon* (64 guns), *Swiftsure* (74 guns) and *Euryalus* (36 guns), all three of which fought at Trafalgar. *Agamemnon* needed 2,000 mature oaks, and elm and beech for planking as well. Buckler's Hard village has been pre-served, and a maritime museum has a model of the yard in its productive years.

But whether or not trees were first systematically planted in the New Forest is another question. The thirteen acres near Cranbourne Lodge in Windsor Great Park, sown with acorns in 1580, are often described as the earliest English plantation. This may be true, but planting of a sort seems already to have occurred in the New Forest.

The crown had first shown anxiety about timber in 1482, when Edward IV extended the period that coppices could be enclosed after cutting from three years to seven. Henry VIII's Act of 1543 not only made compulsory the enclosing for four years of woods in royal forests but ordered not less than twelve standard trees per acre to be left in all coppices, and these not to be felled till they were ten inches square, within three feet of the ground. They were to be oak if possible, but if not 'elm, ash, aspen or beech'. Fifteen years later many of the New Forest's trees would also have been covered by Elizabeth's statute of 1559 which forbade the use of timber trees, as opposed to coppice wood, for charcoal making for the iron industry if they grew within fourteen miles of the coast or of navigable rivers.

The woodland these and other statutes referred to were mostly by definition coppices with standard trees, regenerat-ing themselves from coppice stools, but it seems that some ancient coppice woods were already in part being treated as plantations. When Roger Taverner, the queen's surveyor, reported on her forests in 1565, he described a number of New Forest woods as 'set' with oak, beech and thorn. If this means what it seems to, such trees had been grown from seed or were young transplants rather than single stools.

The New Forest was surveyed again in 1608 by James I's surveyor, John Norden, who reported on another of the uses for the forest's trees. Holmsley Copse, he said, consisted only of 'holly or Holm' which were all decayed because their bark had been taken to make bird-lime. This glutinous substance, which was spread on branches to trap birds, was prepared by boiling holly bark. Despite such depredations, huge old hollies remain a feature of many parts of the forest. The regular cutting of them by keepers to provide winter feed for the deer was a treatment which encouraged them to live to a great age.

James I took an enlightened attitude to his forests, and the way in which the New Forest was managed during his reign shows an understanding of the two sorts of raw material which all mediaeval woods produced: wood from coppicing or pollarding, and timber from standard trees. The oldest surviving record of a felling of New Forest oak for ship building dates from his reign. In 1611, 1,800 oaks were supplied to the navy. After the Civil War, from 1670 onwards, the navy regularly took 300 oaks and 100 beeches each year. Indeed, the really important change in the New Forest during the rest of this century was the felling of its oaks. John Norden had estimated that there were approximately 200,000 loads of mature oak suitable for the navy in the forest, but a hundred years later, in 1707, there were only about 20,000. By the end of the eighteenth century oak was in such short supply that young timber was sometimes used

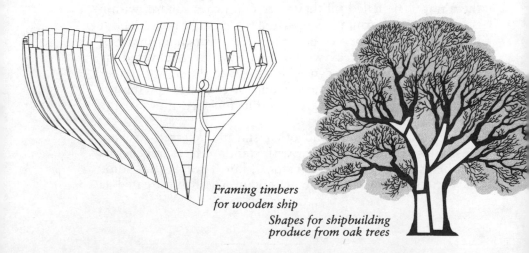

*Framing timbers
for wooden ship*

*Shapes for shipbuilding
produce from oak trees*

(oak must be 100 years old before it is suitable for ship building), and hulls rotted. A notorious example was the *Queen Charlotte*, which lasted only two years from its launch.

In parallel to this decline of mature timber, tree planting became fashionable. One of the earliest publications to recommend it was Anthony Standish's pamphlet of 1613, which was reissued two years later with a royal proclamation by James I asking his subjects to put into practice its 'severall good projects for the increase of Woods'. More influential was the diarist John Evelyn's *Sylva, or a Discourse of Forest Trees and the Propagation of Timber in His Majesty's Dominions,* first published in 1662. An Act of Parliament of 1698 'for the Increase and Preservation of Timber in the New Forest, in the County of Southampton' was in part the result of the tree-planting enthusiasm which such books aroused.

The Act gave the crown the right to enclose 2,000 acres of forest for planting, and for the next 20 years to enclose 200 acres annually, making a total of 6,000 acres. A further right, known as the 'rolling power' of enclosure, became the underlying cause of much future conflict. When the enclosed plantations were large enough to survive grazing, the crown claimed that it could throw them open and replace them with more enclosures, up to a final total of 12,000 acres. At the same time, by taking away the Commoners' rights to coppice or pollard, and forbidding charcoal burning within 1,000 yards of the new enclosures, the Act showed a misunderstanding of traditional wood management.

The crown in fact used only a fraction of the enclosing rights the 1698 Act gave it. Almost 100 years later a mere 3,396 acres had been taken. But the Act remained important because the crown used it to justify enclosures when it had in theory been replaced by later acts.

Early in the eighteenth century a curious development was planned for the forest which Defoe describes in *A Tour through the Whole Island of Great Britain.* He had helped, he says, to draw up a plan for settling 20 families of Palatinate refugees in a rectangular village near Lyndhurst. Each family would be given 200 acres and would easily make a living on the 'undoubtedly good' New Forest soil. The whole scheme, with its confident estimates of returns, has the utopian flavour of urban planning for a misunderstood countryside, and for this reason perhaps, was abandoned.

A far more knowledgeable picture of the forest in the

eighteenth century is the Rev. William Gilpin's. Gilpin was rector of the little village of Boldre in the southern part of the forest for 27 years from 1777 to 1804. His various forest itineraries collect together forest history and legend current in his time, for example the story of the capture of the Duke of Monmouth on 8 July 1685 when trying to reach a Channel port after his defeat at the battle of Sedgmoor. Dressed as a peasant, the duke was found in a ditch near the river Avon, hiding below ferns and nettles.

Gilpin gives vivid pictures of the forest's animals, including cattle the Duke of Bolton had brought from Scotland which had run wild and could not be captured. His account of the way in which the Commoners exercised their right of pannage (he spells it pawnage) gives life to this dusty mediaeval term. A swineherd would collect 500-600 pigs from different farms to take them to the forest for the autumn pannage weeks and would then have the problem of 'reducing a large herd of these unmanageable brutes to perfect obedience and good government'. This he did by erecting an enclosure below a large oak and accustoming them to being fed there.

The next morning he lets them look a little around them—shows them the pool, or stream, where they may occasionally drink —leaves them to pick up the offals of the last night's meal—and, as evening draws on, gives them another plentiful repast under the neighbouring trees, which rain acorns upon them for an hour together at the sound of his horn. He then sends them again to sleep.

The following day he is perhaps at the pains of procuring them another meal, with music playing as usual. He then leaves them a little more to themselves, having an eye, however, on their evening hours. But as their bellies are full, they seldom wander far from home, retiring commonly very orderly and early to bed.

Besides domestic pigs, the forest had a strange half-wild breed, probably a cross between German wild boar introduced by Charles I and domestic pigs.

Gilpin accounts for the forest's lack of young trees by its rabbits 'which breed in the dry sandy hills . . . and which it is difficult, amidst such shelter, to extirpate'. Like other eighteenth-century writers, he confirms that the forest had been plundered of mature trees. 'In all the grand scenery of the forest, which we have just examined, we see little appearance of fine timber. Most of the best trees have been felled . . . Many of the oaks are scathed and ragged.' He confirms, too, the special usefulness of New Forest oaks which 'seldom rise into lofty stems, as oaks usually do in richer soils: but their branches, which are more adapted to what the ship builders call knees and elbows, are commonly twisted into the most picturesque forms'.

For the vegetation of the forest, the most significant event of the eighteenth century was the re-introduction of the Scots pine. Scots pines arrived in Britain soon after the retreat of the ice, about 8,300-8,200 BC, but became extinct in England in neolithic times. Once brought back from Scotland they flourished in the New Forest, as on so many sandy soils of the south. 1776 is often given as the date of their re-introduction; Ocknell Clump and Bolderwood were planted in that year. But there were plantations on private land in the forest nine years earlier at Barnfield near Ringwood, and nineteen years earlier at Bisterne. When, in 1786, the government appointed a royal commission to report on the country's forests, their report on the New Forest strongly recommended pine and larch.

By 1830, after a further Act of Parliament in 1808, these were being planted in quantity. This was the year of one of Cobbett's visits and he describes planting methods of the time.

It was, indeed, a plantation of Scots firs, about twelve years old, in rows six feet apart. Every third row of firs was left, and oaks were (about six years ago) planted instead of the firs that were grubbed up; and the winter shelter that the oaks have received from the remaining firs has made them grow very finely, though the land is poor. Other oaks planted in the *open, twenty years* ago, and the land deemed better, are not nearly so good.

The merits of the locust tree *(Robinia pseudoararia)* was one of Cobbett's obsessions, and the New Forest plantations give him the chance to say that had locusts been planted they would already be worth £50 an acre, while the oaks were still worth nothing.

His general view of the forest was that it was managed by the Office of Woods with deplorable wastefulness. 'This New Forest is a piece of property as much belonging to *the public* as the Custom House at London is . . . never will it grow trees, or anything else *to the profit of this nation* until it becomes *private property*.' Robert Mudie in 1838 described another aspect of its decline: its illegal squatters.

These encroachments are, generally speaking, persons of very questionable character, who live most wretched abandoned lives, and procure much of their miserable subsistence by plunder; while they are ready to enter with eagerness upon any smuggling or plundering expedition to which there may be the slightest temptation. [They established their places in the forest] by means of hovels, the parts of which were prepared in other places, and brought to the forest and erected in the course of a single night. When once the hovel was erected, and a fire kindled, the keepers could not eject the tenant without the formality of a legal process.

Smuggling was certainly common in the forest in the eighteenth and nineteenth centuries. Defoe found that Lymington had no foreign commerce, 'except it be what we call smuggling, and roguing; which, I may say, is the reigning commerce of all this part of the English coast'. A hundred years later, in 1830, Richard Warner described a smuggling party he had met in the forest:

I have myself seen a procession of twenty or thirty waggons loaded with kegs of spirits; an armed man sitting at the front and tail of each; and surrounded by a troop of two or three hundred horsemen, every one carrying on his enormous saddle from two to four tubs of spirits; winding deliberately and with the most picturesque and imposing effect along the skirts of Hengistbury Head on their way towards the wild country north-west of Christchurch.

The Lymington and Beaulieu rivers were obvious entrances to the remote forest inlands, but the convoy Warner describes was circling the extreme south-west corner of the forest and had probably collected its cargo at the small gorge of Chewton Bunny, three miles to the east. From the Bunny goods would also be taken north to the Cat and Fiddle at Hinton or the Queen's Head at Burley, then onwards to Ringwood, Fordingbridge and Salisbury. The forest provided excellent cover for smugglers and there is still supposed to be an underground cellar full of contraband to be found near Picket Post. Smuggling was a capital offence, and smugglers are supposed to have been hanged on Naked Man Tree, once a fine oak, the ruins of which survive near Wilverley Post.

General dissatisfaction with the condition of the forest led to two parliamentary reports in 1848 and 1849, both of which favoured disafforestation. The following years were those in which the New Forest came closest to extinction. They were years when forests all over the country were in danger, when the Commons Preservation Society defended them, when Wychwood in Oxfordshire, for example, was lost, but Epping and Ashdown were in different ways saved.

In the New Forest it was not disafforestation which the act that followed these particular parliamentary reports ordered, but the removal of the forest's deer. About the deer, the crown claimed, it and the Commoners were agreed. They damaged the Commoners' crops and depleted the forest grazing for cattle. In fact evidence given to the 1848-49 select committees by no means entirely favoured removing the deer. As for the crown itself, it calculated that each of the 120 bucks killed annually cost it £100 in compensation, a price far exceeding their value. For good measure the crown claimed that the deer demoralized the local population by tempting it to poach. But even if the Commoners and crown had been agreed about the deer, the Act allowed the crown, in compensation for their removal, to enclose a further 10,000 acres.

The Commoners had good reason to feel aggrieved that the crown was compensating itself so generously for a right which it also claimed was a costly and unwanted one. Furthermore, the Bill had been produced in a great hurry and objectors had had little chance to put their case. They had been able to have the crown's compensation reduced from 14,000 acres to 10,000, and to obtain the inclusion of a clause which forbade it to enclose parcels of land of less than

300 acres—this to prevent it taking the best land from all over the forest—but that was all.

Strong protests followed, some because the Act specifically allowed the planting of other species than oak. As a result pine was now to be used not only as a nurse tree, but to establish whole conifer plantations. There was also a change in the way mixed plantations were managed. Now the pines were either to be cut out later or not at all, with the result that, on poor soil, instead of nursing the oaks they would suppress them. But the Commoners' more serious objection was to the whole principle of enclosure.

Elsewhere in the country Commoners were often divided, the smaller ones against enclosure because they lost valuable common rights, the larger in favour because they wanted to enclose their own lands inside the forest. The big landowners of the New Forest area, however, owned little property in the forest and so stood to gain less, while the common rights which went with the farms of their tenants allowed them to let these at higher rents.

Commoners large and small objected in particular to the authoritarian way in which the Office of Woods made its enclosures. The final provocation came in 1866 when, at one sitting, it agreed to the enclosure of 7,650 acres without any Commoner being informed. From this time there was organized opposition to the Act and to the way in which it was being operated. The Commoners maintained that the provision that no blocks smaller than 300 acres should be enclosed was being ignored, that new plantations were blocking traditional rights of way across the forest so that it was a long and difficult business for animals to reach their grazing grounds, and above all that the crown was still exercising its rolling power of enclosure granted by the 1698 Act. If this continued the whole forest would eventually be enclosed and the Commoners left with no grazing.

They dismissed the argument that they were in part compensated by grazing in plantations which, after a number of years, were re-opened. These were too thick to provide worthwhile grazing below the trees. As for the claim that there would be more grazing for their animals now the deer were being removed, this was proving worse than false. Heather, scrub and furze which the deer had previously eaten in winter were now spreading across the forest's grassy lawns.

The forest's future was still undecided in 1870 when both a

parliamentary committee and the Commoners prepared rival bills. Neither was passed, and Parliament ordered instead that all enclosure and all cutting of old trees be suspended till the future of the forest could be properly settled. Six years later this was what the Act of 1877 effectively did. By this Act the Crown gave up its rolling powers of enclosure, agreed to limit the area it enclosed to 16,000 acres and agreed to register and confirm all Commoners' rights on the forest.

The most valuable of these had always been the right to grazing, known as Common of Pasture. Originally the deer in the New Forest had not only had priority during the midsummer fence month but also during the so-called winter heyning. For some years this restriction continued to be disputed although in theory the deer had gone, but today's Commoners may graze the forest the whole year. Some 350 exercise this right, though many more could if they wished. Of the 5,000 animals they keep on the forest about two-thirds are ponies.

For the visitor the New Forest's ponies are its most picturesque feature, wandering at liberty down village streets and turning it more effectively than trees or deer into a separate world. Professionals, however, consider them to be the least pure of the native breeds, more effectively interfered with by government than other breeds because the New Forest was nearer to London.

At first this interference took the form of trying to breed larger, more horse-like animals, for war. As late as 1765 a thoroughbred stallion named Masque, belonging to the Duke of York, was put into the forest in an attempt to breed for the army. But long before this James I is said to have had a New Forest pony for his children, and in the nineteenth and twentieth centuries Welsh and polo pony stallions were introduced with the aim of producing riding ponies. For eight years from 1852 Queen Victoria loaned her Arab stallion, Zora. The forest guide reports confidently that he was not well patronized, but the fact remains that today's New Forest pony differs in an important way from his ancestors: he has the soft palate of an Arab and as a result is unable or unwilling to eat gorse. After the 1976 drought when there was little other winter feed, ponies were seen dying of starvation next to gorse bushes which they would not touch. Since 1938 the New Forest Pony Society has forbidden outside blood in registered ponies.

The forest ponies can be seen in quantity when they are

Charcoal burner's hut

rounded up in periodic 'drifts', but individuals can be as hard to catch as they were in William Gilpin's time. 'The colts which feed on Ober Green,' he wrote, 'are sometimes taken by the following strategem. In this part runs a long bog, described under the name of Longslade Bottom, which is crossed by a mole thrown over it. With this passage the colt is well acquainted; and, on being pursued, is easily driven towards it. When he is about the middle of the mole, two or three men start up in front, and oblige him to leap into the bog, where he is entangled and seized'.

Besides his grazing rights, the New Forest Commoner retains three other rights, though he uses them less today: the right of pannage, called in the New Forest Common of Mast, once fixed for the period 25 September to 22 November, but now varied according to the acorn fall; the right to cut peat for burning, known as Common of Turbary; and the right to make marl from forest clay for garden dressing, known as Common of Marl. In addition about 80 Commoners have a right to firewood known as Estovers, or Assignment Wood. The wood they get is not dead or fallen, as in other forests, but consists of oak and beech thinnings cut and stacked for them by the Forestry Commission.

The 1877 Act also resurrected the ancient forest Court of Verderers or swainmote. Like all royal forests, the New Forest had had from early times its three forest courts —woodmote, swainmote and visiting high court or forest eyre. At Lyndhurst in 1669 and 1670 Charles II tried to revive the forest eyre, but it was already moribund and never met again. As a result the middle court or swainmote, at which the verderers sat as judges, was left without its high court to which to refer cases. Although it had had its powers increased in 1698 and again in 1800, it had in effect sunk into a kind of limbo.

The resurrected swainmote, now officially the Court of Verderers, who from this time included a number elected by the Commoners, in theory remains the crown's representative judicial body on the forest. It meets every two months at its ancient court house in Lyndhurst, where it has the powers of a petty session. But it also now has administrative functions. It appoints agisters (the other mediaeval forest officers to survive) who have responsibility for the Commoners' animals on the forest, and it raises money by charging the Commoners for grazing. In practice, because half its members are Commoners, it has come to represent the Commoners' interest in the forest.

The 1877 Act left the crown's Office of Woods in charge of the forest enclosures. Most of the history of the forest over the last 100 years consists of conflicts between the new verderers and the Office of Woods, succeeded in 1923 by the Forestry Commission.

One result of these conflicts was a new Act in 1949 which, although it left intact the main principles of the 1877 Act, made important changes. To understand the 1949 Act the differences between the forest's three kinds of land must be understood. First there are the Inclosures, managed by the Forestry Commission. Second, there is the open waste of the forest, also managed by the Forestry Commission but only by agreement with the verderers. Third, there are the so-called Ancient and Ornamental Woodlands (A and Os, in the local jargon) which by the 1877 Act were to remain, apparently unaided, in the condition their name implies, an idea which any forester would consider absurd. In 1949 the Forestry Commission was finally given permission to manage these too.

Another Act followed in 1964. This can best be seen as a response to the motor car which was killing and injuring more and more of the Commoners' animals. It allowed the fencing of the forest's major roads, and by adjusting the forest bounds (the only Act specifically to do this) made possible the enclosing of the whole forest with cattle grids.

In one way the Act of 1877 differed from others which, in the second half of the nineteenth century, preserved some

English forests: it gave the public no right of access. But during the following years the public came to camp and picnic in such numbers that the Forestry Commission eventually decided that it must allow it controlled access. In 1968 ecologists, Commoners, landscapers and foresters were asked to report on which areas they considered essential to their interests.

Taken together their replies left no possible area for recreation, and they were sent away to reduce their needs by ten per cent. From this, gradually over the last fifteen years, enough space has been found for camping and car parking in the forest. The Deputy Surveyor of the New Forest during this time believed that his principle concern was 'putting recreation in its right place on the forest and not letting it ruin the rest'. Considering that over six million visitors come to the forest each year its survival is a compliment to him.

Finally, in 1971, a Mandate presented to the Court of Verderers embodied an important new principle in the management of the forest. The Inclosures as well as the Ancient and Ornamental Woodlands were to be managed 'with greater emphasis on visual amenity' and 'felling limited to single trees or small groups'.

This provision goes to the heart of what remains the central controversy: the way in which the Forestry Commission manages the forest's Inclosures. Nothing was done to solve this controversy by a key phrase of the 1877 Act which the Deputy Surveyor considers to have crept into a clause about plantations when it was meant to apply to the A and Os: 'Care should be taken not wholly to clear or level the woods.'

'What is clear felling?' he asks. 'If we cut down four trees next to each other, is that clear felling?'

From its establishment in 1079 the New Forest's deer have been its best-known wild life, and, rabbits apart, they are still the wild animals most easily seen. Native red deer and fallow deer introduced by the Normans were valued for hunting, but English kings came less often to hunt here than to such more convenient forests as Essex and Windsor, and in later centuries would instead send their huntsmen to kill and bring back deer, or order deer to be sent by the forest's lord warden.

In the seventeenth century the deer had become numerous. If a count of 1670 can be trusted there were 7,593 fallow and 357 red. Between Lyndhurst and Brockenhurst Charles II established a new deer park—its pale can still be seen—for the reception of 'a particular breed of red deer from France'.

The Deer Removal Act of 1851 was never entirely effective. As soon as deer were taken from the forest, others spread back from neighbouring woodlands. Today there are not only about 33 red deer and 600 fallow but 60 sitka —these probably escapes from Beaulieu and living in the south-east corner—and 450 of the small and less-easily seen roe deer. They are culled to keep them to these numbers which are the most the forest can allow without causing unacceptable damage.

Deer find the New Forest an ideal environment, with woods in which to shelter during the day, and open land on which the fallow graze at night. But they damage trees as well as crops, eating out their tops when they are young, and in the rutting season when the bucks and stags need to shed the velvet covering of new antlers, killing them by fraying their bark.

Many other mammals live in the New Forest—eleven out of the twelve British bats have been recorded. There is a similar abundance of birds, plants and insects including such rarities as the New Forest cicada and the wild gladiolus. The New Forest is important for its rarities, but more so for the wide range of species it supports, and for the size and extent of its ecological system in which all play a part. In the words of Colin Tubbs, author of *The New Forest: An Ecological Study*, 'The forest woods are the finest relics of relatively undisturbed deciduous forest in Britain and probably in the lowlands of western Europe.'

They are important because their trees are of different ages, some young, some mature, many senile or dying. Such trees support large numbers of insects and their insects support birds. The forest's size and distance from intensive farming gives it another advantage: it is comparatively free from toxic chemicals. And because game is not reared on the forest it has no game keepers. For these reasons it has large numbers of predatory birds—buzzards, kestrels, sparrowhawks and tawny owls.

Today industry and the ubiquitous car with its noise, fumes, campers and picnickers press in on the New Forest, but it remains the country's finest and most interesting forest.

Bere, Alice Holt and Woolmer

Of the three other important forests of Hampshire, the Forest of Bere, parts of which were called Porchester Forest, has largely disappeared. It lay about eight miles north of Portsmouth, and as late as 1688 extended to 16,000 acres, but by 1792 the parliamentary commissioners reported that the crown was neglecting its woods and large private encroachments were being made. They strongly recommended disafforestation.

A few woodlands from the old forest do, however, survive, and these include the Forestry Commission's 900-acre West Walk, near the small town of Wickham. After the Restoration there were early plantings of oak here, but all had been felled by the mid-eighteenth century, many of them probably when immature. The large oaks growing at West Walk today were planted in the 1860s. There are also well-grown beech trees, and conifers planted in the 1960s. This small forest has picturesque grassy glades, sensational bluebell carpets in early summer and fine views over the Meon Valley.

The chase of Bishop's Waltham, belonging to the bishops of Winchester, was practically an outlying part of the Forest of Bere. Here the notorious poaching gang known as the Waltham Blacks operated. In 1742, twenty years after the 'Black Act' had been passed to suppress them, Bishop Hoadly of Winchester declined to restock the chase with deer, saying that they had 'done mischief enough already'. The chase was enclosed in 1870.

The other two forests, Alice Holt (originally Aelfsige's Holt, after a tenth-century Bishop of Winchester) and Woolmer, lie between Farnham, Alton and Haselmere, on the Surrey/Sussex borders, so close to each other that they were usually considered one and managed by a single lord warden.

Alice Holt was an important supplier of timber for the navy. In 1633, 1,200 oaks were taken to Hamshaw near Chertsey for building *Warspit*. In the 1770s many more began to be supplied. They were taken overland ten miles to Godalming, and then down the river Wey to the Thames and its dockyards. If the trees reached their destination, their branches sometimes did not. Gilbert White, the naturalist, who lived nearby at Selborne, reported in 1784 'a very large fall of timber, consisting of about 1,000 oaks, has been cut this spring in the Holt forest; one-fifth of which, it is said, belongs to the grantee, Lord Stawell. He lays claim also to the lop and top: but the poor of the parishes of Binsted and Frinsham, Bentley and Kingsley, assert that it belongs to them; and, assembling in a riotous manner, have actually taken it all away. One man, who keeps a team, has carried home, for his share, forty stacks of wood. Forty-five of these people his lordship has served with actions'.

White contrasts the two forests. Alice Holt consisted of 'strong loam, of a miry nature, carrying a good turf, and abounding with oaks that grow to be large timber', but Woolmer consisted 'entirely of sand covered with heath and fern . . . without having one standing tree in the whole extent'. Nevertheless, Queen Anne had agreed to visit it. On her way to Portsmouth 'she came out of the great road at Liphook . . . and reposing herself on a bank smoothed for that purpose, lying about half a mile to the west of Woolmer pond, and still called Queen's-bank, saw with great complacency and satisfaction the whole herd of red deer brought by the keepers along the vale before her, consisting of about 500 head'.

The keeper's great grandson, who told White this story, added:

. . . by means of the Waltham Blacks, or, to use his own expression, as soon as they began *blacking,* they were reduced to about fifty head, and so continually decreased till the time of the late Duke of Cumberland. It is now more than 30 years ago that his highness sent down a huntsman, and six yeoman-prickers, in scarlet jackets laced with gold, attended by the stag-hounds; ordering them to take every deer in this forest alive, and convey them in carts to Windsor. In the course of the summer they caught every stag, some of which showed extraordinary diversion; but, in the following winter, when the hinds were also carried off, such fine chases were exhibited as served the country people for matter of talk and wonder for years afterwards. I saw myself one of the yeoman-prickers single out a stag from the herd, and must confess that it was the most curious feat of activity I ever beheld, superior to anything in Mr Astley's riding-school.

Alice Holt Forest had no red deer but a fallow herd. White observed that although there was no pale to separate them, the two herds never mixed or strayed into each other's territory. In 1830 the fallow followed the red to Windsor. But deer can still be seen on the forest, and in the 1960s there was a dramatic increase of roe deer, part of their recolonization of the south of England. They are now kept to about 120.

After the Napoleonic Wars, between 1815 and 1825, 1,600 acres of Alice Holt Forest were enclosed and planted with oak. Many of these were felled in the First World War, but some can still be seen in Goose Green Wood, and the Forestry Commission, which took over its management in 1923, is committed to maintaining oak woods among their plantations of Scots pine, Corsican pine, Norway spruce, western red cedar and western hemlock. As for Woolmer Forest, this is now an army live-ammunition range and best avoided.

FORESTS
OF WILTSHIRE
AND DORSET

There were nine royal forests in Wiltshire. To the north and separated from the others was Braydon (also spelled Braden), a large area of wild country near Cricklade. In the centre were **Melksham** and **Pewsham,** later treated as one. Melksham was between Chippenham and Devises; Pewsham lay south of Chippenham, and was also known as Chippenham Forest. In the south-west was **Selwood,** which extended into Somerset and Dorset. In the east a line of forests started with Savernake near Marlborough, and continued south with **Chute, Clarendon, Grovely** and **Melchet,** the last of these adjoining the New Forest. At times in the twelfth century it would have been possible to travel from Marlborough to Bournemouth never leaving royal forest.

Most of these forests have interesting histories. Clarendon, for example, in 1606 became the sole property of William, Earl of Pembroke, with 'the whole of the offices of keeper, warden, lieutenant and bailiff of the forest with the appointment of all foresters, ranger, launders, palers and stewards of courts of swainmote'. J. Charles Cox continues: 'By this comprehensive patent the earl obtained the most absolute control that probably any one subject ever possessed over a royal forest.' Portions of them survive as woodland, but it is only at Savernake that a large coherent area is still known as a forest, still is largely wooded and still retains in its warden a symbol of its one-time forest organization.

Savernake

There are other reasons for finding Savernake the most interesting Wiltshire forest. It stands beside an old road to the west, known as the King's Way, now in part the A4, and was particularly valued by English Kings as a stopping place. And two of its wardens (and one of their daughters) were nationally important figures. But most remarkably, from the time it was first established in about 1067 until today it has had a continuous line of 30 hereditary wardens. True, the succession three times passed through the female line, and on occasions when the warden was either a minor, inefficient or out of royal favour he was displaced. But the position has always returned to the family and the present Marquess of Ailesbury is a direct descendant of the Richard Esturmy to whom William I originally granted the forest. As a result, when the late Lord Ailesbury moved in 1946 from Tottenham House he found a unique collection of manuscripts which made Savernake probably the best-documented forest in the country.

Savernake is interesting for yet another reason: its early history and institutions are so typical that it can be seen as something of a norm for royal forests. Like many, it was at first of modest size and did not swell to its greatest size till King John's reign.

Just when the additions were made is uncertain; some perhaps by Henry I and some by Henry II, after the confusion of Stephen's reign. Certainly the perambulations ordered by Henry II in 1175 show it to have been enormously increased, and by the time John had added an area north of the King's Way towards Ramsbury, it covered 100 square miles. Its bounds then ran roughly from Marlborough east to Ramsbury and Hungerford, south to Inkpen and Vernham Dean, west to Collingbourne, Easton and Pewsey, north to East Kennet near Avebury, and east to Marlborough again.

Much of the extended forest might well have been lost in 1217 when Henry III agreed in the Forest Charter to reduce all forests to their size in 1154 at the start of his grandfather's reign. But typically at Savernake, as a result of royal procrastination, it was thirteen years before even the additions of King John were abandoned.

Three-quarters of a century later in 1300, when Edward I agreed to new forest perambulations in return for tax revenue, Savernake, like other forests, was again perambulated, but again it was reprieved when the king refused to confirm his promises. Fresh bounds for Savernake were only finally agreed after the accession of the young King Edward III in 1327. The new perambulation of 1330 not only left no forest north of the King's Way, but reduced it to the east and west to about half its previous extent, and removed large portions to the south, leaving three isolated forest areas at Broyle, Southgrove and Hippenscombe. There were other changes to come but the great disafforestation of 1330 was by far the most important in Savernake's mediaeval period.

Its forest organization was equally typical. The king granted it to the warden in return for service, which consisted, at Savernake, of administering the forest and providing one mounted man to serve 'within the seas' at any time the king required. Second to the warden was the lieutenant of the forest, usually managing it for the warden. In control of the different bailiwicks were foresters-of-fee, a position which was much valued, and which those who held it were anxious to make hereditary, often against the warden's wishes. In the 1330s, when de Bilkemore claimed the inheritance of the forestership of the West Bailiwick from his father-in-law, and the warden, Henry Esturmy, opposed him, their quarrel led to petitions to Westminster from both parties, as well as from the Commoners of the forest, and to pitch battles between their respective supporters.

Savernake also had its verderers, woodwards, regarders and ranger, and its three tiers of forest court—woodmote and swainmote, each meeting several times a year, and high court or forest eyre, meeting far less regularly, presided over by a visiting justice. The records of its courts show that in its early centuries it was typically troubled by poaching. Examples could be found in almost any period from the twelfth century to the late fifteenth. Many of the offenders were of no rank or distinction, but at the time of the quarrel about the forestership of the West Bailiwick, the poachers were not only of good family but related to the warden.

They further say that John Sturmy (and others) came into the forest . . . at the hour of twilight at a certain place called Hawkridge in a coppice, and there under cover of night set four and twenty nets for the taking of fallow deer, and with the said nets took one beast and carried it whither they would; but the said John had the numbles [probably the back and loin] of the same, which he sent to his house at Tytcumb.

And thereafter the said four and twenty nets and one great net were found at the houses of Maud Topper, Christina Topper and Edith le Whyte, which nets were deposited at the houses of the said women by the hand of John Sturmi . . .

At the Marlborough eyre of 1380 a sporting parson and his chaplain were accused:

Further they say that Richard, the Vicar of Preschuyte, took a doe with his greyhounds at le Polke Slade within the forest, on the

Monday next after the ending of Lent ... And that Thomas Wytteneye, chaplain to the said Vicar of Preschuyt, took a doe at Crendon with a bow and arrow on the Tuesday of Pentecost week ... And they say that Richard, the Vicar of Perschuyt, took a doe at Cadecroft on the 40th day of Trinity ... And they say that the flesh of the said does was carried away to the house of the said Vicar.

One hundred years later many of the cases were against such local gentry as 'John Wroughton Esquier, Sir Edward Darell knyght, and Sir Cristofre Wroughton', usually coupled with their servants. At this time the Wroughton family, infuriated at being denied the right to hunt in the forest, took 60 ruffians to Marlborough and broke into the Priory of St Margaret where they believed the warden, John Seymour, and his brother were dining, with the intention of hewing them 'as small as fleshe to the potte'. But the Seymours were not there, and John survived to die in office in 1491, when he was succeeded as warden by the third John Seymour.

The first person of national importance to be involved with Savernake was Hugh de Neville. In John's reign, when Henry Esturmy, the warden, had fallen out of favour with the king, de Neville was ordered to manage Savernake in his place. At this time de Neville was constable of Marlborough Castle, but he was soon promoted to be chief forester of all royal forests, in which position he was possibly the most powerful royal official in the country. In 1226, when Savernake was returned to Henry's son Geoffrey Esturmy, de Neville made a special report on the condition of the forest, suggesting that he had kept an interest in Savernake and intended to watch how Geoffrey managed it.

From the succession of the third John Seymour (known as 'John the Worthy') in 1491, Savernake's history becomes less typical, as a direct result of its wardens becoming more dramatically involved with the affairs of the nation. John Seymour was well liked by Henry VIII, who stayed three times at Savernake. His daughter, Jane, became lady-in-waiting to Henry's first two queens, Katherine of Aragon and Anne Boleyn. The day after Anne Boleyn was executed Henry married Jane.

She died giving birth to the child who became Edward VI. When Edward succeeded Henry in 1543, Jane's brother, Edward Seymour, became a member of the regency council, then Protector of the Realm. In this position he accumulated

land and titles, including the absolute ownership of Savernake Forest. In the Le Broyle Bailiwick he began to build a
vast mansion to replace the modest manor of Wolfhall where
the family had lived till now. Two million bricks were made
at the nearby Dodsdown brickworks. A channel, dug to bring
water to the site, can still be traced.

But Edward Seymour (who had taken the title of Duke of
Somerset) fell from power as quickly as he had risen, and in
1552 was executed on Tower Hill. The Le Broyle woods were
granted to the Earl of Pembroke, the bricks were removed
and the great house never built.

The wardens of Savernake never again became so involved
in politics, though two more spent periods in the tower: the
Earl of Hertford, Somerset's son, at the start of Elizabeth's
reign, and, in 1696, the Earl of Ailesbury, a loyal Jacobite
who, when released, exiled himself to Brussels rather than
live under William of Orange.

More serious for the forest were the financial losses which
the family suffered during the Civil War, and again, 200
years later between 1886 and 1894, during the wardenship of
the extravagent third Marquess of Ailesbury. Fortunately
there were other wardens who protected it. First of these was
the same Earl of Hertford who had been imprisoned by
Elizabeth. He moved the family residence from Wolfhall to a
new house at Tottenham Lodge, and created new deer parks.
Small parks already existed, including one at Tottenham. He
now impaled two much larger ones, the Great Park and
Brimslade Park, which together made up all the forest land to
the west of the Marlborough-Salisbury road.

It seems a fair guess that part of the purpose of these parks
was to control poaching. Poachers who would operate in an
open forest seem to have been less willing to cross a ditch and
six-foot pale. Certainly the records of the forest courts during
his wardenship are in marked contrast to those at the end of
the fifteenth century: poaching is scarcely mentioned and
cases typically concern illegal wood cutting or grazing.

These courts were themselves remarkable. Now that Savernake was private property no forest eyre visited it to try
serious cases and confirm sentences. When other forests, for
example the New Forest, lost their visiting eyres, their middle
courts or swainmotes steadily declined in effectiveness, but
Savernake's continued to operate and apparently to com-
mand respect.

The new parks lasted less than a century. After the family's impoverishment during the Civil War they were steadily sold, and they soon became the farm land which they remain today. Hertford's Elizabethan house was lost, probably burned down in the 1670s, and around 1685 its park was also abolished.

As for Savernake's woodlands, these had always included a number of coppice woods, harvested periodically for wood, but by the late seventeenth century productive woods were already being equated with timber-producing woods, and a visiting Admiralty official 'wondered to see so much Timber suffered to decay for want of cutting, and upon a very strict view of the whole could finde but three or four trees fitt for his use'.

It was not till the eighteenth century that Thomas Brudenell (later Earl of Ailesbury) who had inherited Savernake at the age of seventeen from his uncle, transformed the forest, planting the many beeches and oaks which still survive as ancient but splendid trees. Most impressively, he completed planting the beeches of the Grand Avenue, the three-and-a-half mile drive which begins close to Tottenham House and runs the whole length of the forest as far as the King's Way. His period as warden overlapped with Lancelot Brown's 32 years as the leading landscape gardener in the country, and Brown inevitably came to Savernake, where the local agent reported him justifying his name. 'He speaks much in commendation of shady rides, as so frequently agreeable both in summer and winter, a fence both against heat and cold ... Mr Brown thinks there is great Capability about the Loggia and Octogon Buildings ...'

Brown suggested that there should be 'Improvements in the *Forest* so as to make it one *great whole*', and a result was the pattern of intersecting rides—surprisingly geometrical for the period—which still cross it. Behind these, filling the open spaces between the coppices, Brudenell planted large numbers of oaks. Towards the end of his time he erected the monument on Three Oak Hill. It was a memorial to George III who had granted him his earldom.

In 1814 a nineteenth-century warden, the first Marquess of Ailesbury, succeeded, with ideas of the proper style in which a marquess should live. These included enclosing the whole surviving forest with a new sixteen-mile pale, but never planting any new trees. In the late eighteenth century there were said to be no trees at Savernake between the ages of 30 and 300 years. When the first marquess died in 1856 a new gap of 40 years had developed.

As a private forest Savernake never fully recovered from the extravagances of the fourth marquess. This young man, who had been brought up by his grandparents and was known to them as 'dear Willie', had already at the age of 21 accumulated debts of £175,000. To pay these the family estates in Yorkshire were sold, but only on condition that William agreed to extend the entail on Savernake so that he would be prevented, when he inherited it, from selling this too.

But his way of life remained the same. 'Drink and bad company ruined my cousin,' the sixth marquess wrote. 'He would have vigorously denied being a snob but he *was* a snob because he chose deliberately to mix with blackguards having found that in that class alone was he treated with deference.' Compulsive betting was a more serious defect. He once lost a bet that he could recite the Lord's Prayer. Almost his only success was his marriage to a variety hall actress, Dolly Tester, who was considered by the family a better girl than he deserved.

By the time he had been warden for five years he again owed money lenders £230,000, and brought an action against the trustees of Savernake to compel them to accept an offer for the estate of £750,000 from Sir Edward Guinness. His uncle Henry, one of the trustees, violently opposed the sale but after four law suits, including an appeal to the House of Lords, William won his case. Savernake was only saved to the family because Sir Edward Guinness, who had waited five years for his new estate, withdrew his offer.

William, in frustration, planned now to raise funds by felling Savernake's timber, remarking, 'I'll make those damned squirrels jump further.' But before he was able to he died, at the age of 30.

Uncle Henry, who succeeded him as fifth marquess, lived simply and laboured to revive the forest. Before he died in

Vanity Fair cartoon of William, Marquess of Ailesbury

1911 he calculated that he had planted three quarters of a million trees. But by the 1930s the sixth marquess concluded that he could no longer afford to invest the money in Savernake which would make it commercially rewarding, and in 1939 he leased its woodlands to the Forestry Commission for 999 years.

In negotiating this lease the deer were a problem. The marquess feared that, in a commercial forest, they would have to be exterminated. Eventually it was agreed that they should be confined to a park. The deer of Savernake proved no easier to drive than those of other forests, and in 1939 the cadets of the Marlborough Training Corps tried and failed. For their final move in 1946 the small boys of Hawtreys School were recruited.

The late marquess wrote:

> Having at last emerged, the deer paused to take stock of the outer world. They saw, moving slowly towards them from Durley Gate, a line of men and girls on horseback—this gave them a first impulse to move in the direction where their new park lay. Once on the move, they became aware of a stout fence preventing any turn to the right: on their left there was open ground, but it was rendered unattractive by many small groups of boys, stationed at distances of about 100 yards apart.
>
> The obvious course was to move forward; but deer, ever since the first man laid the first trap, have been exceedingly wary of following the obvious course. They advanced a little—then suddenly swung towards the open ground held by the boys.
>
> This was the critical moment—and mercifully everyone did the right thing. The riders halted and remained in line, their horses pawing the ground; the boys no doubt restrained by their masters, stood firm as rocks. If even one boy had begun to run or shout, there would have been a panic and all control would have been lost.

Finally the deer entered the park at Tottenham, where they live today. But not all have been cleared from the open forest, in which about 20 red, 100 fallow and 100 roe deer thrive. The pleasure of watching deer in Savernake has been described by the late marquess.

> At Savernake, the visitor might disturb a fallow buck which had been lying in the bracken's shade, and he could then follow it with his eye as it plunged away into the distance. He would see it pause just beyond bow-shot, turning to eye him mistrustfully—and he could still follow it as it resumed its flight. Maybe it would cross a glade, where sudden sunlight would illuminate its dappled markings, re-entering woodland beyond. Only after some quarter of a

mile would the intervening tree trunks at last close it off from his sight.

The Ailesbury family also feared that the Forestry Commission would transform Savernake into a forest of conifer plantations. Eventually a form of words was agreed by which the Commission undertook to 'use all reasonable endeavours to regenerate the old Forest by natural means'. The important implication of this clause was that natural regeneration would exclude imported conifers. The Forestry Commission used to claim that it had honoured this undertaking, but the owners would not agree.

Most of the forest of Savernake stands on clay with flint over chalk, and the trees which do well here are beech, ash and oak. It is these, sometimes nursed by larch, which make Savernake's final hardwood crop. Among them still stand perhaps 3,000 old beech and 1,000 old oak, including such curiosities as the big-bellied oak beside the Marlborough to Salisbury Road. The Forestry Commission fells these according to their condition, aiming to anticipate their death by five years, when they still have some value.

Outside the forest as it was leased in 1939 the Forestry Commission in the 1930s bought two other woods which once lay within the bounds of Savernake's mediaeval forest: Collinghame to the south and Westwood to the west.

The thirteenth clause of the agreement with the Forestry Commission reads: 'The Hereditary Wardenship of the Forest of Savernake shall be retained by the Marquess of Ailesbury and his heirs.' The position is one he values even if today it carries few of its ancient powers. As late as 1940, when King George VI visited the forest, the warden performed his traditional duty of welcoming him with a blast on his mediaeval hunting horn.

Cranborne Chase

In the southern part of Wiltshire there was yet another area of hunting reserve which, for over 500 years, was forest in all but name. This was Cranborne Chase, bounded to the north at its greatest by a line joining Salisbury, Wilton, Tisbury and Shaftesbury.

To the south this great chase, some quarter of a million

acres in area, extended into Dorset as far as Blandford and Wimborne, while to the west from Ringwood to Downton it marched with the New Forest.

Neither of those two forests, which stretched for some 40 miles across central southern England, conformed to today's idea of a forest, each consisting in large part of treeless open country. But whereas the gravels and sands of the New Forest's plains supported a moor-like vegetation of heath, gorse and bracken, Cranborne's open spaces lay on the ring of chalk downs which surround the New Forest basin and supported downland grasses with privet thickets. And while oak was the main timber tree of the New Forest's woods, beech and ash did better in Cranborne where chalk was never far below a clay topsoil.

For five centuries the chase was regularly in the hands of the king, the queen or some close relative. William I, William Rufus and John held it, and so at various times did all the kings and queens from Edward IV to James I. Indeed, there seems no good reason why, like Ashdown in Sussex which had a similar early history, it should not have been called a forest. Certainly the distinction can have made little difference to those who lived in it, but from the start it was known as a chase, and as such did not come under forest law. Its courts referred serious cases not to visiting forest eyres but to the courts of common law.

The chase finally passed into private hands in 1616 when James I gave it to Robert Cecil, Earl of Salisbury. What the king gave, of course, was not its freehold—though Salisbury like subsequent lords of Cranborne owned large amounts of land in the chase, but its permanent lordship, to be held, passed to heirs or sold, with the right to hunt its beasts of the forest and enforce laws for their preservation.

Its early records, like those of most forests, consist in the main of prosecutions for minor offences against these laws. Only when the Salisbury family became its lords does poaching seem to have become its special vice.

In 1616, for example, Lord Salisbury prosecuted poachers who were said to have gathered at the chase village of Ashmore with 'long-piked staves, swords, "privie coats", jacks, guns, crossbows and other weapons, and provided with buckstalls, gapnets, cords, greyhounds, etc'.

These may have been villagers, operating on their own account, but in 1633 poaching parties of ten consisted of 'persons of good rank', and during the Civil War other poachers were described as persons of quality.

Many such poaching incidents are reported by the Rev. William Chafin whose family were closely connected with the chase and lived in the little village of Chettle, a mile to the west of the Salisbury to Blandford road. William's grandfather, Thomas Chafin, was the head ranger of the chase in the seventeenth century—a position which roughly corresponded to lieutenant or second-in-command of other forests; and his father, George Chafin, was ranger till his death in 1766. At Chettle George had built for him by Thomas Archer the elegant red-brick house with its curved corners, splendid double staircase and terraced lawns which still dominates the village.

William, who lived at Chettle House till he died at the age of 86, was therefore in a good position to write about the chase, which he did in his late years, despite being struck by lightning in the process. His book, *Anecdotes and History of Cranbourn Chase*, was published in 1818, the year he died.

Chafin's anecdotes may indeed explain Cranborne's reputation, but even if similar tales could have been told of other forests, they are the more interesting for bringing vividly to life all such forest crime. The first—which he knew about only by tradition—had occurred at Tarrant Gunville, and consisted of 'a very bloody engagement' at a gate called Bloody Shard at the entrance to Blood-way Coppice, in which several lives were lost.

Whether or not this was before the passing of the Black Act, designed to suppress the activities of a gang called the Waltham Blacks which had first operated around Bishops Waltham at the other side of Hampshire, Chafin does not say. In the chase the Act certainly failed. Here men of good family organized themselves into bands in imitation of the Blacks, and Chafin's book contains a portrait of a band of such gentry, dressed for the sport in a costume they called 'Cap and Jack'.

The cap was formed with wreaths of straw tightly bound together with split bramble-stalks, the workmanship much the same as that of the common bee-hives. The jacks were made of the strongest canvas, well quilted with wool to guard against the heavy blows of the quarterstaff, weapons which were much used in those days, and the management of them requiring great dexterity.

Two straw hats are still kept in a glass case at Chettle House, together with a swindgel, consisting of a truncheon about

Deer hunters

fourteen inches long, hinged loosely to a shorter wooden cylinder about six inches long.

Their sport is described by Hutchins, the historian of Dorset:

A company of hunters, from four to twenty in number, assembled in the evening, dressed in cap, jack, and quarterstaff, and with dogs and nets. Having set the watchword for the night, and agreed whether to stand or run, in case they should meet the keepers, they proceed to Cranborne Chase, set their nets at such places where the deer are most likely to run, then let slip their dogs, well-used to the sport, to drive the deer into the nets, a man standing at each end to strangle the deer as soon as entangled. Thus they passed such portion of the night as their success induced them, sometimes bringing off six or eight deer, good or bad, such as fell into the net, generally of the latter sort, which was a matter of little importance to those gentlemen hunters who regarded the sport, not the venison.

Other gentlemen of good family would poach individually. If discovered, Chafin explains, they 'had thirty pounds in their pockets to pay the penalty, and were then at liberty to repeat their sports the following night if they chose to venture'. He goes on:

I had an uncle much addicted to this sport, but being in general a little too free with his potations after dinner, he was too venturous at night, and so often detected, and so many penalties paid, that his elder brother put a stop to his career in good time. But the amusement was persisted in until an Act of Parliament passed that made a second offence a felony, which not only caused the abandoning of the nocturnal diversion, but converted the names of the sportsmen from Deer-hunters to that of Deer-stealers.

Chafin himself had been present at an equally gentlemanly poaching affair when he and other sportsmen, who were dining together, were brought a report that a buck had been found by reapers in a wheat field. The diners at once set out with two greyhounds, soon killed the deer and had returned to their claret when the keeper appeared and demanded their names. The matter was settled amicably and instead of the standard £30 fine, £15 was given to the poor of the village, three guineas sent to the keeper and a bottle of claret given to Mr Jones of Rushmore Lodge (who had arrived to negotiate) on condition he stayed till he finished it.

Poaching and connected crime of a less gentlemanly kind had also continued after the Black Act, and in 1738 two keepers were murdered. The first, the keeper of the West Walk, was 'most dreadfully beaten and bruised with bludgeons and clubs and his skull fractured' in daylight on his way home from Easter communion. His murderers were never found. The second was killed in Lord Pembroke's walk at Vernditch. One of this man's murderers was executed and hung in chains near the scene of the crime, but soon afterwards his body was cut down and thrown into a well where it sank to the bottom because of the weight of its irons and was 'not discovered till a long time after'.

In 1780, on the night of 16 December, 'a very severe battle was fought between the keepers and deer-stealers on Chettle Common, in Bursystool Walk, which was attended with very serious circumstances. A gang of these deer-stealers assembled at Pimperne, and were headed by a Serjeant of Dragons . . . whose name was Blandford'. Chafin continues:

They came in the night in disguise, armed with deadly offensive weapons called swindgels, resembling flails to thresh corn. They attacked the keepers, who were nearly equal in number, but had no weapons but sticks and short hangers. The first blow that was struck was by the leader of the gang, which broke a knee-cap of the stoutest man of the Chase, who was not only disabled from joining in the combat, but has been lame ever since. Another keeper received a blow from a swindgel, which broke three ribs, and was the cause of his death some time after. The remaining keepers closed in upon their opponents with their hangers, and one of the Dragoon's hands was severed from the arm, just above the wrist, and fell on the ground; the others were also dreadfully cut, and wounded, and obliged to surrender.

Blandford's arm was tightly bound with a list garter to prevent its bleeding, and he was carried to the lodge, where I saw him the next day, and his hand in the window. Peter Beckford, Esq. who was at that time Ranger of the Walk, came early in the morning, and brought Mr Dansey, a very eminent surgeon, with him, who dressed the wound, and administered proper remedies to the poor patient. Two young officers came also in the course of the day to see him. As soon as he was well enough to be removed, he was committed, with his companions, to Dorchester gaol. The hand was buried in Pimpern church-yard, and, as reported, with the honours of war.

Several of these offenders were labourers, daily employed by Mr Beckford, and had, the preceding day, dined in his servants' hall, and from thence went to join a confederacy to rob their master. They were all tried by Sir Richard Perryn at Dorchester assizes, found guilty, condemned to be transported for seven years; but, in consideration of their great suffering from their wounds in prison, the humane Judge commuted the punishment to confinement in gaol for an indefinite term.

Deer stealing continued after Chafin's time, and a young keeper, James Barrett, was involved in the arrest of a notorious poacher named Thomas Amy in 1822. After a four mile chase he came up with Amy and charged him, knocking aside his pointed gun. A bloody wrestling match followed, in which Amy lacerated Barrett's shins with boots fitted with 'iron kicking-plates which projected from the tips . . . and were filed up sharp'.

The Pitt family, who were Lords of the chase during the 100 years when most of these episodes occurred were cousins of such better known Pitts as the Earl of Chatham and Pitt the younger. They had acquired the chase in 1714. Forty years earlier the Salisburys had finally lost interest in it—their main family seat was at Hatfield—and though they had kept and still keep Cranborne Manor, in 1671 they had sold the lordship of the chase to the Earl of Pembroke. Eight days later he in turn had sold it to Lord Ashley, soon to become Earl of Shaftesbury, and the Shaftesburys in their turn had sold it in 1695 to the Freke family.

By then Vernditch Ward had passed to the Pembrokes and Alderholt Ward had been detached and kept by the Shaftes-burys—the best explanation of these complex changes of ownership is that the two families wanted to suppress the deer in the wards nearest to their other lands. Whatever the reason, when in 1714 the Pitts acquired the chase by mar-rying into the Freke family its centre had effectively ceased to be Cranborne Manor and become Rushmore House.

Of the eighteenth-century Pitts, George, the third of that name to be lord of the chase, who held it from 1745 till he died in 1803 at the age of 83, was the most eccentric. In 1760 he became convinced that squire Harbin of Gunville Park was using pomance (crushed apple pulp from cider making) to attract deer from the chase into his park, from which they could not then escape. Pitt and his ranger broke down the pale to make a way into Harbin's park for his hounds and his friends' carriages. Harbin took Pitt to court, but they seem to have settled privately.

Eleven years later, when Horace Walpole described Pitt's wife as 'all loveliness within and without', he contrasted her with her 'brutal, half-mad husband'. It was this George Pitt who was granted a peerage and took the name of Lord Rivers.

In 1790 he began to negotiate seriously about the disfran-chisement of the chase. He was not against it, but his own and his successors' claims for compensation delayed matters for forty years. By then the family had lost a law suit against a farmer of Alvediston, which by implication much reduced the value of the chase. The farmer, Thomas King, who had set his dogs on deer found grazing on his land, based his chase on the proposition that the chase did not extend into Wiltshire. The jury found in his favour. Lord Rivers eventually accepted £1,800 a year in compensation, to be levied on the disfran-chized land. For his part, he undertook to remove the deer before 1830.

The deer had been at the heart of the dispute, and the Pitt-Rivers were claiming compensation of just the sort which the crown was granted twenty years later by the New Forest's Deer Removal Act, which gave it the right to enclose 10,000 acres of forest. All four beasts of the forest, red deer, fallow deer, roe deer and wild boar, had at one time been hunted at Cranborne. Wild boar survived till the sixteenth century. Red deer there must have been—certainly there was a herd in the park at Wardour Castle—but records which distinguish between red and fallow are scarce. Fallow were the species mainly hunted and preserved.

In the first half of the seventeenth century they probably numbered 1,500. As elsewhere in the country, they were much reduced during the eighteen years of Civil War and Commonwealth, but after 1660 increased steadily again, until the Pitt-Rivers, when negotiating for compensation in 1828, could seriously claim that there were between 12,000 and 20,000. William West had suggested twelve years earlier the more realistic figure of five to eight thousand.

Once disfranchisement had been agreed, the Pitt-Rivers seem to have set about disposing of the deer profitably while they were still theirs, and in 1828 nearly 2,000 were either killed or sold alive. After 1830 when the chase was thrown open, villagers of the chase organized parties to hunt them, and throughout the nineteenth century they steadily declined. About 150 survive today.

The history of roe deer at Cranborne almost exactly reverses that of fallow, and is of great interest because it provides a key to their fortunes in the rest of the country during the last few hundred years. Until 1800 they declined all over the south of England and in Cranborne probably became extinct. Then some were released at Milton Abbas by Lord Dorchester, some in the west of the country by Lord Ilchester, and others at Charborough. These aristocrats were interested in them as hunting quarry, and from the 1830s roe deer are commonly reported as kills by Dorset hunts. In 1857 there was a notable run when a roe buck was followed from Charborough to Poole, across the Stour at Badbury Rings, then back to Wimborne, till finally after four hours in continuous rain it was brought to bay below Julian's Bridge where it stood with head and antlers just above the water.

There seems little doubt that the roe deer released in Dorset in the early nineteenth century were the ancestors of those which have recolonized the south of England, spreading through Hampshire, Surrey and Sussex to Kent. Though they were first brought for hunting, they have prospered because Forestry Commission plantations provide them with an ideal habitat, and because on the whole they do less damage to farm crops than the grazing fallow deer.

Today in Cranborne they have been joined by some of the small barking muntjak deer, and by Japanese sika deer, these last probably escapes from Brownsea Island in Poole Harbour or Hyde Park near Wareham.

Though the Pitts were the last lords of the chase, the family's influence on its history did not stop with its disfranchisement in 1830, indeed it reached something of a climax during the last quarter of the nineteenth century. Then, in 1880, Rushmore descended to that fine eccentric and still admired archaeologist, General Pitt-Rivers. It was a prosperous inheritance, and the general, now retired from the regular army and suffering from diabetes and bronchitis but already a Fellow of the Royal Society, decided to devote the rest of his life to exploring the antiquities of the chase. His underlying intention was to develop for human artefacts a chain of descent similar to Darwin's evolutionary chain for living creatures.

During the next 20 years he investigated two Romano-British settlements (Woodcutts and Rotherly), two Bronze Age camps (South Lodge and Martin Down), the neolithic long barrow near Hadley Hill, and—his best-known site —the four-mile-long earthwork known as Bokerley Dyke, which crosses the A45 at Bokerley Junction. Later archaeologists have confirmed his conclusion that this was built towards the end of the Roman occupation (and finally closed about AD 405) perhaps as a defence work against attack from the north-east.

It was a period of agricultural depression, and the general was popular in the neighbourhood for the work his excavations provided. He also provided local entertainment, in the form of pleasure gardens at Tollard Royal, set around an ancient wych elm known as the Larmer Tree. Here he built a temple, a half-timbered cottage and bandstand, a theatre, a dining hall for 200, two Indian houses and an Indian room, and imported Mesopotamian deer, yak, Pembroke, Highland and Kerry cattle, reindeer, South American parrots, the Australian bower bird, lama, emu, prairy dogs, impeyan pheasants and Aden sheep.

Friends, relations and his nine children who knew him more intimately were less indulgent towards his eccentricities. The general favoured cremation, not only for himself but for his wife. When she protested, he told her, 'If I say you'll burn, woman, you'll burn.' The whole family, according to Nancy Mitford, had a sort of downright passion for quarrelling.

If the chase was never a great timber-producing forest, trees formed an important part of its economy, and its hazel coppices have continued to be cropped longer than most others except the chestnut coppices of Sussex and Kent and a few oak coppices in the West Country.

The Act of Henry VIII of 1543 which ordered the enclosure of coppices for four years after they had been cut is often considered one of the most important forest statutes, and it certainly marked a new royal concern with timber. But whatever its effect elsewhere, the practice at Cranborne never precisely conformed. Both Chafin and West describe this in detail. 'On the third autumn,' Chafin writes, 'these hedges are in divers parts lowered down, to give entrance to the start deer, and creep-holes are made for the fawns and weak ones; and this operation is called "leaping and creeping".' In the fourth autumn the coppice fences were entirely removed so that cattle and sheep could also feed.

In mediaeval times, no doubt, such coppices were sources of wood for burning, house repairs and other farm and domestic purposes, but gradually over the years they came to be valued for two purposes only, the cutting of 'spars' for thatching and the making of hurdles for sheep.

Such work used to be done at home, and Chafin describes its setting:

While the master of the cottage is attentive to his work, the children are employed in picking up the chips and shreds of the gads as they are called, and with handfuls at a time feed the lingering fire underneath the little crock, containing a few potatoes or other vegetables, the produce of their small garden or plat, so as to keep it in a constant simmering and the little blaze from each handful adds a temporary lustre to the dimness of their farthing candle, and the gleam from it illuminates the placid countenances of the groups of happy offspring round the fireside.

Hurdles are still made in the chase, and many of its cottages are thatched. As a result coppices survive. On the

Rushmore estate, on either side of a fine avenue of beech which runs from the Pitt-Rivers' Larmer Tree gardens as far as the old Bloody Shard gate, there are textbook examples of coppice-with-standard, hazel and oak woods in various stages of their cycles. In spring and early summer the ground below them is gay with primroses and wood anemones, then carpeted with bluebells. Till 1970 the right to cut such coppices was sold by annual auction. A hurdle-maker needed three or four acres for his year's work, which he bought in so-called lugs. Ten paces by ten paces made four lugs and about 200 lugs made an acre.

Many of the other broadleaf woods of the chase were felled and not replanted during the First World War and the countryside is now mainly used for corn growing and dairy farming. Approached from the east through Hinton it rises ahead, a line of rolling downs with isolated hilltop clumps, but the best idea of its magnificent rolling quality can be had from the top of Wyn Green Hill. This is the highest point of the chase, and although many of the hills and ridges are capped with clay and grow oak, here there is a clump of weather-slanted beech. The 360-degree view is as impressive as any in the south of England; Salisbury, the Mendips, Bournemouth and the Isle of Wight can all be seen on fine days. Closer are the villages of the chase, of which Ashmore with its picturesque central duck pond is typical. More than in other forests, such villages have kept the quality of isolated communities in an expanse of empty countryside.

In the 1930s Balfour-Gardiner, who owned woods at Fontmell, attempted to revive neglected coppices on his land, and in 1938 he gave the two woods of Verndown and Stonedown to the Forestry Commission. Today these, and a number of woods on the Rushmore estate, have been planted with various mixtures of hardwood and conifer. Preferable as such orderly plantations are to most other possible developments, they seem to have little connection with the chase's ancient coppiced woods, let alone with the untamed eighteenth century countryside where keepers fought poaching gentry in beehive hats, or with the nineteenth-century chase of General Pitt-Rivers' excavations and follies.

FORESTS OF THE WEST

Exmoor

Exmoor National Park today corresponds approximately to the original Forest of Exmoor. Its 170,000 acres lie mostly in Somerset—it was by far the largest of Somerset's five mediaeval forests—but extend into Devon. For 25 miles it is bounded by the Bristol Channel, to which it falls steeply, and two small coastal towns—Porlock and Lynton—lie on its borders. Though it is the smallest National Park, three times since the Second World War it has provided national news, first and most dramatically in August 1952 when nine inches of rain fell on the moor in 24 hours, and the accumulated torrents of the East and West Lyn swept down Lynton's narrow comb, carrying large parts of the town into the sea and drowning 172 people.

The moorland itself made news on the other occasions, when in 1958-59 the Forestry Commission planned to plant a particularly bleak and characteristic central area known as the Chains with conifers, and when in 1976-77 there were plans to plough large new areas of moorland, in particular Stowey Allotment near the village of Oare. On both occasions the people of Exmoor, represented by the Exmoor Society, tenaciously defended their moorland. The Forestry Commission was frustrated, and Lord Porchester's report on the 1976-77 enclosure proposals has given the remaining 40-50,000 acres of moorland better protection.

Of the rest of the park, the greater part is enclosed farmland, as much of it has been for over 100 years. Only 17,000 acres are wooded and there is no evidence that there was any more woodland in the mediaeval forest. It was, however, a royal hunting ground from Saxon times—the Domesday Book records that Withypool was held by three foresters during the reign of Edward the Confessor—and was formally afforested by the Normans who imposed their rule on it from such centres as Bampton Castle, Bury Castle near Dulverton and Holwell Castle near Parracombe. Holwell

—today a large gorse-covered hillock at the centre of a field—has been described as 'a text book model of the earthwork of a Norman private fortress'.

The Plantagenets expanded the forest. Like many others, it grew to its largest in the 60 years from the accession of Henry II in 1154 to the death of John, and in spite of nominal concessions by John in Magna Carta (1215), and by Henry III in the Charter of the Forests (1217), remained the same size for another 80 years.

Then, typically, it was much reduced when Edward I around the year 1300 finally conceded what John and Henry III had promised, becoming an island at the centre of the older forest, something like the shape of North America. Unlike many other forests, it kept these boundaries more or less intact for 500 years, and when it was finally disafforested between 1815 and 1820 it still measured 18,500 acres.

Throughout mediaeval times it had similar officers to those of other forests, administering the same forest law. Though J. Charles Cox makes much of the fact that in one part of Somerset—the Warren of Somerton—the hare was a beast of the forest (in addition to red deer, fallow deer, roe deer and wild boar), there is no evidence that this was so on Exmoor. As he points out, it would have been impossible to pursue every hare poacher, or to account for every hare found dead, and Somerton's hares were probably unique. But if Exmoor's officials, courts and game were typical, its Commoners and their rights were unusual.

They were known as Suitors, and divided into two classes: Free Suitors, and Suitors at Large. The Free Suitors—who were the owners or tenants of 52 holdings in the forest parishes of Hawkridge and Withypool, had considerably greater rights but also more duties. They could graze certain numbers of animals on the forest, take turf, fern and heath from the forest and fish the river Barle, all without charge. In return they had to drive the forest nine times a year for ponies, cattle and sheep, act as jurymen at coroners' inquests on bodies found on the forest, and perambulate the forest every seven years with the warden. Thus they performed some of the stock-minding and perambulating duties which agisters and regarders performed in other forests.

Suitors at Large either held land abutting the forest or represented communities known as 'tithings' bordering the forest. Their grazing rights were not free, but they paid less per animal than 'strangers'. Those of them who represented tithings kept their parish branding irons for marking the beasts of the parish. Unbranded beasts were impounded or charged fully. The Suitors were important in the forest's history. They resisted enclosure and though in the end they were unable to prevent it, the many thousands of sheep, cattle and ponies which have *de facto* grazing rights on Exmoor today represent a form of success.

Three families, James Boevey's in the seventeenth century, Sir Thomas Ackland's in the eighteenth century, and John Knight's in the nineteenth century, were mainly responsible for transforming Exmoor from a wild and largely uninhabited mediaeval hunting reserve to today's picturesque but comparatively bland mixture of moorland and field. None is so well-known as a family which probably existed more in the imagination of a Victorian novelist than in reality: the Doones of Badgworthy Water in the parish of Oare. To millions of readers, R. D. Blackmore in his novel *Lorna Doone* made them so real that numerous pamphlets and thousands of earnest walkers have treated them as historical fact and spent much time and energy trying to identify the sites of their exploits.

Certain things are now clear. Blackmore did not invent the Doones. There are a number of references to them which date from well before he wrote. He was brought up on Exmoor and heard stories of them from his grandfather who had been Rector of Oare. Later he lived at Charles, Withypool and Oare, and continued to collect stories for his novel. But it also seems likely that the Doone legends exaggerated the facts, and that Blackmore made vague legend into specific incident. So the search—which is entertaining enough—is more for the places of his imagination than those of real events.

For a long time there was argument about the Doone valley itself, where this robber band held out for many years, terrorizing the countryside, and from which they were eventually driven by gallant John Ridd with the help of a regiment of local troops. The valley of the Badgworthy, still often called the Doone Valley, is far too open ever to have been defended in the way Blackmore describes. It is much more likely that he was thinking of Hoccombe Combe, a small tributary valley of the upper Badgworthy. The ruins of old cottages have been found here. But even Hoccombe Combe has no Water Slide of the sort John Ridd scaled when he first found his way into the Doone Valley. Another tributary of the Badgworthy, Lank Combe, does have a small-scale version of such a slide, and Blackmore probably transferred it to Hoccombe.

Other incidents of the story are more easily and convincingly placed. The little church of Oare, for example, is set on a steep hillside which would have given Carver Doone just the elevation he needed to shoot Lorna Doone on her wedding day through one of its windows.

Internal evidence suggests that the tale is meant to have taken place in the second half of the seventeenth century. But those who doubt the historical basis of the whole Doone legend argue that if it were fact there would have been some figure in the story to represent James Boevey, the London merchant of Dutch extraction, who was warden of the forest for 43 years from 1652, holding this position longer than any other warden, even succeeding in retaining it at the Restoration. For the whole period he was not only the most powerful man in the forest but worked vigorously to civilize it. The Doones, if they existed, could of course have come to some arrangement with him, and their valley in any case lay outside the reduced forest, but the fact that Blackmore describes no conflict between the Doones and anyone like Boevey suggests either that they were mainly invented or that he exaggerated their power and importance.

John Aubrey gives a vivid picture of Boevey—pronounced Boovey. He was five foot high (cautious historians suggest that Aubrey missed out the inches) and frenetically active. From the age of fourteen he kept a lighted candle by his bed to allow him to jot down ideas he might have in the night. He had 'alwaies a weake stomach, which proceeded from the agitation of the braine'. He had retired at 32 to live in the country because town air didn't suit him, and to write 'Active Philosophy . . . wherin he enumerated the Arts and Tricks practised in Negotiation'. He was highly litigious—Aubrey says that one of his law suits lasted eighteen years—and he almost at once became involved in legal actions against the forest's Suitors. He tried, but failed, to get all the Free Suitors' rights abolished, and later to question their perambulations and have included in the forest all the commons which bordered it. Here again he failed but he did have confirmed his right as warden to fix grazing rates. After an initial boycott, he successfully raised these. Today the most visible of his achievements is Simonsbath Lodge (1654). It was the first house to be built on the forest, and Simonsbath itself became from this time the forest's centre. Around it he enclosed a farm of 108 acres, and to the north he planted a new Hoar Oak Tree. Its successor is still the forest's best-known boundary mark.

During the eighteenth century the wardenship passed to the Ackland family, and it was they who ultimately preserved for today's National Park the most important of its woodlands. But in the eighteenth century the Acklands were more interested in stag hunting, which the first Sir Thomas Ackland revived. When his house was burnt down, he is said to have been more distressed about the loss of his collection of stags' heads than his pictures or silver.

Fallow deer, introduced by the Normans into many English forests, have never been found on Exmoor. About roe deer there is some doubt. In the records of the forest eyre of 1257 three roebucks (*caprioli*) are mentioned, but they appear in no other document then or later, and may in fact have been red deer calves which the court scribe misdescribed. During the last ten years, however, roe deer have finally begun to arrive, spreading north-west from Dorset where they were re-introduced in the early nineteenth century, just as they have spread east to Kent.

It is red deer which were always the beasts of the forest on Exmoor, and today 600 to 900 make the finest collection of herds in England. Although there are so many, they are not easily seen, staying in the wooded combes in daytime, only emerging to feed at dusk. For nine or ten months of the year the stags live apart, singly or in groups of two or three, but in the autumn rutting season each collects around him a harem of five to fourteen hinds. At this time the stags 'bell', a sound like a cow in agony, and rivals fight each other with clashing antlers.

During the winter the sexes drift apart again and in the spring the does drop their calves. At the same time the stags shed their antlers to grow new ones. These increase in size each year but not precisely by one point. As the new antlers grow the stags rub off their velvet on trees, so damaging the bark. For this reason, and because they are the largest British deer and can only be excluded from plantations with eight-foot fences, they are a considerable nuisance to foresters.

The centre from which Sir Thomas Ackland re-established stag hunting in the mid-eighteenth century was Exford. It is still the headquarters of the Devon and Somerset Stag Hunt, and remains the horsiest village in a horsey part of the country.

By the time the third Sir Thomas Ackland to be Warden of Exmoor applied in 1810 for his lease of the forest to be renewed England had been at war with France for the greater part of 20 years, and politicians were anxious, as they had periodically been since the reign of Elizabeth, about the supply of oak timber for warships. A surveyor, Richard Hawkins, was sent to the forest and found a total of only 37 trees, seven of them lime pollards. Simonsbath Lodge was being used as an inn. He recommended disafforestation and the planting of oak. If he had visited the Hoar Oak and seen how slowly oaks grow on Exmoor, even in one of its combes,

he might have given different advice. However, Parliament accepted the idea of disafforestation, in compensation awarding each Free Suitor 31 acres, each Suitor at Large a smaller parcel of land, Sir Thomas Ackland 3,201 acres, Sir Charles W. Bampfield 1880 acres and the crown 10,262 acres.

The crown land was to be planted, but there seems to have been an immediate change of policy because it was soon put up for tender. The highest bid came from John Knight, an industrialist who owned iron works in Shropshire and Worcestershire. So a second businessman became master of the forest and set about establishing his family here as aristocratic owners of a great estate.

Knight intended to make his forest pay, but his agricultural experiments mostly failed. Though he broke 2,500 acres of moorland, his crops did not grow. The Highlands cattle he imported were too wild, and could not winter on the moor without being fed—though the Herefords were more successful. He attempted but failed to improve the moorland ponies with Arab blood which produced foals with the same lack of hardiness. Even the great new house he started at Simonsbath was never finished. He did, however, metal many miles of moorland road and build a 29-mile wall round the forest. Long stretches of this survive, and there is no better way to see Exmoor than walk its course.

John Knight's son, Frederic, who took over the estate in 1841, was more successful, and it was largely his work which produced the mixed farm and moorland of today's National Park. He gave his tenant farmers low rents and long leases in return for undertaking to plough up areas of moorland. He imported 5,000 sheep from Scotland—Blackface and Cheviot—together with their shepherds, which did well and are still kept in large numbers on Exmoor, alongside the local Exmoor Horns. Foresters are less pleased, because Blackface, in particular, are as agile as goats and difficult to exclude from plantations. Frederic Knight is also responsible for one of Exmoor's most delightful features: its dozens of miles of beech hedge, perched on stone walls. They are cut and laid about every fourteen years, and because they provide shelter they are subsidized by the Ministry of Agriculture. Why they do well is a mystery, for the soil of the moor is acid and not particularly suitable for beech. Possibly the stones of the walls provide the alkaline environment it needs. Exceptional, too, is the beech wood which Knight planted near Simonsbath, probably using overgrown seedlings from his nursery there. In one year he spent £16 on beech nuts for sowing.

He was less successful with the moor's minerals. His father had bought the right to these with the forest and a number of mines were started between 1846 and 1860. At Weal Eliza on the Barle, where iron ore was found instead of the expected copper, the early signs were so promising that Frederic Knight himself took over the lease, but the veins of ore gave out and later mining just before the First World War was also unsuccessful.

Though Richard Hawkins in 1810 may have underestimated Exmoor's trees, it remained throughout the nineteenth century largely treeless. Any there were formed coppice oak woods on the coast, or grew in the shelter of combes. Even today's 17,000 acres of woodland consist largely of Forestry Commission plantations in the Bredon Hills at the eastern end of the park, and the National Park itself owns a mere 1,000 acres of woodland. There is, however, one important area of woods and plantations, rare in the park for its size and of unique scientific interest. The Ackland family had continued to own the large Holnicote estate near Porlock in the north-east corner of the original forest. In 1919 they leased the estate's moorland to the National Trust and in 1944 gave the Trust the whole estate.

Today, with other gifts and purchases including Dunkery Beacon, the highest point on Exmoor at 1,705 feet, Holnicote includes about 12,500 acres. Many of these remain open moorland, and Exmoor is at its most characteristic on the windswept heath-covered slopes of Dunkery Hill. But lower down there are 1,800 acres of woodland, consisting of a collection of plantations and ancient woods of unusual variety.

Most interesting and ancient are those closest to Dunkery, in the Horner and East Water valleys. The rest form an approximate horseshoe around the Vale of Porlock, which reaches inland from Bossington Beach as far as the villages of Blackford and Tivington. At the northerly point of the horseshoe, above Bossington, is a plantation, less ancient than the Horner Woods, but in its way of equal interest, entirely composed of holm-oak (*Quercus ilex*). A painting of 1809 shows this hill bare, but from that year onwards Sir Thomas Ackland, the tenth baronet, began to plant it with ilex to celebrate the births of his nine children. Though probably unique, these trees are now old and of value only as firewood. Furthermore, their thick evergreen foliage creates a plantation with almost no undergrowth. The Trust plans to keep a part of the plantation as pure ilex, but elsewhere to fill gaps with other broadleaf species to create a more varied plantation.

Seven hundred acres of other plantations around the Vale of Porlock are dedicated woodland (committed to timber growing in return for government assistance), and it is these which consist largely of such conifer species as Douglas fir and larch. Luccombe and Little Headon plantations are typical. They were first planted between 1921 and 1924 by the fourteenth baronet, a keen forester and one of the original Forestry Commissioners in 1919. These were probably the earliest conifers (ornamental ones apart) to be planted at Holnicote, though it is difficult to be sure for the estate's records were lost in 1944 when a German bomb destroyed a solicitor's office in Exeter. Plantations like these produce a total of about 700 tons of wood and timber a year and make the estate nearly self-supporting.

Little Headon is fringed to the south with oak, as what the National Trust's warden calls 'a sop to broadleafery'. Some of the other plantations—Tiverton for example—are mainly broadleaf and will remain so. Great Headon Wood is of interest in another way. It is a typical example of an old National Trust plantation, intended ultimately to be broadleaf but grown with conifer nurse trees—a technique which unfortunately produces a coniferous effect for 20-30 years and which the National Trust is now abandoning.

On the steeper sides of the Vale of Porlock there are many acres of ancient oak, once coppiced for firewood, building material and bark for the tanning industry. It is the view of the warden, that these should be managed too. 'You can't wrap woods in cotton wool.' Dead trees are removed and natural regeneration encouraged, though the red deer make this a problem. These are the woods which suffered most severely in a great storm in 1981. There was no known history of windblow at Holnicote, but in mid-December of that year a north-west wind of hurricane strength blew up the Vale of Porlock then turned north. Three hundred oaks of substance were blown down, and it took seven men five days working with lorries and tractors to clear the roads and rivers. The locals were inclined to blame the warden for thinning the woods, but his view is that the Lord was weeding out the weak.

Finally there are the Horner Woods, forming part of a

7,500-acre Site of Special Scientific Interest (S.S.S.I.), of which the National Trust owns 5,000 acres. These are also oak woods, last coppiced before the First World War, and the National Trust believes that they, too, must be managed. A few years ago it began to single the coppice stools, with the aim of producing a mature oak wood consisting of trees of more various ages. So far a disappointingly small area has been found suitable—only 35 acres out of 900—these lying half way up the valley sides between 500 and 700 feet above sea level. The trees below, where ash, rowan and hazel are mixed with the oak, are forming high forest without assistance, and the 200 acres which fringe the tops of the valley sides are too windswept.

About a third of the National Park's red deer habitually live or take refuge during the day in these woods. Deer apart, they are rich in wild life, from many kinds of lichens to fritillaries. Webbers Post, half way up the long climb to Dunkery Beacon, has fine views to the west over both the wooded Horner and East Water valleys, which can be seen from here to be divided by the round hill named Cloutsham Ball, and of the beacon itself, standing formidably on the southern skyline, topped by its modern cairn. Here, as elsewhere on the moor, it is common to see groups of buzzards circling high in the sky above prey or carcass. The views from Webbers Post are so fine that in 1807 Richard Fenton tried to persuade the tenth baronet to build a house here; fortunately he failed.

Though oaks on the Holnicote estate were traditionally cut for the tanning industry, there is only a little evidence of charcoal burning. But this industry thrived until about 70 years ago in the coastal oakwoods west of Porlock. In the Middle Ages the burners were a colony of lepers, and there is a lepers' window in the tiny church of Culbone which lies close above the woods. The lepers were not allowed to cross Culbone water, and may have partly survived on the products of a herd of feral goats which lived in these woods until shortly before the First World War.

Today an uneasy truce exists between the Exmoor Society and the moor's farmers about the ploughing of moorland. Certainly the Porchester Report shifted the grounds of the argument from whether or not moorland was being lost (it was) and whether or not it should be conserved, by accepting that it should be and discussing ways of compensating

farmers for the loss of their right to farm their land in the
most profitable way. Since then the National Park has itself
purchased about 2,500 moorland acres and entered into
management agreements protecting 2,000 acres. The problem is that these agreements are for only 20 years, and that
they are increasingly expensive to maintain.

The question of forestry in the park is less settled. In 1971
the moor was mapped and out of its 170,000 acres only
3,075 found suitable for tree planting. This map remains the
basis of the National Park's forestry policy, but a new plan is
due and at the moment being vigorously discussed. Farm
shelter belts are one subject of argument. The National Park
wishes any new ones to consist of broadleaf trees, matching
those which already exist, but many of these were originally
established by planting Scots pines alongside them as nurse
trees.

Whatever the outcome, Exmoor will remain largely a
treeless expanse of upland grazing and moor. This is its
principal charm. Charm is the appropriate word to describe,
for example, the enclosed valley of the Barle, near Landacre
Bridge, where the twelfth-century forest courts were held,
and where a car will pass only once in half an hour and this
perhaps the crumpled Ford of a farmer who stops to check
his sheep on the hillsides through binoculars. On a summer
day even the Badgworthy and its tributaries—Doone country
—can seem peaceful and fertile. But the coastal moorlands,
where driving snow will coat the heather in May, blanketed
by mist in winter for days on end, are another matter. In the
early nineteenth century Southy reported that Porlock was
known locally as 'The End of the World', because 'all beyond
is inaccessible to carriages or even carts'. Leave the comfort
of a car and struggle on foot up and down the steep combes
of the moor in a westerly gale and Exmoor still seems as wild
and remote as it must have done to Saxons and Normans.

Dartmoor

Dartmoor is separated by 40 miles from Exmoor, though
both it and the western end of Exmoor are in Devon. If
Exmoor is bleak, Dartmoor, the highest of its granite tors
rising to over 2,000 feet, is even more so. In 1786 a surveyor
of the Duchy of Cornwall recorded that 'within the last

twenty years there were only three or four very blind roads across the whole, insomuch that going over the moor in *winter* was always considered not only an arduous but really dangerous undertaking'. Before the building of the eighteenth-century turnpikes there are many tales of locals becoming lost in Dartmoor's notorious mists and dying of exposure. The climate has not changed.

Granite is not only the material of the tors, but the underlying rock of the whole moor. It forms the most easterly and highest of a succession of granite outcrops which continue west through Bodmin Moor, St Austell, and West Penwith, ending with the Isles of Scilly. Granite is also central to the moor's history. It was quarried for stone to build, among other things, the old London Bridge (now in Arizona). It held the mineral lodes which made Dartmoor at one time the largest tin producer in the world. A different type of granite weathered into material for today's vast china clay mines which will ultimately form a crater in the south-west corner of the moor measuring one and a half miles by two and a half miles.

The moor's granite may also explain why mesolithic, neolithic, Bronze and Iron Age communities *seem* to have inhabited Dartmoor more extensively than any other area in southern England. The moor is littered with their monuments, circles, forts and ruined dwellings. Granite lasts better than other rock.

They lived in what was probably, up to at least 1,000 feet, a forest of scrub oak. For many years historians believed that Wistman's Wood, that strange belt of stunted, lichen-covered oak lying on one valley side of the West Dart near the centre of the moor, was an untouched remnant of this forest, but recent studies have shown that its history is more complex.

In about 400 BC, however, perhaps because the climate grew temporarily colder, Dartmoor became an uninhabited waste, and it was only around AD 700 that the Saxons began to use it again. From this time onwards farmers from all over Devon (and until AD 850 from Cornwall too) would drive their flocks on to the moor for summer grazing. During the eighth or ninth centuries it became a customary hunting ground of the Saxon kings, and after the Conquest the Normans placed it, with the whole of the rest of the county of Devon, under forest law. Although there is no record of Norman or Plantagenet kings hunting on Dartmoor, they clearly believed they might—the Manor of Skerraton, for example, was held in return for the service of providing the king with three barbed arrows.

At the comparatively early date of 1204 King John disafforested the whole of Devon except Dartmoor and Exmoor. For 35 years Dartmoor remained a royal forest, then Henry III gave it to his brother Richard, Duke of Cornwall, and it became in effect a chase. From this time Common Law applied, and cases were tried in the local manor courts.

The change roughly corresponded with a new development on the moor. There had been earlier attempts to settle the high ground around the edges of the forest, but all had been abandoned by about 1100 and none had been on the forest itself. Now, 150 years later, the duchy seems to have encouraged the settlement of certain areas in the valleys of the East and West Dart and its tributaries. These holdings came to be known as the ancient tenements, and their holders (there were 35 of them, later reduced to seventeen) formed the class of Commoners with the most valuable rights on the forest. In return for serving on the juries of manor courts and helping with cattle drifts they were entitled to free grazing.

Different rights were held by so-called Venville Commoners. They were the occupiers of certain lands in certain manors, mainly those which bordered the forest. They paid a fixed rent to the king or duchy, and in return could pasture their animals on the forest *and* on their commons by day, but had to pay if they kept them there at night. The animals they could pasture were limited (as they were in other forests, such as Ashdown in Sussex) to those they could support on their holdings in winter. If they pastured more they paid the rate which 'strangers' paid. Venville Commoners could also take materials for fuel, building and hedging from the forest.

'Strangers', also called 'foreigners', were householders of the rest of Devon (except Totnes and Barnstable, who were strangely left out). They could graze the commons round the forest free, but had to pay for each beast they pastured on the forest itself.

Alongside these stockfarmers who used the forest and its commons for grazing there grew up another class of men even more important to the king: the tin miners. Tin had been worked in Cornwall in the Bronze Age, and was clearly being worked again in AD 950 when Athelstan received tin dues from a stannary court, but the earliest record of tin mining on Dartmoor occurs in the Pipe Roll of 1156. Only a few years later, between 1171 and 1189, the output from Dartmoor had risen to an average of 343 tons a year, overtaking Cornwall.

By the end of the next century, however, the position was reversed, Dartmoor producing a mere 33 tons annually, Cornwall 300. Dartmoor production recovered in Tudor times—in 1524, 252 tons were produced—and again after 1800, but mining finally ceased in 1914, and in 1939, when the last Dartmoor tin was produced from the material of earlier mine dumps, it was taken to Wales for smelting.

The explanation of these changes is simple: the tin ore gradually became harder to recover or exhausted. At first it could be found in river valleys where tin-bearing rock had accumulated after being washed out of the lodes. The ore was then so rich that it would flow like quicksilver when heated in a simple peat fire. As the miners exhausted the river bed deposits they pursued the tin back to its sources and drove adits into the valley sides. When, in the eighteenth and nineteenth centuries, these became unproductive, they sank deep mines, of which the deepest, Vitifer, went down 460 feet. Ultimately deep mining also grew uneconomical.

Tin has been a key metal in the steps man has taken towards material prosperity and industrial civilisation. It was the discovery that copper could be hardened with tin to make weapons and tools with sharper cutting edges which created Bronze Age civilization. In mediaeval times tin was used for pewter, bell casting, adulterating coinage and many other purposes. There is no need to look further for the king's special interest in it, but by chance in Devon it was largely found on royal, later duchy, land. This made it simple for the king to tax all tin produced. He also on several occasions bought the whole tin production for the year and, acting as middle man, resold it at a profit. Richard I made £352 in this way in 1197, and in 1367 the Black Prince did a similar deal, buying at 20s a hundredweight and selling at 26s 8d. To regularize the trade the king, in the early fourteenth century, established the stannary towns of Tavistock, Chagford, Ashburton and Plympton (*stannum* is latin for tin) through which all tin had to be sold.

To encourage tin mining he gave special privileges to the miners. These were probably granted earlier and were certainly more valuable than those of the miners of the Forest of Dean, and for its miners Dartmoor became virtually a state within a state. They could mine where they chose in the forest and—except for murder, bodily injury and the stealing of land—were tried in their own stannary courts. They were exempt from almost all taxes. Such privileges were resented and landowners claimed that miners blackmailed them by threatening to mine on their property. The stannary courts in return accused the landowners of trying to avoid taxation by claiming to be miners.

Tin was mostly found in the central and southern parts of Dartmoor. Elsewhere, copper, arsenic, lead and iron were mined, though never so extensively. From the mid-twelfth century to the early twentieth, when all except china clay mining ceased, mining was more important than any other forest activity, and the local population rose and fell as it prospered or declined.

It was not the only industry which flourished on the moor. Wool and cloth making first developed at much the same time that the tin mines were at their most productive. The wool then came from sheep kept by the Cistercian abbey at Buckfast and the Benedictine abbey at Tavistock. Dartmoor was able to provide not only the wool, which was corded in its cottages, but streams to power mills for weaving it. There were mills at Ashburton and Moretonhampstead before 1300, by the mid-sixteenth century there were fifteen mills around Tavistock, and during the next century others at Sticklepath, Bridestowe, Belstone and Dean Prior. In the eighteenth century the Belstone mill made the scarlet serge ordered by the Nizam of Hyderabad for his bodyguard. The industry declined more slowly than mining. It lasted longest at Buckfast and Dartington Hall, and the wool of the moor's sheep—now mainly Scottish Blackface—is still valuable and easily marketed.

The water mills which made cloth were often adapted to other uses. The mill at Belstone, for example, ground corn before and after it made cloth. Water power has also at different times been used in the making of edge-tools, paper and gunpowder on the moor. But the industry most closely connected with its surviving trees was leather. There were tanyards at Okehampton, Moretonhampstead, Tavistock and Plymouth. The oak bark they needed was taken by rippers from coppice oak woods in the moor's sheltered valleys.

In spite of its long history of exploitation, Dartmoor remained a remote, infertile area, of little interest to those who, everywhere else in the country, were trying to enclose forest land, until the second half of the eighteenth century. Then new roads, especially the Moretonhampstead to Tavistock turnpike opened in 1772, encouraged the improvers, as they were called on Dartmoor, to move in.

They based their operations on the ancient tenements. The occupiers of these had always claimed the right to enclose new land, known as 'new takes', up to eight acres in extent on succession to the tenement, provided it had been held for at least two generations, and at first the improvers on various pretexts extended this practice. Later they obtained permission from the Duchy of Cornwall to enclose further huge areas of forest. During the Napoleonic Wars the duchy considered it patriotic to allow development of this sort which could produce food for the nation. One of the foremost improvers was Justice Francis Buller, who came to hold a group of ancient tenements with a total area of 2,000 acres, and who tried in 1791 to have a bill passed for enclosing the whole forest. Though this failed, by 1802 the ancient tenements amounted to 2,876 acres and the new takes to 5,274 acres—and these figures seem not to have included some of the duchy grants to men like Thomas Tyrwhitt.

Of all the improvers, Tyrwhitt, secretary to the Prince of Wales, had most permanent influence on the forest. Some of the moor's best-known places were given their names by him in honour of his patron. He operated from Tor Royal, just south of Two Bridges, built an inn called the Plume of Feathers and created a settlement nearby called Prince's Town (now Princetown).

Tyrwhitt's arable farming failed. The site he had chosen was 1,300 feet above sea level and hopelessly exposed. His failure was typical of many of the other Dartmoor improvers, and forms a close parallel to the agricultural failures of John Knight on Exmoor at about the same time. All that happened agriculturally during these years on Dartmoor was summed up by Tyrwhitt's contemporary, the Rev. J. P. Jones of North Bovey, who wrote, 'The Gentlemen and adventurers who commenced improvements were altogether mistaken with respect to the soil and produce of Dartmoor.'

But this was by no means the end of Tyrwhitt's effect on the moor. When a prison was needed for French prisoners during the Napoleonic Wars he used his influence to have one built at Princetown. This turned the settlement there into a thriving community, which only declined in 1816 when the war had finished and the last prisoners left.

Tyrwhitt had died before Princetown became a prison again, but he schemed so industriously to have it reopened that he managed to have a railway (horse-drawn, of course) built to connect it to Plymouth. When there was a railway, he argued, convicts could be sent up and down more easily, and meanwhile it would bring up lime, fertilizers, timber, coal and groceries, and take down granite, peat and in due time flax and hemp. The full 25 miles of this remarkable line were finally completed in 1827, and it worked spasmodically, though never at a profit, till 1878.

Meanwhile an even more remarkable line had been proposed, built and failed. This was the Haytor Granite Tramway, designed exclusively to take granite down from the moor, running on a track of flanged granite blocks. It was completed in 1825 and carried to Bovey Heathfield 300,000 cubic feet of stone for London Bridge, as well as stone for a number of other well-known buildings and monuments, including the vast block on which George III and his Copper Horse stand at the centre of Windsor Great Park. Though it was closed over 120 years ago (1858) long stretches of track can still be found.

It was promoted by George Templer, of Stover House, who is connected with the forest's history in another way: as a huntsman. Red deer had been the original beasts of the forest on Dartmoor, but they were exterminated before 1780 by the Duke of Bedford's hounds, imported for the purpose. Forty years later, foxes were the usual quarry, but since they were scarce George Templer kept a yard full of them, chained and kennelled. They were released 20 yards in front of the hounds, then pursued, but the hounds were so well controlled that they were normally prevented from killing. In 1824-25 one fox survived 36 hunts. Hunting on the moor was always hazardous. During a hunt in 1892 the South Devon had six horses sunk to their bellies in bog at the same time, and the whole pack of the Eggesford hunt was once lost for several days in the northern forest.

In the late eighteenth century the Dartmoor improvers were also the first on the moor to attempt modern forestry. In this they were later than those who planted conifers in the New Forest, for example, or on certain Welsh estates, but began soon after the first turnpikes opened up the moor. At Prince Hall around 1785 Francis Buller planted 40,000 trees. Tyrwhitt planted at Tor Royal and Edward Bray at Beardown. None of these plantations were sufficiently successful to produce commercial timber, though parts of some survived as shelter belts.

During the Napoleonic Wars some broadleaf plantations were established around Dartmoor for patriotic reasons —Bagnor Woods at Ilsington, for example—and in 1854 there was a proposal (which came to nothing) to forest 50,000 acres of the moor. Many of these early foresters were under the misapprehension that plantation, once established, would modify Dartmoor's climate.

The first plantations to reach maturity and be successfully harvested were established around 1862 at Brimps. They were largely felled during the First World War. It was only at the end of this war that large-scale forestry on the moor was again proposed and became the subject of fierce argument.

Here the history of forestry on the forest and moor merges with that of the Dartmoor Preservation Association. This body was founded in the early 1880s, exactly the period at which the Commons Preservation Society and a number of other associations were belatedly trying to save from enclosure the country's commons and forests. Soon after it had been founded the DPA set about establishing the legal basis of the Commoners' rights. They were able to prove that almost all the eighteenth- and nineteenth-century enclosures had been illegal, and as a result to prevent a number of further ones which were being planned.

So when, in 1931, the Forestry Commission took over all the duchy plantations, and an area of 1,900 acres for further planting including Bellever and Laughter Hole, the DPA led public protest. By this time Brimps had been replanted, a large 800-acre site planted at Fernworthy and smaller ones at

Frenchbeer near Chagford and at Beardown. Sitka spruce and Douglas fir were used. The Plymouth Corporation had also begun to plant some 700 acres with conifers around its Burraton reservoir.

The DPA argued that the original new takes, on which the new plantations were to be established had been largely shown to be illegal, that the public would lose its right of access and the Commoners their grazing, and above all that the whole landscape of the moor would be changed by big blocks of conifers which were entirely out of keeping with its scenery and vegetation.

The argument has continued for 50 years with victories on both sides. Today, to summarize, the Forestry Commission has 3,180 acres of plantation on the forest itself (and some 2,050 acres to the south-west in the Plym area). The plantations on the forest now consist very largely of sitka spruce, although there are small amounts of Norway spruce and Japanese larch. And Plymouth Corporation retains its plantations at Burraton. But at present there are no plans to enclose or plant new areas.

As for the plantations themselves, because of Dartmoor's high rainfall, they are the most productive in the country. And aesthetically, those around Fernworthy Reservoir, for example, edged with birch and rowan, would seem delightful anywhere except on Dartmoor. Even on Dartmoor they provide habitats for a wider variety of wild life, and seem less scenically objectionable than most of the other uses to which the moor has been put over the last 1,000 years.

Apart from its conifer plantations, the moor has a number of broadleaf woods of exceptional interest, including Wistman's Wood, already mentioned, Black Tor Beare and Piles Copse, which are similarly composed of stunted English (pedunculate) oak, mixed with small amounts of holly and rowan; and Yarner Wood and Holne Chase where durmast (sessile) oak predominates.

Dartmoor's National Park Officer believes that such woods cannot simply be left to look after themselves but must be managed. 'Some of my colleagues,' he says, 'are bitterly opposed to felling anything. They have to be educated.' For Holne Chase the National Park and other interested bodies have been recently preparing a management plan. This fine and extensive area of woodland which fills a bowl-shaped section of the Dart valley contains—as well as coppiced oak—silver birch, coppiced lime, hazel and invading beech and sycamore. Singling, planting, encouraging natural regeneration and selective felling will all form part of this plan. If private broadleaf woodlands need to earn some financial return, the National Park would not oppose the planting of a small proportion of conifers. But coppicing on Dartmoor can also be profitable, coppiced oak selling well for burning and hazel for thatching spars.

Today forestry on Dartmoor, if not a dead issue, is at least a sleeping one. So are reservoirs, even if these in the past have done more permanent damage to the landscape than anything else. No new ones are planned. Nor are there any plans for new roads which would cross the park, though the Okehampton bypass may, if agreed, cut off a few yards. The National Park on principle has argued against this infringement.

Four live issues remain and involve the National Park and the DPA, still led by Sylvia Sayer, the veteran campaigner who has done more to save the moor than anyone else, in a series of skirmishes. Of these the most complex concerns Commoners' rights. A new Dartmoor bill is needed, the National Park Officer believes, and hopes that recent publicity about the welfare of the moor's ponies will encourage Parliament to pass one. But the last attempt in 1979 failed, and there is now disagreement about, among other things, the Venville Commoners' claim to grazing rights not just on their own commons but on the forest and other commons.

Simpler—because it is insoluble—is the question of china clay mining. China clay is such a valuable export—there are few other sources in the world—that it must continue to be mined. All that can be done is conceal the devastation. This has become easier since the Aberfan tip disaster; waste tips are now less steep and can be planted sooner. The National Park Officer tells the more vehement objectors that they use it every day themselves—in their toothpaste.

Also simple is the question of the Okehampton bypass, which a recent public enquiry has agreed to allow south of the town, thus, in Lady Sayer's words, 'dismembering the ancient deer park of Okehampton with its downland and woodland rich in prehistoric and medieval sites, and straddling the lovely valleys of the East and West Okement rivers with vast concrete viaducts'. Because no land can be found to replace the loss this will cause to the National Park the D.P.A. has been able to take the issue to Parliament and a joint committee of both Houses will consider its petition shortly.

Finally, and most unfortunately, there is the army, which still occupies 30,000 acres of the forest as a training area. These cover much of the northern half of the forest and include several firing ranges. The army began to use the moor regularly in 1873. A firing range for nine- and sixteen-pounders was established in 1876 and annual camps began the next year. Strangely, the army used the moor rather less than in previous years during the First World War, but in the Second World War it took over vast areas and in 1946 asked to be allowed to retain 70,000 acres. Only fierce local opposition forced it to accept less, and from 1970 its leases have been restricted to seven years. It needed a new one in 1984, but at the time of writing this has still not been agreed. Meanwhile the National Park can only work to prevent the army entrenching itself too deeply. It has lately opposed the modernizing of one rifle range and the building of one new permanent camp.

Perhaps it is no coincidence that Dartmoor, once the most remote and rugged of all English royal forests, has been more vigorously and consistently exploited than any other. It seems likely that exploiters of all sorts will continue to wish to despoil this conveniently out of the way piece of wild country. The Duchy of Cornwall has a poor record for preserving the natural qualities of its unique property, and those who want such areas to survive in an overpopulated country should be grateful to the Dartmoor Preservation Association for its long and on the whole successful defence of moor and forest.

Picnic in Epping Forest

THE FOREST
OF ESSEX

'The Epping Hunt is now entirely discontinued,' wrote the author of *English Forests and Forest-Trees* in 1853, 'as it had for many years become a mere pretext for a holiday to all the idle, dissolute, vagabondish people of London.'

The right of the people of London to an annual hunt in the Forest of Essex was believed (incorrectly) to go back to Henry III's reign. By the eighteenth century much of the county had been disafforested, but the substantial remaining forest—about 60,000 acres, including today's Epping Forest—lay in its south-west corner, conveniently near to London, and here the Easter hunt survived. It seems to have been a Derby Day of its time. Writing in the *Illustrated London News,* 'a Cockney sport', describes a typical hunt.

'Easter Monday was a glorious day . . . to the whole class of bold riders from every part of town who could procure anything in the shape of a horse to "carry them up to the hounds".' They came not only on horseback but 'in a vast variety of conveyances . . . to that beautiful spot in the Forest, Fairmead Bottom to see the deer let loose from the cart and join in the labours of his re-capture or death'.

They paused first for refreshment at the Eagle at Snaresbrook, then continued to the Bold-face Stag at Buckhurst Hill (both survive) where 'Thomas Rounding Esq., huntsman in ordinary', in hunting cap and coat, buckskin-breeches and top boots, took charge. 'The animal, on being released from the cart . . . made its way for the thickest part of the forest.' As a result 'all four-wheeled and all two-wheeled carriages were soon *hors de combat* . . . As the chase increased, a series of accidents was inevitable: some fell from their horses; many horses fell from their riders; some were engulphed in mud and mire; some were knocked "up", others were knocked "down"; and before half an hour had elapsed, not a tithe of the original "field" were to be seen in the forest. The deer had a trick which was to some peculiarly annoying, though others thought it capital fun: he would betake himself to one of the herds of his species grazing in the forest, and then, instead of one quarry, the hounds and hunters had their choice of a score or two which to pursue. Here was perplexity, and that not a little increased by the hallooing of Tom Rounding, the yelping of dogs, the cursing of men, the cracking of whips, and the blowing of horns.'

Eventually the right deer 'was for the most part . . . driven to bay, when, after a contest with the dogs, he was secured, and taken back to the place from whence he came, not to immediate but to ultimate execution, *i.e.* to another day's sport at a subsequent anniversary. All this was followed, indeed accompanied, by eating, drinking, singing, speechifying, and so forth; and if no great encouragement to stag-hunting in its more legitimate sense, was the means of amusement to hundreds of people, excited mirth and merriment, enforced good-fellowship, and furnished good exercise and diversion.'

The great Forest of Essex, in which these Cockney Easter hunts took place, had declined in size and importance in parallel with other royal forests, but, perhaps because it lay close to London and successive kings and queens took a particular interest in it, had retained something of its mediaeval character longer than most. It continued to survive into the nineteenth century when its future was finally settled.

William I and his immediate successors seem to have afforested, in the legal sense, virtually the whole county of Essex; only a small north-western fragment beyond the Roman road of Stane Street which ran from Bishop's Stortford to Colchester was excluded. But just when this afforestation occurred was sufficiently uncertain for Henry III, in signing the Forest Charter of 1217, to agree to a perambulation of the forest. In 1225 two perambulations recommended the disafforestation of all except the forests of Kingswood (north of Colchester), Felsted (east of Great Dunmow), Hatfield Broadoak (south-east of Bishop's Stortford), Writtle (south-west of Chelmsford) and Waltham. The grounds of their recommendations were that the rest of the county had been first afforested by Henry II. But three years later Henry III reclaimed for the crown all the previous forest, arguing that Henry II was only taking back what had been lost during the civil war of Stephen's reign.

The king's recovery of most of Essex for forest was only temporary. When Edward I, in 1301, agreed with the Commons that, in return for a tax of one fifteenth on his subjects there should be a pardon of all offences against the king's deer and new perambulations of royal forests, the forest of

Essex was again reduced to the 1225 limits. From then onwards the different forests of Essex had different histories.

Waltham

Waltham was now considerably the largest, including not only today's **Epping** and **Wintry** forests but also the forests of **Hainault** and **Havering**. The greater part remained forest for over 500 years, but Havering, which lay close to the town of Havering-atte-Bower, was lost quite quickly. Edward II assigned it to his queen, Isabella. And though the crown continued to claim it as late as 1617, it had clearly by then become a purlieu of the forest. It had a ranger—foresters in charge of purlieus were called rangers. And the 1641 perambulation defined the bounds which separated it from the rest of Waltham Forest. The destruction of its woodland occurred over many centuries, and to the west of the town woods which once formed part of it still survive.

The remainder of Waltham Forest was administered much like other royal forests. There were three courts: the court of attachment or woodmote, which met every two months and recorded accusations against forest offenders, then passed them on to the swainmote. The swainmote, which met three times a year, decided whether the offences had been committed and fixed the punishment. And the Court of Justice Seat, or forest eyre as it was called elsewhere, held periodically by the visiting Justice for the forests south of the Tyne, which alone could decide if the offences *were* offences under forest law and actually hand out the punishments.

The chief administrative officer or steward of Waltham was alternatively called the lord warden. His deputy was the lieutenant of the forest. From the thirteenth century, lord wardens were able to leave or grant their office to others. There continued to be lord wardens and lieutenants of the forest till the nineteenth century and the doings of Lord Mornington, who was warden from 1812 to 1857, will be described presently.

Next came the forest verderers. They were gentlemen or esquires, and from 1306 at latest were elected by the freeman of the county. They were judges at the courts of attachment and presided at the swainmotes. Their original function was to protect the king's rights in the forest but in Waltham

Forest by a curious irony (and an Act of Parliament in 1812) they were given power to take action against unlawful enclosures. They should thus have become its protectors against those, including the king and warden, who were allowing or actively encouraging enclosure.

The practical work of protecting the woods and deer of the forest was carried out by foresters or riding foresters. There were also three foresters-in-fee in Waltham, who paid with cash or by service for their office. Each forester had his bailiwick, but these by 1580 had become known as walks.

Waltham also had its regarders—approximately twelve knights—who were to make a regard or general survey of the forest every three years. But no full regard of the forest survives from before 1489, and just how irregularly they carried out this duty in later times is shown by the regard of 1630, when some of the 400 offences they reported had occurred between 40 and 60 years ago.

Beyond the forest, rangers managed its disafforested purlieus. The purlieus of Waltham formed an arc enclosing it to north, east, and south, and, as well as the liberty of Havering, included Ongar Park, Stapleford, Wealdside, Bentry Heath and Leyton. The king claimed the right to hunt in the purlieus and though forest law did not apply the lord warden of the forest appointed the chief ranger.

All these officials were directly or indirectly responsible to the king, but the woodwards were appointed by the owners of land inside the forest, and had dual responsibilities to the owners of protecting their interests and to the king of ensuring that the woods were not felled or assarted, so depriving the deer of their habitat.

Finally, Waltham's reeves were of particular interest; they were appointed by the parishes of the forest and had responsibility for the Commoners' cattle grazing on the forest. One of their duties was to 'drive the forest'—go through it once or

twice a year, commonly at Michaelmas, to catch and impound any cattle which had no right to be there. Such cattle, if not claimed, were sold by auction at Romford market. The forest still has two pounds, but today they rarely contain more than a stray horse or pony. The reeves, to help them supervise the Commoners' cattle, had the duty of branding them. The brands were seven to nine inches high and each parish had its own mark, representing a letter of the alphabet with a crown on top.

The right of the Commoners to pasture animals in the forest became of great importance when Epping Forest was threatened with destruction in the 1860s and 1870s. It was of long standing. Typical of the feuds it caused between Commoners and landowners was one between the people of Waltham and Simon the Abbot of Waltham Abbey in 1245. On two occasions the people killed or drowned the abbot's mares. In retaliation he excommunicated them, and ultimately won his case at the King's Bench.

But in 1512 the rights of the inhabitants and tenants of Waltham Manor to graze their animals on the Great Common Marsh of Waltham were confirmed. More importantly, in 1620 the regarders confirmed the rights of all inhabitants of the forest to pasture their animals in the forest. Goats and geese were always excluded, and, after a series of court cases in the seventeenth century, so were sheep. In 1877 the Epping Forest Commission found that forest inhabitants also had pannage rights for their pigs, but there is only occasional evidence of their exercising it.

The deer which the verderers and foresters protected were both native red and the fallow which the early Normans had brought with them. Bones of wild boar and roe deer have also been found, but there is no written evidence of them until roe were introduced by E. N. Buxton in 1884.

Norman and Plantagenet kings hunted in the Forest of

Cattle brands in Epping Forest

Essex, and the Tudors in particular favoured it for their sport. Henry VIII is said to have hunted here on the day of the execution of his second wife, Anne Boleyn. The occasion was dramatized in the early nineteenth century by Dr John Nott.

On the fatal morning Henry went to hunt in Epping Forest; and while he was at breakfast his attendants observed that he was anxious and thoughtful. But at length they heard the report of a distant gun—a preconcerted signal.

'Ah! it is done!' cried he, starting up; 'the business is done! 'Uncouple the dogs, and let us follow the sport.'

In the evening he returned gaily from the chase; and on the following morning he married Anne's maid of honour, Jane Seymour.

The hunting lodge at Chingford, now called Queen Elizabeth's, suggests that even if Henry VIII rode to hounds in pursuit of his deer, the later Tudors preferred to shoot at them as they were driven past. At this time, Camden wrote, 'Near the Ley . . . spreads out a chase of vast extent, full of game, the largest and fattest deer in the kingdom; called heretofore, by way of eminence, the Forest of Essex, now Waltham Forest.'

James I took a particular interest in his deer. The year after he became king he 'violently scolded his subjects for their ill-manners in interfering with the sport of himself and his family'. In the early months of 1615 there was such severe weather that, before the following winter, he issued a proclamation which began, 'For that great number of Deere both Red and Fallow have been destroyed by the last great Frost and Snow, and those that remaine and have escaped the hardnesse of the weather have beene so weakened and surfeited by the extremetie of the colde, so as they will hardly hold out this next winter,' and continued to forbid pannage and other practices which might deprive the deer of winter feed.

Both the deer of Waltham and their protectors suffered regularly from poaching. One night in 1593 John Porter and others from Kelvedon were found coursing deer in the forest. 'The keeper's man coming in unto them did charge them in God his name and the Queen's to stand; then the said John Porter did slight his horse, and mainteininge his mastief upon the keap's man, with a bill did very sore hurt him.'

Poachers not only coursed the deer with hounds and shot them with long bow, cross bow and musket but also netted them. One type of net was known as a 'thief net'. It was 'baited with bottles, flowers, looking glasses etc; an apparatus designed to practise upon the curiosity of the deer'.

In the eighteenth century many deer survived, as the description of the Epping Hunt shows, but all red deer were transferred to Windsor in 1820, and during the nineteenth century the fallow deer steadily declined till by 1870 there were only ten to twelve does and one buck.

After the 1878 Act they increased again and by 1902 there were about 270, but today not more than a dozen are likely to be found on the forest at any one time. There is, however, some evidence that they still breed on the forest, and a much larger number visit it from the estates of Copthall, Worley Park and Woodredon to the north.

The fallow deer of Epping are special. They are entirely 'black'. Black, or rather dark-brown, deer occur in any fallow herd from time to time, as do albinos, but are elsewhere often culled. In Epping black deer are preserved and lighter ones eliminated. When the herd seemed in danger a 100-acre reserve was created near the forest at Theydon Bois, where about 100 Epping deer now live and breed.

There were no agisters for Waltham Forest to supervise the grazing of the king's land because the king had no land here until the Reformation. It was only then that he recovered the estates and rights which had been granted to such religious institutions as Waltham Abbey. In 1635 Charles I, as one of his money-making schemes, made a more dramatic attempt to re-establish his forest rights by having the Forest of Essex extended again to include the whole county south of Stane Street. By 1640 he was so successful that in this year landowners who wished to have their lands again disafforested paid him sums amounting to £300,000. But such extortions made him increasingly unpopular and in the same year he agreed to an Act of the Long Parliament which set aside the 1635 decision, and, after a new perambulation, Waltham was reduced again to the boundaries of 1301.

These remained its legal limits till the disafforestation of Hainault in 1851. But much had happened by then to alter its character. Throughout the eighteenth century its land was extensively enclosed, assarted and much built up on. 'Gravel and sand pits were open in all directions, and the material removed without restraint; large spots of ground from which the turf had been removed for use in gardens both near to and distant from the Forest; bushes and underwood cut and removed at pleasure; deer-stealers so numerous, that there was barely a small house in and for miles round the forest which did not contain one or more; greyhounds and lurchers kept by most of the poor inhabitants, and by unqualified farmers round the Forest; encroachments by inclosures and buildings in various parts; workpeople trespassing in all directions, and at all seasons; oak timber shamefully destroyed; young trees and tellers wasted; and pollards and underwood lopped and carried away'.

This was the description of Long Wellesley, later Lord Mornington, who became lord warden in 1812. But within 20 years he was openly supporting enclosures. In E. N. Buxton's words, he was a man who 'saw more profit in breaking his trust than in keeping it'. When Hainault Forest was disafforested by Act of Parliament in 1851, the lord warden received £5,250 in compensation.

The crown, for its compensation, was allotted 1,917 acres of woodland, containing over 100,000 oaks, hornbeams and other trees. The sale of this timber paid for the destruction of the rest of the forest. Ninety-two per cent was almost instantly felled and grubbed out. A manufacturer of the newly invented steam plough did the work in six weeks, driving anchors into the ground to enable him to drag out the ancient oaks by their roots.

Hainault Forest contained the famous Fairlop Oak, which is often said to have been destroyed at this time and was claimed to be the largest in the country. The first claim is incorrect and the second ignores the Doodle Oak at Hatfield.

It was, however, a formidable tree, its trunk measuring 48 feet in circumference at the ground and 36 feet at three feet above the ground. Nineteenth-century drawings show that it had by then become a typical stagheaded tree. This condition is often thought to be fatal, but in fact it merely indicates that its annual 'commitment' to cover with new wood the surface area of its trunk and branches has exceeded the 'income' of nourishment provided by its roots and foliage. At this stage outer branches die, but those which survive are often in good health and stagheaded trees can live for many decades.

The Fairlop Oak had probably once been a pollard—hence its great age. Above its short trunk it divided into eleven branches, each ten to twelve feet in circumference. In the early eighteenth century an annual fair was held here, at which no stall was allowed beyond its spread. The fair

Fairlop Oak

originated in a forest picnic at which Daniel Day would entertain his friends to beans and bacon. By 1725 it had become a public occasion, taking place every 2nd of July, but Day still provided beans and bacon for the general public, distributing them from the tree's hollow trunk.

The 'orgies annually celebrated to the honour of the Fairlop Oak' did it no good, nor did a family of gypsies who took up residence inside it, and it was treated by the Hainault Archery Society with 'Mr Forsyth's composition', who hung a board on it saying that a plaster had been applied to its wounds. Around the middle of the century, however, a large branch was torn off by a storm, and when Daniel Day died in 1767, aged 84, his coffin was made from this.

Still more severe damage was done in 1805 by a party of cricketers who lit a fire close by. At eight in the evening the trunk was found to be alight and although it was doused with buckets of water, it smouldered till morning. Even so it survived another fifteen years and finally blew down in the high winds of February 1820. The pulpit for New Church, St Pancras, was made from its timber.

Nine years after the disafforestation of Hainault the Lords of the Manors of the parishes in which the rest of the forest of Waltham lay (now reduced by the loss of Hainault and by other enclosures from 60,000 to 7,000 acres) were allowed to buy the crown's rights in their parishes. They at once set about enclosing their portions. The Rev. John Maitland, Lord of the Manor of Loughton and its newly appointed rector, obtained the largest share: about a third.

The Commoners of Loughton had traditionally had the right to pollard hornbeams in the forest for fuel. On 11 November, the day on which the annual lopping season began, one of these named Thomas Willingale was discovered lopping, arrested for trespass and theft and sent to gaol for two months.

The Commons Preservation Society took up Willingale's case, but failed to get his rights confirmed, and in 1870 a bill was prepared for Parliament which would have reserved 400 acres to be sold to compensate the Commoners for the loss of all their rights, and a mere 600 more for the general public.

E. N. Buxton describes the meeting of the Commons Preservation Society at which this proposal was discussed. 'So dark was the outlook that it was seriously debated by the committee whether this so-called compromise should be accepted. It is not too much to say that the fate of the Forest trembled round the table where this committee sat. If weak-kneed counsel had prevailed, the Bill would probably have passed without opposition and the Forest, as we know it, would have ceased to exist. Happily a spirited policy carried the day.'

At this point the Corporation of London came to the support of the forest, and provided money needed for expensive legal proceedings. It was able to do so because a closely connected body, the Commissioners of Sewers of the City of London, owned a cemetery and farm at Wanstead which entitled it to common rights. The Corporation took the advice of the forest historian, W. R. Fisher, who believed that Commoners of each parish had common rights not just on the lands of their particular manors but over the whole forest. It was on this point that the case turned, since it made agreements between the Commoners and their Lords of the Manor to give up their rights insufficient justification for enclosure.

Fisher also prepared a scheme for the forest which formed the basis of the 1878 Epping Forest Act. By this the Corporation of London were made Conservators of the forest with the duty of preserving it as an open space for the recreation and enjoyment of the public. They were to buy up and pay compensation for the Commoners' lopping rights, but to preserve their grazing rights. In 1882, 22 years after the first of the enclosures which began these troubles, Queen Victoria arrived at Chingford Station, decked out with evergreens for the occasion, to open the forest formally to the public.

The Act required the Conservators to 'preserve the natural aspect of the forest'. It is these words which have caused much argument over the years, because the condition of the forest in 1878 was a highly unnatural one. In the opinion of the Superintendent of the Forest, it was this that the Act essentially wanted preserved. If nature alone was allowed to take over, the forest would become 'dark, cold and bloody awful'.

At the same time he believes that Parliament may not have fully realized, when it required the Conservators to keep the forest in its 1878 condition, how much maintenance this would mean. Many centuries of use had produced a wood-pasture vegetation, in which the Commoners' animals, helped to a small extent by the deer and to a larger extent by the forest's rabbits, kept much of the land unwooded, and the regular fifteen-year lopping of the trees allowed enough light into the woodlands for many and various plants, shrubs and small trees to grow below them. Today far fewer cattle or deer use the forest and the rabbits have been decimated by myxomatosis. And although the Conservators have done a small amount of lopping since the last war, to do it on a large scale would be hopelessly expensive and impractical. As a result, and despite much grass cutting and scrub clearance by the Conservators, large areas of grassland have reverted first to birch and thorn scrub then to oak or beech wood, and the wooded areas, now about 4,000 out of 6,000 acres, often consist of standard trees or grown out pollards with only a carpet of brown leaves below.

Conservationists regret these changes, saying that although the Act specifically requires the Conservators to 'protect the timber and other trees, pollards, shrubs, underwood, heather, gorse, turf, and herbage', they have favoured the timber trees at the expense of other vegetation, and much of the forest has become undistinguished secondary woodland. Their point is both that the character of the forest has been allowed to alter, and that the average age of the trees has been reduced. A tree, to quote Rackham, 'needs to be at least 300 years old and preferably a pollard before it will harbour many of the more distinctive wood-pasture organisms'.

In the Conservators' defence it must be said that they consider a forest with trees of more various ages to be more interesting. To encourage the natural regeneration of young trees, some old ones are felled, so letting light into the forest. In time they would anyway have fallen and this policy could be described as merely 'speeding up nature'. As for the grasslands, where it is not too late the Conservators are continuing to do what they can to prevent their reversion to scrub.

Insufficient as they may be, Epping is lucky to have a staff of 52. Four manage the forest's playing fields, three its golf course, and eighteen are Special Constables with powers of arrest and prosecution for general as well as forest by-law offences. But these spend half their time on physical management, as do fourteen other full-time forest workmen.

All are paid by the Corporation of London from private City funds. The Corporation appoints twelve of the sixteen members of the Forest Committee. The remaining four are the new verderers of the forest, elected by the Commoners. Though only five Commoners now turn out cattle on the forest, many hundreds of inhabitants of the forest parishes are Commoners, and, provided they have half an acre of unbuilt-on land, have grazing rights.

The earthworks of two Iron-Age forts are the earliest evidence of Epping's history to be seen on the ground today. Most is known about Ambresbury Banks, which lies in the northern part of the forest, close to the A11. It dates from between 300 BC and AD 10 and according to legend was the base from which Boadicea set out to fight her last battle with the Romans. Three miles to the south, Loughton Camp is better placed for defence, at the top of a south-facing slope, but less is known of its history. Both camps are entirely covered by trees which form part of the surrounding woodland, and need some hunting.

Far more obvious, indeed by a long way the most impressive single feature of the forest, is Queen Elizabeth's Hunting Lodge at Chingford. This timber-framed building is not only remarkable in itself but has wider interest. As the best-preserved hunting lodge of its period in the country, it gives the clearest picture of the hunting practices of the Tudor and Stuart kings and queens.

Perhaps it became known as Queen Elizabeth's because of the unconfirmed story that she was here when she heard of the defeat of the Armada, and in celebration rode her white palfrey up the broad staircase from the ground to the upper floor. K. J. Neale, who had published a study of the lodge, writes that this would have been possible, and that in the nineteenth century a pony was kept here for hire by anyone who wanted to imitate her. But the lodge was built before her time, probably about 1543, possibly a 100 years earlier. A recently discovered document of 1444 charges the Steward of the Forest of Essex to construct a forest lodge with a pimfold.

On balance Neale believes this document to refer to another lodge, now demolished, but the addition of a pimfold or pound suggests the form of hunting which the Stuarts and Tudors probably favoured. It supports a detailed description of repairs required by Queen Elizabeth's Lodge in 1589, which contains the words, 'The second [storey] ... for convenient standing to view the game. The Th[ird] serveth likewise.' Their construction, with floors sloping outwards to shed the rain, shows that they were unenclosed. Here the hunters would stand and shoot with musket or crossbow at the driven game, while their ladies and courtiers watched from alongside or above.

For 100 years during the eighteenth and nineteenth centuries it was lived in by the bailiffs of the manor, whose families served refreshments to picnic parties. Then in 1878 it was vested in the Corporation of London, along with the rest of the forest. Fifteen years later, as a result of the efforts of, among others, E. N. Buxton, it was opened as a museum of the forest, which it remains today.

From the upper floors of the lodge there are fine views north over Chingford Plain to High Beech and east towards

Queen Elizabeth's Hunting Lodge
at Chingford

Warren Hill. Closer in this direction is Connaught Water, among the larger of the 150 ponds which are one of Epping's features. They are also one of its problems. Now that gravel is no longer taken from them they are silting up.

Not far to the north of the lodge lies Fairmead Bottom, where the Epping Hunt used to meet, and which was once sufficiently open to be a horse training ground for Newmarket. Much of it was later colonized by thorn which nursed up oaks that are now well-grown trees. Because oak leaves hang downwards they allow some light to penetrate and permit a certain amount of undergrowth. Beech, on the other hand, forms a light-excluding canopy of horizontal leaves and the ground below it is commonly bare. Perhaps because it must be able to contend with such conditions beech regenerates readily and already beech seedlings are growing below the oaks of Fairmead Bottom. Ultimately it may become a beech wood.

North-east again, Staples Hill, where in 1866 Thomas Willingale went lopping to assert his Commoner's rights so starting the long battle which saved the forest, the hornbeams he lopped are an even more direct link with the forest's history. They have not been touched since and, destructive as they have been to all undergrowth, they have become one of the forest's most remarkable sights, their 100-year-old poles reaching up from massive gnarled pollard tops. No wood in other English forests can equal them.

The beech woods on Jacks Hill near Ambresbury Banks are a forestry parallel and equally interesting if they seem at first sight less unusual. They consist entirely of standard trees grown from coppice stools. Though it was normal practice to grow standards in this way in ancient coppice woods, complete high forest of this sort is uncommon.

The so-called Pillow Mounds near the Kings Oak public house are connected with another aspect of the forest's past; they were probably eighteenth-century rabbit warrens. In modern times rabbits have been considered a menace by foresters—Epping, because it wanted to retain its open land, was exceptional in finding them useful. But they were systematically introduced into many forests and kept for their meat. The Warren, today's forest administrative centre, almost certainly got its name for the same reason.

It lies a mile south of the Robin Hood roundabout, and among offices, workshops, stables for the horses of the riding foresters and the forest Superintendent's house there is one strange delapidated building: T. E. Lawrence's hut, moved here from Pole Hill on the western edge of the forest where he once lived in it.

Today the Superintendent of the Forest considers that the greatest threat to Epping is internal, a result of the pressures of nature on something which has to appear natural but is not. Against this he works hardest. But the forest is also threatened from outside, from London and its suburbs which press continuously on it. Any one pressure may not seem significant in itself but in combination he sees them as an insidious rot. The southern part of the forest has today been engulfed by buildings, but the northern half remains an astonishing enclave of countryside in which, after a few hundred yards, the noise of traffic fades and it is easy to wander lost for half an hour. The Superintendent and the Conservators mean to keep it that way.

Hatfield Broadoak and Writtle

Of the other parts of Essex which remained forest after 1301, **Felsted** was lost in late mediaeval times, and virtually none of it remains wooded today.

At Colchester, not only **Kingswood**, but Kingswood Heath, Mile End Heath and the town itself with its castle were subject to forest law. The forest was granted to the burgesses of the town by Henry VIII in 1535 for a payment of £100, and they in turn sold it as farmland. The forest land outside the town had consisted partly of heath and partly of coppiced woods in which limes were characteristic. North of the town small areas of this woodland can still be seen.

Hatfield and Writtle also passed by various stages into private hands. It is about these two small forests that Oliver Rackham writes so enthusiastically, describing Hatfield as 'of supreme interest in that *all* the elements of a mediaeval forest survive: deer, cattle, coppice woods, pollards, scrub, timber trees, grassland and fen, plus a seventeenth century lodge and rabbit warren. As such it is almost certainly unique in England and possibly in the world . . . Hatfield is the only place where one can step back into the middle ages, to see, with only a small effort, what a forest used to look like.'

The king's rights at Hatfield were first granted to the Duke

of Buckingham in 1446 but in 1483 reverted to the crown
when the duke's grandson was beheaded for High Treason.
Rather more than 100 years later in 1592 and 1612, Lord
Rich, who now held the manor and forest of Hatfield, took
the two apparently irresponsible actions which saved the
forest. First he sold the forest to Lord Morley, then he sold
the manor to Sir Francis Barrington.

For over two centuries the Morleys and their successors
quarrelled with the Barringtons. The Barrington family had
been hereditary woodwards of the forest for 500 years and
although they had lost this office they had been recompensed
with rights to cut wood in 350 acres of the forest. They had
also acquired many more rights over the whole forest, in
particular the right to pasture their animals, when they
bought the manor. It was these rights which prevented Lord
Morley from enclosing Hatfield Forest. A feud developed
between the two families, who lived in fine houses on
opposite sides of the forest, in which Barrington's servants set
an ambush for Lord Morley's son, and this young man
threatened to 'hack to pieces like dogs' two justices of the
peace who tried to settle the dispute.

In 1666 Sir John Turnor, Speaker of the House of Commons, bought the Morley estate, including the forest, and
continued the quarrel. Dogs of the Barringtons' tenants were
caught and hung alongside the way through the forest known
as London Road.

The Houblons, a Huguenot family, acquired the forest in
1729 and made efforts to turn it into the sort of landscape
garden fashionable in the second half of the eighteenth
century. They created the lake and built the Shell House. But
again the rights of the Barringtons and their tenants frustrated the owners and forced them to preserve the forest's
mediaeval character. Animals still grazed there, and locals
gathered nuts and held picnics. Finally in 1836 John Archer
Houblon bought the Barringtons' rights. The forest now
belonged entirely to the Houblons and they enclosed it,
blocked forest tracks and planted ornamental trees but by
great good luck held to the general purpose of re-establishing
it as a deer park.

In 1923 Hatfield was most seriously threatened. The
Houblon estate was sold and a timber merchant began to fell
the trees. By this time E. N. Buxton, who more than anyone
else has been responsible for saving Epping Forest, was old
and ill, but set about the rescue of Hatfield. With the last

cheque he signed he bought a large part of it, and the next year his son gave this to the National Trust.

For 50 years the National Trust managed Hatfield with good intentions but no coherent plan. Areas of woodland were clear felled and inappropriate plantations of beech and Spanish chestnut established. Finally the Nature Conservancy council reported on the forest and, in the words of today's warden, rapped the National Trust over the knuckles.

Fortunately most of the forest survived in its earlier form, including twelve out of seventeen coppice woods. Coppicing is at the centre of today's management plan. Standard trees are left among the stools, but not so many that they inhibit the coppice trees—about ten or fifteen to the acre. The fashionable wood burning stove has come to the rescue of the forest and whereas a few years ago coppicing was an expensive museum exercise, today contractors will pay for the right to coppice.

As in a mediaeval forest, grazing goes alongside coppicing. Three farms now graze Hatfield's rides and plains. Some of these are treeless, some have ancient hornbeam pollards which are now again being lopped. The forest deer survive too. As well as a herd of 60 to 70 fallow deer there are muntjak deer, thought originally to have escaped from Woburn, and sika deer. Four years ago a red deer stag was seen, the first on the forest since the 1914-18 War.

The lake is the forest's central feature, no doubt chiefly responsible for the 200,000 visitors who come each year. Beside it, the Shell House is another quaint eighteenth-century survival, and a nearby grove of horse chestnuts was planted at the same time. They are treacherous trees for a public forest, liable to shed heavy branches with no warning. But of the forest's mediaeval features, London Road is most impressive. This grass way, as wide as a field, runs through the forest from north-east to south-west, and gives a clear idea of what a drovers' road must have once looked like. About it stand ancient ash pollards, hollow with age, their branches nourished by veins of new wood, and thorns, many of them tinted green in winter with patches of mistletoe.

Coppices of hazel, maple, ash, oak and birch edge the London Road. To the west the standard trees of Round Coppice were elms, as was 25 per cent of the forest. They died in the 1970s of Dutch elm disease, and when recently taken out, locals told the warden that the nightingales, for which this coppice was famous, would never return; it was here, the following year, that he heard them first.

Currently, Wall Wood, a detached coppice wood to the south, is being coppiced for the first time for many years. The forest has few bluebells, but as soon as light was let on to the floor of this wood a carpet of them grew, from seed which must have lain in the soil for decades. The forest was always famous for its oaks, and many fine ones survive, though none to compare with the Doodle Oak, which stood near the north-west corner. The rim of its trunk can still be seen in the grass. When it fell in 1924 it measured 60 feet in circumference.

Hatfield Forest is at its most picturesque in summer when the horse chestnuts are in flower, the woodland in full leaf and the banks of the lake gay with picnic parties, but at its most evocative out of season when half a dozen fishermen huddle below umbrellas, the green rides are bare except for their contorted pollards and the leafless copses alive with winter birds.

Parts of Writtle Forest also survive, though more has been lost. The park divides the old forest into two, with coppices on either side. These were not fully compartmented till the eighteenth century, later than at Hatfield. Oak and hornbeam were the principal standard trees, but beech also grew in the park and in Highwood.

About Writtle Rackham writes, 'Nearly everything one sees there is of the fourteenth century or earlier: the great assart surrounded by hornbeam springs and alder slades; the heathland, pollard oaks, and woodbanks; the lonely cottage, with a palfrey in its pightle [paddock], on the site of the hermitage where a solitary monk dwelt. This astonishing survival from the depths of the mediaeval countryside is within 25 miles of St Paul's Cathedral'.

THE HOME COUNTIES

Windsor

Alexander Pope wrote the first part of his 434-line poem, *Windsor Forest*, in 1704, when he was sixteen and living at Binfield, where his father, a linen draper, had retired.

> Thy forests, Windsor! and thy green retreats,
> At once the Monarch's and the Muse's seats,
> Invite my lays. Be present, sylvan maids!
> Unlock your springs, and open all your shades.

Binfield lies nine miles west of Windsor and was then still on the borders of the royal forest. Earlier the forest had been of vastly greater size and was at one time estimated to be 120 miles in circumference.

Around Windsor itself it had included a large piece of Berkshire, reaching as far west as Hungerford. To the east it took in a small part of Middlesex and extended to the borders of Huntingdonshire. To the north it included part of Buckinghamshire, and to the south most of Surrey. In the Surrey part were Chertsey, Cobham and Guildford.

As with many forests there are suggestions that the Saxon kings had customary hunting rights over much of this countryside, but Windsor Forest was only formally established by William I. Here he built Windsor Castle, as one of a circle of strongholds to protect London and keep in subjugation the conquered Saxons. For its site he chose, not his manor of Old Windsor, but a chalk ridge which reaches out into Berkshire from the Thames to dominate the river. There may have been accommodation at the castle from the start, but William I and his immediate successors valued it primarily as a fortress. They also valued the hunting its forest provided. William hunted obsessively, and Pope suggests that he laid waste the countryside to create this royal forest.

> Not thus the land appear'd in ages past,
> A dreary desert, and a gloomy waste,

> To savage beasts and savage laws a prey,
> And kings more furious and severe than they;
> Who claim'd the skies, dispeopled air and floods,
> The lonely lords of empty wilds and woods . . .
> In vain kind seasons swell'd the teeming grain,
> Soft show'rs distill'd, and suns grew warm in vain;
> The swain with tears his frustrate labour yeilds,
> And famish'd dies amidst his ripen'd fields.
> What wonder then, a beast or subject slain
> Were equal crimes in a despotic reign? . . .

In fact there is no more evidence that William I depopulated any parts of Windsor Forest to make it a hunting reserve than that he did anything similar in the New Forest where the tradition is stronger. Large parts of Windsor Forest were always open common—rather than woodland—and today some of the sandy commons around Camberley give an idea of what much of it must have been like, though there would have been birch scrub rather than pine. When, in the thirteenth century, Henry III made many gifts of timber from his forests, few were from Windsor in comparison with those from his forests in Northamptonshire, Wiltshire, Hampshire and Essex.

But in some sense Windsor does seem already to have been a special forest. It is one of the few mentioned in Domesday Book, which also records that people of the county who failed to turn out to drive the king's deer when summoned to do so would be liable to a 50s fine, a large amount for that time.

The forest which William I established was only the nucleus of what it eventually became. In his own reign he extended it, and major extensions were made soon afterwards, probably by his son, Henry I. It was Henry I who, about 1105, first took up residence in the castle.

His own grandson, Henry II, began to build here in stone. The passion for hunting of this short, bow-legged, frenetically active man at least matched that of William I, and Windsor was a favourite forest. His son John also came here frequently to hunt. On the forest, at the Thamesside meadow of Runnymede, he was forced to negotiate and finally sign Magna Carta, with its important concession that he would disafforest all areas afforested during his reign. When he subsequently obtained the Pope's nullification of the charter, the barons, helped by the French King Louis, besieged Windsor Castle, which held out successfully for three months.

In these early centuries there are some records of hunting at Windsor. There are also descriptions of the supplies needed for vast feasts and tournaments, for example one held by Edward I in 1278. And in 1222 the woodlands of Windsor Forest were devastated by the great storm of that year. When Henry III sent special orders to 27 forests to have the fallen timber recorded and sold—the foresters would normally have had a right to it—Windsor was one of them.

In the same century Windsor Forest became the hide-out of the notorious outlaw, Richard Siward. When Henry III crossed the forest between Reading and Windsor in 1234, it was only because the king was one of the party that Siward refrained from attacking it. The sheriffs of ten counties were urged to arrest him if possible, and to take great care when sending money through the king's forests to the Exchequer. Forests were a natural place for outlaws of this sort to hide, and whether or not Robin Hood was a real character, there were certainly real-life Robin Hoods. Soon afterwards Siward, finding England too hot for him, set off for the wilder country of Wales, and since there are no records of his capture, probably reached safety there.

Throughout this period more of the surviving records of Windsor Forest concern such less dramatic matters as the granting of land, timber or hunting rights to religious institutions. The houses most favoured were the friaries of Oxford,

Windsor Forest and Castle

Reading and London, the Abbeys of Chertsey and Westminster, the priories of Ankirk and Merton and the nunnery of Bromhall.

Alongside these grants which referred to land, trees and game *inside* the forest went the disafforestation of certain parts of it, of which Surrey was the most seriously contended. In 1327 Edward III confirmed a perambulation of 1299-1300 which had excluded it entirely—though he allowed himself 40 days to have all the deer in the county chased into the remaining forest. But six years later he annulled Surrey's disafforestation, and 300 years later again, in 1607, the topographer John Norden's survey of the forest confirms that the king still claimed parts of the county.

The forest had by then, according to Norden's reckoning, been reduced in circumference to 77½ miles. Nevertheless, on his map he states: 'This Foreste lyeth in Barkshire and Surry. Wilteshire also extends into it. It confineth Surrey, Hampshire, Barkshire, Oxfordshire, Buckinghamshire, and Middlesex. The Tamise boundes it north, the loddon weste, Brodforde [Blackwater] Riuer and Gulddown South, and the Waye Riuer Easte.' Windsor Forest continued to contract, but at the time of its disafforestation by the Act of 1817 its bounds still measured 56 miles.

Meanwhile Windsor Great Park had developed as a deer park. In 1246 Henry III built a manor house on land at the south end of today's park, about 400 yards north of Five Arch Bridge which now crosses the upper end of Virginia Water, and it seems likely that land around this manor was the first to be impaled. In 1275, however, verderers were still selecting oaks and beeches for the park's pale, and a park of anything like today's extent was not completed till 1278. It included roughly the present southern half, but excluded Home Park and other areas near the castle.

In John's reign there was clearly no shortage of deer. In 1202 he gave 100 live bucks and does from Windsor to Richard de Muntfechet for his own park. And in 1215 he ordered 64 deer for the great feast to celebrate the consecration of the bishop-elect of Coventry and Lichfield, at Reading. But to stock the new park Edward I sent one of his yeomen to take as many fallow deer from Chute Forest, Wiltshire, as could be spared. And three years later, when the bishopric of Winchester was conveniently vacant, he had the bishop's pond at Frensham, Surrey, fished and 'forty female and fat bream, twenty other bream, forty great pike, and three or four hundred of other sorts of fish . . . sent alive in order to stock the stew of the King's Park at Windsor'. Up to this time there seem to have been wild cattle—probably not genuine but escaped—in the park, for in 1277 the constable of the castle was ordered to capture and sell them to pay for the expenses of the king's children living at the castle.

The park was extended in 1313 to include its present north-western parts, between Snow Hill and Sheet Street. A north-eastern area, the manor of Wychmere, was added in 1359. Soon afterwards records mention the Little Park, which reached to the castle itself, and by 1365 the name New Park was being used to include both the Little Park (now the Home Park) and the earlier park. There have been a number of later additions and subtractions, but this is the date at which the Great Park as we know it today essentially came into being.

In Tudor times the records of the uses to which kings and queens put Windsor Park and Forest become more frequent. Henry VII entertained Philip, King of Castile, here for twelve days in 1505, in an attempt to secure his daughter Eleanor as a bride for his son, later to become Henry VIII. Here one evening after dinner 'eyche of the kyngs kylled certene deare, to theire owne hands, with theire crosbowes'.

In Henry VII's reign Cranbourne Lodge, the park's oldest surviving building apart from the castle, was built. At this time it was sometimes referred to as the new tower or lodge, and only its tall brick tower with gothic windows now survives. Near here, in 1580, a thirteen-acre plantation of oak grown from acorns is often said to have been the first plantation in the country. The gnarled and delapidated survivors of this plantation can still be seen to the right of the present approach road to the lodge.

At first, like other lodges, it was the residence of the keeper of a part of the park—Cranbourne Walk—but later various people lived in it, including Charles II's treasurer to the Navy Board, Sir George Cartaret. Here Samuel Pepys visited him on 19 August 1665, to tell him of the failure of the British attack on the Dutch fleet off Bergen. By the time he reached Staines it was dark and his guide lost his way in the forest till Pepys put him right with the help of the moon. When he eventually reached the lodge he found it being rebuilt and had to climb to Sir George's bedroom by ladder. 'And there in his bed I sat down and told him all my bad news, which troubled him mightily, but yet we were very merry and made the best of it; and being myself weary, did take leave ... So to sleep—being very well but weary, and the better by having carried with me a bottle of strong water—whereof now and then a sip did me good.'

In the morning Pepys observed that the lodge was 'a very noble seat, in a noble forest, with the noblest prospect towards Windsor and round about over many Countys that can be desired. But otherwise a very melancholy place and little variety save only Trees.' Pepys came again to Cranbourne the following year soon after the Great Fire of London and found that 'an abundance of pieces of burnt paper' had been carried here from London by the wind.

During the reign of Henry VIII, yet another obsessive royal hunter, there are more vivid glimpses of royal hunting at Windsor. Here Henry would hunt with such companions as Sir William Fitzwilliam and Richard Weston, to both of whom he gave forest appointments. In 1526 Fitzwilliam wrote that he had brought letters for the king 'but as he was going out to have a shot at a stag, he asked me to keep them until evening'. Two years later, on a day when the king hunted from nine in the morning till seven in the evening, he killed the greatest red deer killed by him or any of his hunters that year. In January 1534/5 Lord Sandys wrote to Thomas Cromwell 'in sore dread of the king's wrath, for young Trapnell had killed twenty of the king's deer on the borders of Windsor Forest'.

The king was keen enough on his sport to wish, when he was living at Hampton Court, to have forest closer than Windsor, and for this purpose tried to afforest all the country from here to his new palace of Nonsuch near Epsom. By 1539 he had achieved this, despite legal problems, and named the new area the Honor of Hampton Court, but it was dechased soon after he died and its deer taken back to Windsor.

Queen Mary, though less keen on the chase than her father, was prepared to be entertained by mass killings. On the Tuesday after her marriage, when she was at Windsor, a novel method of wholesale sport was introduced. 'Toils [nets] were raised in the forest four miles in length, when a great number of deer, driven therein by the hounds and huntsmen, were slaughtered.' Elizabeth, on the other hand, hunted keenly all her life, and in 1602, the year before she died, killed 'a great and fat stagge with her owen Hand'. Despite the evidence that she and other Tudors enjoyed having deer driven past them which they shot from the upper stories of such lodges as Queen Elizabeth's Lodge at Chingford, Epping, she also rode to hounds, often with her favourite, Sir Henry Neville, decked out in fine jewellery.

James I was no less keen, and brought to hunting his own idiosyncratic practices. When a deer had been killed he would personally cut its throat, open its belly, and put his hands and occasionally his feet inside, before daubing his companions with blood. He was delighted, on his arrival from Scotland, by Windsor's well-stocked forest and tried to add to its game by releasing six wild boars at Egham. In 1617 he hunted boars at Bagshot, though with what success is not recorded, and they do not seem to have become established. Early in James's reign, Norden's survey of the forest estimated that the Great Park was stocked with 1,800 fallow deer. Elsewhere in the forest Norden reported many red deer, and in Bagshot Park about seventeen roe deer, which, typically for these small nocturnal animals, 'lie covertlie and are hardlie discovered'.

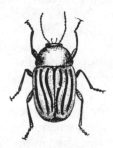

Though Charles I hunted at Windsor, it was his attempts to re-establish his forest rights which were more interesting, and which aroused so much anger at the time. At Windsor they took a particularly exaggerated form. On the advice of Noy, his attorney-general, called by Carlisle 'that invincible heap of learned rubbish', he revived the highest forest court, or forest eyre. At eyres held at Bagshot and Windsor 'every old formality was strictly observed; at the opening each forester had to present his horn on bended knee to the chief justice in eyre, and each woodward his hatchet; and these insignia of office were not returned until a fine of half a mark had been rendered'.

In Surrey this revival of forest law was particularly resented, though here as elsewhere it was the king's deer themselves and the damage they did which caused even more ill feeling. A grand jury of Berkshire of 1640 complained about 'the innumerable red deer in the forest, which if they go on so for a few years more, will neither leave food nor room for any other creature in the forest'. In 1641 riots broke out in the New Lodge Walk of the Surrey part of the forest and spread next year to Berkshire. In February the House of Lords was told that 100 fallow deer as well as red deer had been killed, and in the same year the pale of the Great Park was largely destroyed by rioters. Several were arrested and imprisoned at Newgate, but during the Civil War which soon followed, all the fallow deer and most of the red in the forest were poached. Many of the great oaks were also felled at this time to provide timber for warships.

Charles II at his restoration made efforts to restock a number of his forests and Windsor had a share of 300 deer which various noblemen gave him. Hunting in Windsor was revived. In 1680 his wish for a drive which would connect the castle with the park was the origin of the Long Walk, now one of the park's main features. Extra land was bought and a three-mile double avenue of elms planted, most of which survived for 250 years. In the 1920s, however, they began to suffer from Dutch elm disease and they were eventually felled in 1940 when they were replaced with alternating London planes and horse chestnuts. The idea of this mixture was that the avenue would never again need total felling since the planes will have a longer life than the chestnuts.

James II's passion for hunting was as great as that of his grandfather, James I. The year before he became king he took part in a famous run which began on Windsor Forest, crossed Middlesex and ended in Wintry Forest in Essex. He was the first king to hunt fox—never beasts of the forest and previously considered fit quarry only for the lesser gentry. Some fifteen years later, Queen Anne, the last monarch to hunt enthusiastically at Windsor, did so in the most eccentric style of all. When she grew too fat to ride she would pursue her quarry in a single-horse carriage with enormously tall wheels, dismaying farmers of the forest by driving across their standing corn. On occasions she would travel 50 miles a day in this contraption. When a deer was killed horns were blown and its head ceremonially cut off by the senior man present.

During her reign several avenues, in the formal style made fashionable on the continent by the French landscape gardener André le Nôtre, were laid out in Windsor Park, including Queen Anne's Ride, which diverges from the Long

Walk and leads to the gate of the park nearest to Ascot Race Course. The main local race meeting was moved here in 1711 from its previous site, Datchet Mead.

Though the first two Georges took little personal interest in hunting or Windsor Forest, it was still of some economic importance to the Crown, and according to Sarah, Duchess of Marlborough, there were at one time four to five thousand deer in the Great Park for the supply of the royal household with venison.

It was a time when there was much poaching in many parts of the country, and the notorious 'Waltham Blacks', so named for their blackened faces and because they first operated around Bishops Waltham in Hampshire, moved from forest to forest, poaching deer and fish and extorting money with threats. At Windsor a young keeper who looked out of his window to protest was shot and killed. In 1722 the 'Black Act' authorized severe punishment for such crimes, and soon afterwards over 40 of the gang were caught in Windsor Forest. They were tried by a special assize at Reading, four of them executed and their bodies hung in chains like scarecrows in different parts of the forest. The deer at Windsor nevertheless declined. In 1731 there were estimated to be only 1,300 in the whole forest, and by 1806 only 318.

The Duchess of Marlborough had lived at Byfield House (now Cumberland Lodge) from 1702 when she and her husband, the Duke, were made joint rangers, till she died in 1744 at the age of 85, and it was here that she schemed to marry Frederick, Prince of Wales, to her granddaughter, Lady Diana Spencer. To succeed her she appointed, as she was entitled to do, her grandson, John Spencer to be the next ranger, but he died at the age of 36 or 37, according to the *Gentleman's Magazine*, 'merely because he would not be abridged of three invaluable blessings of an English subject, brandy, small beer and tobacco'.

George II's son, William, Duke of Cumberland, succeeded John Spencer as ranger. It was the Duke who undertook the most dramatic of all landscape projects in the Great Park. Despite his name, 'Billy the Butcher' of Culloden, and his reputation for slaughtering Scots, he proved when not engaged in warfare to be a man of taste and compassion. It was to give his discharged soldiers work that he proposed the creation of Virginia Water. One hundred years later this was still described as 'the largest piece of artificial water in Europe'.

His designers were the deputy ranger, Thomas Sandby, and his brother the painter, Paul Sandby. They made the great lake by diverting the small streams which crossed the southern park into a natural basin and damming the outlet. To complete the scene a yacht, the *Mandarine*, 'above forty foot in the keel', was brought ashore at the Bells of Ouselay and floated on the lake. The work was finished by 1753, and included the High Bridge, a wooden single-span bridge of 165 feet, believed to be the largest in the world. Mrs Delany, who visited it with a party four years later, described it as 'desperately steep', and was afraid to be driven across it, 'though carriages of all sorts go over it every day'. The Duke's other memorable achievement at Windsor was to breed one of the best-known of all racehorses: Eclipse. This animal was foaled at Cranbourne Lodge, where he was staying while Cumberland Lodge was enlarged; the event is commemorated by a plaque in the nearby paddock.

William had been succeeded as ranger by his nephew, Henry, Duke of Cumberland, when, as a result of a torrential rain storm on 1 September 1768, the Virginia Water dam carried away. The same Mrs Delany wrote on the 6th. 'I suppose the newspapers have informed you of the extraordinary inundation caused by only one night's rain on Thursday last. The Virginia Water broke head and is entirely gone, fish and all, and a house in its way carried off as clean as if no house had ever been built there.'

Thomas Sandby had apparently made the dam only of sand and clay, and as a result became known as 'Tommy Sandbank', and celebrated in rhyme:

> When Tom was employed to construct the pond-head,
> As he pondered his task to himself thus he said,
> 'Since a head I must make, what's a head but a noddle?
> So I think I had best take my own for a model.'

Though George III did not at first live at Windsor, he was residing there by 1791 when Henry died, and he took control of the park himself, making his son nominal ranger. In and nearby he established several farms, including Flemish Farm (400 acres) to the north-west of the park, and Norfolk Farm (1,345 acres), towards its southern end. Here he indulged his farming interests, and was often to be found dressed as a farmer. The farms were soon afterwards let to tenants, but Norfolk Farm, an undistinguished small red brick building now standing among conifer plantations, became a royal farm again during the Second World War.

When the king declined into madness in 1811, the Prince Regent, later George IV, took up residence in the park at the building known today as Royal Lodge, and closed the Great Park to the public, much to its annoyance. Close to the northern shore of Virginia Water near Five Arch Bridge, which in 1790 had replaced the High Bridge, he built the Fishing Temple. About this lakeside folly the author of *English Forests and Forest-Trees* wrote 25 years later: 'The notion seems to have been to realize the idea of a Chinese Pagoda. The design has been accurately copied from the willow-pattern plate, whilst the colouring has been taken from a gingerbread-stall. The Fishing Temple is probably the most tasteless article we ever saw.' Sadly it was demolished in 1867 and two armed frigates which George IV had moored on the lake were also removed.

Further down the southern shore a curiosity known as 'The Ruins' survives. Already by the mid-nineteenth century these appeared to be the genuine ruins of a Roman Temple. Today they are crossed by a road bridge, but still seem convincingly real. They were in fact made up from classical columns and

The Fishing Temple, demolished in 1867

statues placed here by Sir Jeffrey Wyattville, including, according to tradition, some of the Elgin collection, and were named The Temple of Augustus, 'probably because Sir Jeffrey thought the name would do as well as any other'.

Despite George III's farming enterprises, much of the land of the park remained waterlogged at least till 1822. When he crossed it that year William Cobbett wrote, 'Started at day-break in a hazy frost for Reading. The horses' manes and ears covered with the hoar before we got across Windsor Park, which appeared to be a blackguard soil, pretty much like Hounslow Heath, only not flat. A very large part of the Park is covered with heath or rushes, sure sign of execrable soil. But the roads are such as might have been made by Solomon.' Four years later, however, George IV ordered extensive drainage works, producing 'a great local advantage in the regular employ of many industrious labourers'.

Virginia Water

His last memorable act was to put in hand the erection of a monument to his father to stand at the park's centre on Snow Hill. This was to be an equestrian statue, and the four-ton block of granite from Dartmoor on which it would be mounted was ceremonially lowered into position in 1829, to the accompaniment of a double royal salute of guns fired from Fort Belvedere (another folly which survives in the woods beyond Virginia Water).

The king had died by the time the statue itself, today known as the 'Copper Horse', arrived. On its way through Staines it fell from its wagon and a forge had to be constructed there to repair it. When finally set in place the local Windsor paper comfortingly reported that 'the fractured parts appear to have been so cleverly mended as not to be perceptible at the height it is now elevated'. Here it stands today, on the hill which provides the most dramatic views, not only of the Great Park, but of the distant forest land beyond, and of the castle itself, on its opposing hill top, where distance gives it back its one-time power and dignity.

Meanwhile the forest itself, in its legal sense, had gone. Dr William Mavor had written in a survey of Berkshire in 1808 that although the crown woodlands of Windsor were in good condition, 25,000 acres of unenclosed forest were deplorable. By this time Parliament, too, was concerned, and set up investigations in four successive years, each of which advised the enclosure of the forest. Finally an Act of Parliament of 1817 disafforested Windsor.

Under this act the crown was granted 6,665 acres, of which 1,454 were added to the Great Park, so making up for George III's disemparkments. However, 1,900 acres of the crown's grant had to be sold to pay for the act and to compensate forest officials who lost their positions.

The novelist, Thomas Love Peacock, who had lived many years close to the forest, describes, in what was probably his last essay (c. 1862), what happened during the following years. At first the deer in what had previously been forest were hunted by enterprising farmers, one of whom set himself up as Robin Hood, with assistants named Scarlet and Little John.

Peacock witnessed some of the confrontations between Lord Harcourt, Deputy Ranger, and 'Robin Hood', 'Lord Harcourt threatening to ruin Robin Hood by process in the Court of Exchequer, Robin Hood setting him at defiance, flourishing the Act of Parliament, and saying: "My Lord, if you don't know how to make Acts of Parliament, I'll teach you."'

Eventually a troop of the Horse Guards and a detachment of the fifth regiment of the line were called in to settle the problem by driving the deer into the Great Park. Peacock watched.

My position was on a rising ground, covered with trees, overlooking an extensive glade. The park was on my left hand: the main part of the forest on the right and before me. A wide extent of the park paling had been removed, and rope fencing had been carried to a great length, at oblique angles from the opening. It was a clear calm sunny day, and for a time there was profound silence. This was first broken by the faint sound of bugles, answering each other's signals from remote points in the distance: drawing nearer by degrees, and growing progressively loud. Then came two or three straggling deer, bounding from the trees, and flying through the opening of the park pales. Then came greater numbers, and ultimately congregated herds: the beatings of their multitudinous feet mingled with the trampling of the yet unseen horses, and the full sounds of the bugles. Last appeared the cavalry, issuing from the wood, and ranging themselves in a semi-circle, from horn to horn of the rope fencing. The open space was filled with deer, terrified by the chase, confused by their own numbers, and rushing in all directions: the greater part through the park opening: many trying to leap the rope fencing, in which a few were hurt, and one or two succeeded: escaping to their old haunts, most probably to furnish Robin Hood with his last venison feast. By degrees, the mass grew thinner: at last, all had disappeared: the rope fencing shut up the park for the night: the cavalry rode off towards Windsor: and all again was silent.

This was, without any exception, the most beautiful sight I ever witnessed: but I saw it with deep regret: for, with the expulsion of the deer, the life of the old scenes was gone, and I have always looked back on that day, as the last day of Windsor Forest.

In the Great Park itself the deer—red and fallow—survived for over 100 years—they were supplemented in the nineteenth century by red and fallow deer from Alice Holt and Woolmer forests, and in 1820 by the last of the red deer from Epping—but during the Second World War, when 2,000 acres of the park were ploughed up by royal order, 800 members of the local garrison drove the 1,000 survivors into a 300-acre enclosure. No contemporary man of letters watched this replay of the 1817 drive. Here they survived till 1950, when, in the words of the official guide, 'it was decided to disperse the deer'. Many went to Richmond Park and their progeny are still there.

Today red deer are back at Windsor, in a 1,000-acre enclosure lying mainly to the north-east of Snow Hill. After an absence of 30 years they were re-introduced in 1979, partly from Balmoral, partly from other Scottish forests, and have now increased to about 400. They can be easily found, grazing among scrub and bracken, raising their huge antlers to gaze curiously at visitors.

Other deer have also returned to the park and to the countryside which was once forest. None are fallow, and sika are only occasional visitors, but there are many roe, and the Chief Forestry Officer of the Crown Estate could take you any day to places where you would see the small muntjak.

As Chief Forestry Officer, his responsibility is to manage

all Windsor's trees and woodlands. The operation is essentially a commercial one. At Windsor he, two assistant
foresters and 50 forest workmen, carry out every forestry
operation from seed collecting and planting to felling and
marketing. The woods and trees in his charge can be divided
into those within the Great Park and those without. These
two areas are managed with different aims.

Within the park there are only 800 acres of woodland, and
though there are conifer plantations, the general aim is to
maintain a traditional park-like environment, preserving
ancient clumps and trees which are long past maturity. Some
of the most spectacular are hilltop clumps of Spanish chestnut. Though this species can live longer than oaks, at
Windsor they have tended to break up sooner, and
apparently ancient stands often date only from the nineteenth
century.

The oaks at Windsor are much older. They stand everywhere, as individuals, in groups, or in long avenues, many of
them far beyond the stagheaded stage, vast ruined trunks
topped by a few green boughs, but still alive. Best known was
Herne's oak, and a tree in Home Park has been given this
name. Almost 400 years ago Shakespeare referred to the

Herne's Oak

legend of Herne the Hunter in the Merry Wives of Windsor.

> There is an old tale goes that Herne the Hunter,
> Sometime a keeper here in Windsor Forest,
> Doth all the winter time at still midnight
> Walk round about an oak with great ragged horns.
> And then he blasts the tree and takes the cattle,
> And makes milch kine yield blood, and shakes a chain
> In a most hideous and dreadful manner.

But by 1853 there was already doubt about which was the correct oak, and the present candidate is not much more remarkable as a tree than dozens of others in the park.

The history of the rest of the Crown Estate at Windsor, which today, in a woodland sense, forms the largest part of the old forest to survive, is obscure, partly because of the destruction of the estate office with its records in 1906. Here, at 5am on 1 December, a fire broke out. The police at Windsor remained unaware of it because the alarm bell rang in a police station which they had abandoned. The Windsor Park fire brigade was a mile away at Cumberland Lodge and would normally have been drawn there by horses, but H.R.H. Prince Christian's head coachman refused to wake the prince at such an hour to get his permission for them to be used so it had to be dragged there by hand.

Some of these 7,000 to 8,000 acres adjoin the Great Park to the west of Cranbourne Walk, and some lie to the south of Virginia Water, around Fort Belvedere. But a larger area forms a big block of woodland between the four towns of Bracknell, Ascot, Bagshot and Camberley.

This block can again be divided into northern and southern sections. The southern section lies on the Bagshot sands where birch is indigenous and Scots pine has become naturalized since it was re-introduced, probably by James I. Taking advantage of this, the Crown Estate planted large blocks of Scots pine in the 1930s, and as a result much of the area is as monotonous as most conifer plantations. Though Scots pines regenerate freely here, Corsican pine has recently been found to do better and this is now being planted, as well as other exotic conifers: western hemlock, Norway spruce, the giant fir *Abies grandis* and European and Japanese larch.

The northern section lies on London clay, and has a greater variety of trees. Most of the stands consist of a mixture of hard and soft woods, and the fast-growing southern beeches from Chile, *Nothofagus obliqua* and *Nothofagus procera* are now being widely planted. In general these plantations are no longer clear felled, but progressively thinned, so producing a much more attractive woodland. Among the plantations a number of very old oaks and Spanish chestnuts of no commercial value have been preserved. This part of the forest is of particular interest to entomologists. Thirty-four butterfly species have been recorded, and 2,000 out of the native 3,600 beetle species.

If the Crown Estate plantations at Windsor bear little resemblance to the woods and commons which would have been found here when Windsor was a royal forest, they are at least still forest in the woodland sense, and with the advice of the Nature Conservancy Council are being managed in a way which will in future increase their value as a wild life reserve.

Ashridge

In early mediaeval times there were other royal forests or private chases in the Home Counties to the north and west of London—**Enfield Chase**, for example, a big stretch of wood-pasture reaching north nearly as far as Hatfield, which was almost entirely enclosed in 1777. Ashridge Forest, on the other hand, lying partly in Hertfordshire and partly in Buckinghamshire, was apparently never a royal forest, but today is one of the most varied and interesting small forests in a silvicultural sense of the south of England.

It stands high on the Chiltern Hills, just north of Berkhamsted, and consists of 4,000 acres of woodland, farmland, open grassland and once open land reverting to birch or thorn scrub. It includes 1,000 acres of commercially managed plantations, producing mainly hardwood.

The little that is known of the early history of Ashridge suggests that it was enclosed in 1286 by the Earl of Cornwall when he gave it to the rector and brethren of Ashridge College. The college was suppressed at the Reformation, and soon afterwards makes a brief appearance in history as the place where Edward VI and Elizabeth spent much of their childhood. The long ride which extends west from the house was perhaps named 'Prince's Ride' after Edward. When Mary became queen, Elizabeth retired here, and here she was arrested to be brought to London on suspicion of being involved with Wyatt's rebellion.

Early in the following century (1609) it passed into the

hands of the Egerton family who became earls of Bridgwater, and from them in 1849, by indirect succession to the Earls of Brownlow. Finally, in 1921, Ashridge was sold and the National Trust bought the part of the park which forms the core of the present forest. To this a number of other areas have been added, including Ivinghoe Beacon, Berkhamsted and Aldbury Commons, Moneybury Hill with the Bridgewater monument and Frithsden Copse, the last two given by the historian G. M. Trevelyan.

Whenever they are mentioned during these later centuries the woods of the park excite admiration. In 1681 Thomas Baskerville visited Ashridge and remarked on herds of red and fallow deer and on the 'lofty groves of trees, so thick set together that the like is scarce anywhere to be seen'. In 1908 the surroundings of the house were 'exceedingly beautiful, both as regards the garden and the park beyond and round it. The beech trees are perhaps the most notable feature, several growing up to a most unusual height before throwing out side branches, and the undulating character of the ground sets off the groups of trees to great advantage. The park contains a large herd of deer, red and fallow, as well as some white Cashmere goats, which appear to thrive in their unaccustomed surroundings.'

Of the woodland with historical interest, Frithsden Beeches is most remarkable. Here once pollarded beeches have grown so vast that the public is warned not to walk below them since they are liable to split and fall. They were probably last pollarded in the middle of the nineteenth century, when the village of Little Gaddesden was built, largely of brick. Near Frithsden Beeches the estate had its own brickworks and wood from these beeches could well have provided its fuel. Though they are at present not being touched, similar outgrown beech pollards in another area are being experimentally pollarded. Some may not survive but the stumps will be left. Throughout the ancient woods of the forest fallen trees and branches are intentionally allowed to lie, providing habitats for wild life and preventing any suggestion of a park-like tidiness.

Close to Frithsden Beeches is one end of Berkhamsted Common, which circles from here to the north, then west then south, forming a big horseshoe that bounds the forest. The inhabitants of Berkhamsted had common rights here which they exercized to such an extent during the hard times of the nineteenth century that the common was not only stripped of gorse but even the roots grubbed out. The common passes close to Ashridge House, and in 1866, the year that the famous Epping Forest law suits began, the second Earl Brownlow enclosed a section of the common with a fence in order to add it to his deer park. Soon afterwards a trainload of navvies, led by one Augustus Smith, came by night and uprooted the fence. Here, too, prolonged law suits followed before, in 1870, the Commoners won their case.

During both World Wars the commons and woodlands were used by the army as training grounds and birch scrub spread. Today this survives, judiciously thinned, in the form of picturesque areas of silver birches, now tall trees some 50 years old, with grassy walks below. In places the walks can be clearly seen to have been created by wartime tanks.

Commoners' rights no longer survive on Berkhamsted Common, though they do on Aldbury Common, which lies on the western side of the forest. Here Commoners still collect certain sizes of fallen wood. Across Aldbury Common runs Prince's Ride, the wide avenue lined with fine oaks and chestnuts of considerable age which begins at Ashridge House and ends at the monument to the Earl of Bridgwater, 'father of inland navigation'.

Elsewhere in the forest there are a number of woods which were once coppiced for firewood, fencing wood and other rural needs. Most of these have been allowed to grow out, but a small area of hazel above Dunscombe Farm is still coppiced by the National Trust. This, at least in the earlier years of its cycle, keeps open the view to the south-west, down a deep green valley with the little village of Aldbury lying on its lower slopes and the hills above Tring forming the horizon. Here there are also plantations of beech, at present nursed by 75 per cent Corsican pine, a method of establishing a hardwood plantation which for 30 years after the last war was considered one of the best by the National Trust, but is now being abandoned. Higher up the valley sides, where there will one day be another view point, the Trust is establishing an arboretum devoted exclusively to varieties of four species: lime, oak, ash and chestnut.

As in so many broadleaf woodlands, grey squirrels are a serious pest. They attack sycamore, beech, birch and oak in roughly that order. Lime, cherry and ash they leave comparatively untouched, and *Nothofagus,* today's much favoured southern beech, is believed to be immune, though this

remains to be proved for certain. There is no general agreement about why they prefer one species to another but the
head forester at Ashridge believes that they are attracted by
sap with a high sugar content. Here they have even been
known to ring-bark conifers.

Of the forest's other wild animals, the 200 fallow deer,
with at least one fine white buck, are most dramatic. Many
were killed in the Civil War, but they never entirely died out.
Red deer, on the other hand, finally disappeared in the
Second World War. Among the fallow deer there is an
unusually high proportion of 'black' deer, and these may be
related to Epping's 'black herd'. When the Epping herd was
in danger a number were sent to Whipsnade and some of
these are believed to have escaped and interbred with those at
Ashridge.

The deer are culled—not very scientifically—by passing
traffic, which kills 50 to 60 a year. To protect their crossing
point on the only large road which runs through the forest
there are posts with angled stainless steel plates which reflect
approaching headlights into the trees. Though these seem to
work, the deer are adept at finding alternative crossing
points. The National Trust preserves and values its fallow
deer, but recognizes that the herd must be kept to a reasonable size to prevent excessive damage to neighbouring farms.

Because of its many different habitats, Ashridge Forest has
an unusually large and varied bird population, many nesting
on the forest, others visiting. Almost every English woodland
bird can be found here, from common tits, thrushes, blackbirds, woodpeckers, nut hatches, gold crests and chaffinches
to the rare warblers, redstarts, black caps and lesser red polls.
On the open parts of the forest, 40 species breed regularly,
and hoopoe, great grey shrike and red-backed shrike have
been occasional visitors. For botanists it is the open grasslands towards Ivinghoe Beacon which are of special interest.
Sheep grazed them for centuries, producing a short turf of
fescue grass which provides a favourable habitat for a large
number of species. Here it is usually possible to find two
dozen different plants growing in a square yard of ground,
some common, some rare, among them hairy violet, rock-
rose, kidney-vetch, horseshoe vetch, bird's foot trefoil,
orchids (fragrant, pyramidal, spotted, frog and bee), tway-
blade, squinancywort, fairy-flax, pasqueflower, dropwort,
two varieties of wild thyme and field fleawort.

Since sheep ceased to be economic in the 1930s some areas

have reverted to scrub, chiefly hawthorn with occasional juniper bushes. Among this oaks are now growing and many areas will eventually become oak wood unless interfered with. Meanwhile the scrub has produced yet another habitat in which small mammals have increased and where other varieties of birds nest.

Ashridge, to sum up, has a number of surviving ancient woods of interest to ecological historians, and elsewhere a wide range of plantations and secondary woodland of general interest, which support an unusually rich animal and plant life. Its setting, high up on the Chiltern plateau, is unique.

THE WELSH BORDERS

Dean

For 60 years the Forest of Dean has been managed by the Forestry Commission. Though still nothing like its mediaeval size, it has been enlarged during this time by new purchases and now amounts to some 27,000 acres. Of these about 150 are clear felled each year, producing an annual crop of 55,000 tons of wood and timber and making it one of the largest and most effectively managed of modern English forests. Yet of all English forests, the Dean is the one where a visitor seems not just to arrive among trees, but to move into a piece of ancient and foreign country. As for its inhabitants, those who live around it consider them, with some historical justification, to be ferocious and slightly mad.

'Those men here who are not black'd by coals and furnaces are redded by the iron-ore,' the Hon. John Byng wrote in 1781. Certainly coal and iron have given the Dean its special character. Sometimes they have been closely connected. Near the village of Radnor, Byng came to a furnace where he was 'well receiv'd by the devils who bear the infernal heat, which soon drove me forth: they shewed me the iron melting, and the immense bellows moved by water, eternally keeping alive the monstrous fire; for they work by day and night, and make about four tons in 24 hours'. Such a furnace at this date would have been using the forest's coal to smelt its iron-ore.

Both iron-ore and coal had always been connected with the forest's trees. For many centuries the wood (and sometimes the timber) was the raw material for the charcoal which the furnaces and forges used. And the forest's mines, both iron and coal, at one time depended on its timber for props.

But if, as a result, the forest's history consists in part of conflicts about timber between the miners and the king or other landowners, its most dramatic incidents were conflicts between the king and landowners, and the Commoners, who fought to preserve their common rights with as much tenacity as those of Epping or the New Forest, and with more violence than even those of Ashdown. To complicate matters further, the forest contains valuable deposits of stone.

The Dean lies in the western part of Gloucestershire. Here the rivers Wye and Severn, which both rise in the Plynlimmon mountains of Wales, rejoin each other shortly before they reach the Bristol Channel, and form a V which—as far north as a line from Gloucester on the Severn via Newent to Ross-on-Wye, was once all forest. Roughly at the centre of this triangle an oval-shaped area eight miles from north to south and five miles from east to west contains the coal measures. Fringing this on all sides except the south-east is an area of carboniferous limestone which yields iron-ore.

The ancient Britons were the first to discover the iron-ore deposits, which come to the surface near Lydney. Here they smelted the ore in primitive bloomeries, producing blooms of soft iron for hammering into tools or weapons. When the Romans came they exploited the same workings, using the same techniques. Nearby they built a temple to the Silurian river god, Nodens. They also established iron workings at

Miners in the Forest of Dean

many other places in the forest, supplying iron to their settlements across the Severn in the Cotswolds, to Monmouth, and to the vanished town of Ariconium near Ross. The route to Ariconium was along the Dean Road, which ran north from Lydney through Littledean and Mitcheldean. It can still be seen at several places, and a particularly well-preserved section lies south of Soudley, near the old railway line at Blackpool Bridge. There are mysteries about this road. It is eight feet wide, not the usual Roman width, and made of large stones without top dressing, not normal Roman practice. Furthermore, unlike the Roman roads of every history book, at this point it is clearly bending.

Though the Saxons, who were keen agriculturalists, cleared many parts of the forest for crops, there is no definite evidence that they mined its iron-ore. Domesday Book (1086) refers to iron-ore workings in the county of Gloucester, but does not say where. Only during the twelfth and thirteenth centuries when the Dean was a well-established royal forest with typical forest courts and officers, is it certain that iron was again being mined, smelted and forged in the forest.

Though king, miners and iron workers were later in conflict, at first the king's attitude was ambiguous, because he too owned forges in the forest. At different times in the 1200s up to eight royal forges were at work, some stationary, some itinerant. In total between 40 and 70 forges were usually working in the forest by the end of the century.

How much permanent damage all this did is uncertain. Cyril Hart, today's authority on the forest, takes the traditional view that producing charcoal for smelting iron-ore and forging iron 'probably impoverished the woods more than all other operations together'. Timber as well as wood was certainly taken—the eyre-roll of 1270 specifically says so, and can be trusted because the distinction at this time was important. The same eyre-roll reports that charcoal burners used not only what they had bought but also what they 'took furtively'.

Perhaps, because the Dean was more remote than other forests, its timber in mediaeval times was less valued. Elsewhere there were strong economic reasons for selling timber rather than making it into charcoal. In Ashdown Forest during the seventeenth century timber had four times the value of wood. But in earlier years the using of oak, beech, ash and chestnut for charcoal in the Dean had been forbidden, suggesting that timber was considered important here too. The forest would indeed have been 'impoverished' by extensive felling of its timber. But even if all its standard trees had been taken it would not necessarily have been destroyed, because woodland which is cut, grows again. Significantly, Hart adds that natural replenishment would have followed had animals been fenced out. The responsibility for any permanent loss of woodland lies less with the charcoal burners and iron workers than with the Commoners, who were more interested in grazing for their animals than in trees.

As in other iron works of the time, hammers, levers, horseshoes and nails were made. In the Dean iron was also put to one special use: the making of projectiles for cross-bows, known as quarrels. These had four-sided heads which were usually pointed but sometimes blunt with small projections at each corner to prevent them glancing off armour. They were hollow at the rear end to take a shaft which was normally of yew, about twelve inches long and winged with feathers, horn, leather or strips of wood. They were made at the castle of St Briavels, residence of the warden of the forest, which for 70 years was one of the great arsenals of the country. Between 1223 and 1293 a total of half a million to a million quarrels were produced at St Briavels.

Around 1230 a workman called John Malemort was employed here at a wage of 10½d a day, and he continued to work here for at least the next 27 years. By then he was being paid £50 a year and perhaps sub-contracting the work. At first he was expected to make 100 quarrels a day, using in the process (besides iron and charcoal) lard and bran. Throughout this period the king sent orders to St Briavels for quarrels to be delivered to his wars or castles in every part of the kingdom. The first recorded order was for 6,000 to go to Montgomery, the last for 3,000 to go to Corfe Castle. The Dean was an especially convenient source of supply for his Welsh ventures, and in 1257, 30,000 were to be delivered to Chester 'with all speed, by night and day as the king is about to depart with his army for the parts of Wales'.

Coal, meanwhile, was also being mined in the forest, but only in a small way, where the seams came to the surface. The first certain records date from around 1250 when Blakeney, Staunton and Abinghall each had mines. It was the fuel of the poor and remained so for many hundreds of years.

The iron and coal miners of the Dean both provided the king with a certain revenue, but he found them useful in another way: as special troops. Woodsmen he needed too. In 1282, to clear the passes for another Welsh expedition, he ordered 100 of the strongest woodcutters to be sent from the Dean to Chester, each with 'a great and strong axe or hatchet to fell large and small trees'. But these he could have got elsewhere. It was the miners of the Dean with their tunnelling skill that, judging by the calls he made on them, he found irreplaceable.

In 1222, 40 were sent to London, the next year 20 to Montgomery, the year after 30 to Bedford and eleven again to London. One of these, John de Standon, seems to have become well known for his proficiency and the king rewarded him with twelve acres of land near Sitegave, before he was killed at the siege of Bedford. For 300 years the king continued to call on Dean miners for service not only in England, but also in Scotland, Wales and France. Twelve took part in the siege of Berwick-on-Tweed in 1319, and in 1522 Henry VIII ordered 300 to be sent to Dover.

The local, self-taught poet, Kitty Drew, described one of their exploits in verse in 1835, though she does not say which.

> A foreign army did our land invade
> And blood and carnage, then was all the trade,
> They pitch'd their tents, and then without delay
> They waited anxious for the bloody fray;
> But our bold miners underneath did get
> And many a ton of powder there did set,
> So up they blew the unsuspecting foe,-
> Their shattered limbs came rattling down below . . .

A few lines later she gives the traditional view of the way in which the miners gained their special privileges:

> The King with honour did them so regard,
> Made them free miners as a just reward . . .

When and why they in fact got their privileges is uncertain. The earliest surviving document listing these dates from 1610 and refers to a grant by King Edward III, but he may well have only been confirming established traditions.

To become a free miner it was necessary to have been born in the forest and to have worked in a mine there for a year and a day. The miner could then start a mine where he pleased in the forest. When he had dug 'three steps deep' he

had to inform an officer known as the king's graveller, pay
him a penny for himself and for each other workman, and
allow a 'king's man' to become one of the partners (called
'verns') in the mine concession (called a 'gale'). The share this
man earned (called a 'dole') was the king's share. The free
miner in return had a right to timber for props, to a way
across the forest to his mine, and to trial of cases affecting his
mining rights in the Mine Law Court, a court entirely
separate from other forest courts. Here twelve of his fellow
miners would sit as jurors, or on appeal 24, or on a second
appeal 48.

Remains of early surface workings, known as scowles, can
be seen in many parts of the forest, for instance south-east of
Staunton. They consist of labryinthine trenches, passages,
caves and huge rock masses, today overgrown with ancient
yews, mosses and ferns. Millions of tons of ore must have
been taken from such workings. But as the surface ore
became exhausted, the miners tunnelled deeper, creating the
sort of workings described by the Rev. H. G. Nicholls,
perpetual curate of Holy Trinity, Drybrook, in the mid-
nineteenth century.

Occasionally they are found adorned with beautiful incrustations
of the purest white, formed by springs of carbonate of lime,
originating in the rocky walls of the limestone around. Sometimes,
after proceeding for a considerable distance closely confined in
height and width, they suddenly open out into spacious vaults,
fifteen feet each way,—the site, probably, of some valuable 'pocket'
or 'churn' of ore; and then, again, where the supply was less
abundant, narrowing into a width hardly sufficient to admit the
human body.

Mining and iron working apart, the early history of the Dean
differs from that of other royal forests in the south of
England chiefly because of its remoteness. The old view that
the king valued his forests mainly as hunting reserves seems
even less plausible in the Dean. There were deer and wild
boar in the forest, and sometimes he came to hunt them, but
more often he sent orders for certain numbers to be killed and
delivered to himself or as gifts. In the fourteenth and fifteenth
centuries even orders of this sort ceased.

The Dean's poaching problems, however, were typical, and
not confined to the laity. Records of the forest eyre of 1270
show that the prior of Lanthorny was imprisoned till he paid
a fine of 20 marks for taking supplies of venison from one

Jordan Hok, a notorious poacher. The canons of Hereford at Lydney had bought from another well-known poacher, Walter Kappe, and half a deer was found at their house, hidden under straw. The other half had been sent to the Dean of Hereford. As for the Abbot of Tiverton, he had employed a regular band of poachers to supply his table.

The Dean's position beside the Severn gave its inhabitants opportunity for a special kind of lawlessness. In Henry VI's reign the people of Tewkesbury complained that forest dwellers had stopped, pillaged and seized their boats on their way to Bristol. Despite letters of privy seal ordering such piracy to stop, it continued and 'the said trespassers came to the river with greater routs and riots than ever they did before, there despoiling at divers times eight trowes of wheat, rye, flour, and divers other goods and chattels, and the men of the same cast overboard, and divers of them drowned'. The ships' owners were told that if they were 'so hardy as to cause any manner of victuals to be carried any more by the same stream, much or little, for lord or lady', they would have their craft hewn to pieces. An Act of Parliament of 1429 ordered all goods to be returned and the offenders imprisoned.

In Tudor times the crown began to be seriously alarmed about a possible shortage of timber for warships. Elizabeth's Act of 1559 forbidding the felling of oak, beech and ash timber for charcoal making for the iron industry within fourteen miles of the sea or of a navigable river was in part no doubt aimed at the Dean. But the reserves of timber in the Dean seem to have remained large throughout the whole of the sixteenth century—so large that even the Spanish knew of them, if the diarist Evelyn can be believed. He wrote that the admiral in charge of the Armada was given orders to destroy the forest even if the whole country could not be conquered. Hart considers that the Spanish may have wanted to cripple the country's iron industry, though this would not explain why they thought the Dean's more important than the much more advanced industry of the Sussex Weald. Suspect though Evelyn's story is, for this and other reasons, it provides interesting evidence of what he and his contemporaries *believed* the forest to have been like, before the Civil War, the Earls of Pembroke and the Winter family decimated it.

Why the Dean's iron industry remained so backward is uncertain. Though there is no description of a Dean furnace of the sixteenth century, it seems a fair guess that they were of the sort being worked by men from the Dean in Glamorgan in 1531. With four men to pump the bellows, who worked a twelve-to-fourteen hour day, this produced a daily two hundredweight of iron—a fortieth of the amount produced by the furnace Boyd saw in 1781. At Hartfield on the Ashdown Forest the first furnace with water-powered bellows had been working for 38 years.

Eventually, however, water power arrived, and in 1612 the Company of Mineral and Battery Works set up four blast furnaces with three associated forges at Lydbrook, Cannop, Parkend and Stourley. Together these were known as the 'King's Ironworks', though they were in fact run for several powerful landowners, including Sir Edward Winter and the Earl of Pembroke. It was these furnaces, consuming vastly greater quantities of charcoal, which set off the violent events of the next 60 years. They were the most dramatic in the forest's history, when it came closer than ever before to destruction as a royal forest, and closer than ever again to destruction as a forest in the tree-growing sense.

The first to riot were the miners, who feared for their traditional right to free timber. To avoid a confrontation with them, the Earl of Pembroke, a much disliked man, cut timber while they were at church. But 'fifteen desperate knaves set it on fire . . . and dancing about the fire cried "God save the King!" They still walk about the woods with weapons, and as I hear with shot; they call their neighbours cowardly for not assisting them'.

Various law suits followed, and for the time being the miners recovered their timber rights. The Earl of Pembroke was ordered to cease felling and send his timber men home to their own counties. He remained Constable of St Briavels, however, and a few years later was again felling oaks marked for the king. When one of his workmen was asked how he dared cut a marked tree he replied 'that for two pots of ale he would cut down that tree or any other so marked.'

In 1627 the earl was granted a new lease of the king's ironworks, together with the right to cut further huge numbers of trees. But it was less tree felling than enclosure by the crown against grazing—which from this time onwards the king began to realize was essential if the forest's timber was to survive—that provoked new protest. Now it came from the Commoners whose rights to grazing and pannage were affected far more seriously by enclosure than by felling. Their protests were part of a series of riots which, along with others in the Dorset forest of Gillingham and the Wiltshire forest of Braydon, are known as 'The Rising in the West'. Together they formed the largest outbreak of public violence in the 35 years before the Civil War.

They were connected because all were provoked by enclosure of forest land, and because all were directly or indirectly led by the mysterious John Williams, who operated under the name of Lady Skimmington. A skimmington, in Wiltshire dialect, was the word for the communal punishing of a hen-pecking wife. A procession of men in white caps and smocks would approach the guilty woman's house led by a horse carrying in front a stuffed man and behind a man in woman's clothing beating the dummy with a wooden ladle. When the wife was persuaded to emerge she would be ducked 'to the sounds of drums, horns, dancing and shouting'.

The Dean riots began in 1629, and were provoked by enclosures of land at Mailscot Wood near Bicknor, made for the Villiers family by their agent, Sir Giles Mompresson. At first 20 Commoners threw down the fences, but when Mompresson continued to enclose, 'this did exasperate their giddy brains and [they] seconded their first attempt by sound of drums and ensigns in a most rebellious manner, carrying a picture or statue apparelled like Mompresson'.

Soon afterwards 500 rioted in front of the house of another of the Villiers' agents, 'marching with drums and colours displayed', and threw down 100 perches of fence. By April the sheriff had been ordered to muster the trained bands, but in August he had to withdraw from the forest because of 'multitudes of people arrived to withstand him'. Eight hundred and eighty-six rioters were indicted but few could be brought to trial. Lady Skimmington was not finally arrested and sent to Newgate prison till 1632.

Worse, for the forest, was to follow. In 1640 Sir John Winter, son of Sir Edward, was granted 'all the coppices, wood, ground, and waste soil of the said Forest . . . with the

Wood and Timber, and all the Mines of Iron and Coal, Tin and Lead, and Quarries of Millstones, Grindstones, and Cinders in the forest'. Eleven blast furnaces and eleven forges had been at work for the last twelve years and large amounts of wood and timber had been consumed, but during the eighteen months of this, Winter's first lease, he felled and enclosed with new vigour, reducing the remaining forest trees from about 129,000 to about 88,000. The Civil War soon followed and Winter, after defending the forest for the king, was deprived of most of his property and sent to the Tower.

This was by no means the end of his connection with the forest. After the Restoration, in 1662, he was not only paid £30,000 for surrendering his original lease, but granted a new one for eleven years, which included the right to 30,000 trees provided he reserved 11,000 tons of timber for the navy. He soon had 500 woodsmen felling in the forest and so alarmed the House of Commons that within a year it tried but failed to stop all further felling. Four years later a new and third grant was made to Winter. In this he was given 8,000 acres for himself, and allowed to manage a further 10,000 as a nursery for naval timber.

By now, however, he had felled all but 200 of the trees

St Briavel's Castle from the north

previously granted to him and delivered to the navy only 1,000 of the agreed 11,000 tons of timber. What he had done with the rest is a mystery. Huge amounts of wood had been used for charcoal, but there are no records to show whether or not the timber trees were also used for this purpose. 'During his felling operations,' Hart writes, 'the Forest must have been a hive of industry, with the almost continuous sound of axes and falling trees, and with many hauliers lugging timber to the sawpits or to the local pills and creeks. The inhabitants, except those finding employment under Winter, looked on with disgust.'

To add to the devastation, during these years the forest was struck by two great storms. In 1662 in a single walk 1,000 oaks and 1,000 beeches were blown down, and 'in some great orchards' it was 'possible to go from one end to the other without touching the ground'.

All this led finally to the important Act of 1668. This was the equivalent of the New Forest Act of 1698, and in its different way, to the settlement in 1693 of Ashdown Forest's disputes between the Commoners and the Lord of the Manor. In Dean, too, it effectively settled the affairs of the forest for 100 years. On the one hand it gave the crown the right to enclose 11,000 acres for timber growing. The Commoners lost all rights in these enclosures, and their firewood rights in the rest of the forest. In return, however, they were confirmed in all rights of pannage and grazing in the rest of the forest which had been lawfully theirs in 1635. Just what these rights were has never been decided, and the crown still maintains that the Commoners graze and take pannage in the forest by the crown's kind permission and not as a right.

All was not totally peaceful, however, and in the years soon after the Act the Commoners of Dean continued to justify their reputation for obstinacy and violence by pulling down enclosure hedges and starting fires. In 1688 they destroyed two of the forest's lodges and damaged the new Speech House, where the Verderers' and Miners' Courts now met. The miners still considered that they had a right to free timber and continued to take what they wanted.

Throughout this period—the fourteenth to the seventeenth centuries—there are fewer records of the forest's coal mines, but they had steadily increased, and gradually over the next 200 years they became more numerous than the forest's iron-ore mines. An early and important development occurred

in 1674 when King Charles II ordered his iron works in
the forest to be pulled down. 'If the iron trade was unpromis-
ing,' Nicholls wrote, 'owing to the course which the government felt constrained to take lest the development should
endanger the timber, it was not so with coal, the getting of
which the crown would obviously regard with favour in the
hope that it would relieve the woods from spoilation'.

As the surface coal was exhausted, the coal miners, like the
iron-ore miners, pursued deeper seams. This they did by
sinking so-called bell-pits, which were narrow at the top,
swelled out below ground, and went down perhaps 30 feet.
From their bottoms short galleries were sometimes dug
outwards, but the miners usually preferred to dig a succession
of pits next to each other. Boys carried up the coal on trays.
Hot air rose continuously from their narrow mouths and
there are stories of how this parachuted those who
accidentally fell into them safely to the bottom on inflated
smocks or skirts.

Extensive remains of bell-pits can still be seen on the forest,
for example where the Forestry Commission recently clear
felled an area south of Parkend. All are now collapsed and
resemble the craters of a string of small bombs, some filled
with felling debris, some with dark-green water.

In spite of the good intentions of the 1668 Act and the
comparative peace it brought, the Dean as a timber forest
steadily declined during the eighteenth century. In 1781 the
woods were said to be 'suffering and have suffered much
lately from the axe: and can never recover, owing to the
flocks of sheep which will prevent the growth of young
timber'. Seven years later parliamentary commissioners, in
one of their seventeen reports on royal forests, found that the
Dean was reduced to an 'unprofitable and wasted condition'.
There had been still heavier felling for the French Revolution-
ary War by 1803, when Nelson took an interest. Vast droves
of hogs were allowed in the woods in the autumn, he
reported, 'and if any fortunate acorn escapes their search,
and take root, then flocks of sheep are allowed to go into the
Forest, and they bite off the tender shoot. There is another
cause of failure of timber: a set of people called Forest Free
Miners, who consider themselves as having a right to dig coal
in any part they please'.

But it was not till 1808 that a new Act of Parliament was
passed. Though this did little more than confirm the Act of

1668, it marked the start of systematic planting. At the time only 676 acres of the 11,000 which the crown had been allowed, were enclosed, but in the next ten years the whole of the remainder was taken, and planted with four million oak trees and 880,000 ash, elm, sweet chestnut and 'fir'. Protecting the young trees was a problem. They were attacked by mice, moles and rooks, and in one year alone 100,000 mice were killed, but by 1819 all these plantations were flourishing. A visitor in 1823 wrote that she 'rode about the Forest, which 50 years hence will be a *real* Forest; at present it consists of about 11,000 acres of young plantations six or seven years old, but where the oaks are growing luxuriantly'.

The Commoners were less pleased, and in 1831, when they considered that certain of the new plantations should have been thrown open for grazing, 2,000 of them took pickaxes and spades to the fences and walls and demolished almost every yard of them, then drove in their sheep. They were only suppressed by the Royal Monmouth Militia and the Third Dragoons.

It is ironic that the millions of oaks planted between 1808 and 1818 for the navy were never wanted by it. Before they were half the proper age of 100 years, iron ships had replaced wooden ones. The last large deliveries of oak to the navy (cut from earlier plantations) were made in 1855. It is a further irony that, after years in which the miners had taken such damaging quantities of its timber for nothing, they and the country's other miners now became valuable customers. The Dean miners had finally lost their free timber rights in 1808.

By the end of the century professional foresters were realizing that the post-Napoleonic planters had made other serious mistakes. The oaks which had seemed so fine when young were now poor. In 1896 the forestry expert Sir William Schlich wrote, 'Any person with a pair of eyes ... found on by far the greater part of the area a thin crop of oaks from 80 to 90 years old, of poor height growth, with rounded or flat tops, and the branches coming down low, so that only clear boles of small length were formed ... Presently the wanderer would probably come across a solitary old oak of magnificent dimensions, towering high over the 80 or 90-year-old crop; the idea would at once cross his mind that the flat-topped younger generation could never grow to the height of the few remaining old trees, and he would be sure to ask, "What has brought about the change?"' Schlich's answer was that the large old oaks had grown in a forest composed two parts of beech to one part of oak. Planting oak alone had ruined the soil's fertility.

Again the Commoners were infuriated by attempts to correct this error, because these involved re-enclosing all 11,000 acres for various forms of felling and replanting. In 1898 fences were torn down and a steam sawing machine near Blakeney Hill blown up. But the new work went ahead, and in 1910 Schlich reported that the effect of keeping the sheep out of the new enclosures had been remarkable. Many of the 90-year-old oaks which he had found so poor were being replaced successfully with larch. It was from this period, rather than from 1919 when the Forestry Commission began to supervise the forest, that the woodlands of the Dean for the first time for many centuries were successfully managed. About 3,000 acres of the post-Napoleonic oaks remain today, but the rest of the forest area which was wooded in 1900 has been replanted or transformed by interplanting with other species. To this have been added about 12,000 acres of conifer plantation.

It is no use pretending that the character of the forest has not been affected. Apart from the oak plantations, before the present century there were extensive areas of heath with gorse, heather, bracken and birch scrub with only the occasional isolated tree. Now little of this forest waste remains and dark plantations stand on every side. And although in theory the Dean remains half a broadleaf forest, conifers are also used as nurse trees in over 5,000 of the 12,000 broadleaf acres, increasing the sense that it is primarily a conifer forest. The Deputy Surveyor, Dean, admits that in some plantations the broadleaf trees will never take over, and for this reason officially commits the Forestry Commission only to a proportion of 45 per cent broadleaf to 55 per cent conifer.

Given the Forestry Commission's brief to operate commercially, there is no alternative. Large areas of the Dean are too high or infertile to grow broadleaf trees economically. Even on the least promising sites Corsican pine does well, and elsewhere larch and Douglas fir can be grown. These species are now even more valuable than before since large-size timber cannot be imported in container ships, and the Forestry Commission fells them as they are needed, but for the most part the conifers are felled after 50 to 60 years.

The oaks are now managed on a 150-year rotation. At this age, young for an oak, only 20 per cent of Dean oak timber is suitable for the upper end of the market: furniture making, or the building of herring-fishing boats. If the trees are left till 180 or 190 years old the proportion falls to ten per cent.

Dean oaks, when growing in all-oak plantations, suffer heavily from oak leaf roller moth, which can entirely defoliate them, but less severely when growing in mixed plantations. It seems that the roller moth's chief predator goes through two life cycles in a season while the roller moth goes through only one. The predator therefore finds no prey during its second cycle and dies out unless it has the alternative preys which other species of tree provide.

Grey squirrels are an even more serious pest, to all broadleaf trees. Large forests like Dean control them with Warfarin, but this is less successful for small areas of woodland because the squirrels breed on neighbouring land. Sentimental suburban ladies who feed them are, in the Deputy Surveyor's opinion, also to blame. Furthermore, about 20 years ago, during one of those changes of government policy which undo decades of forest planning, conifers were considered to be all that mattered and insufficient protection given to broadleaf woodlands. Trees damaged then will not recover.

One menace to successful forestry in the Dean *is* under better control today: the Commoners' animals. Up to 5,000 sheep graze the forest, but they are excluded from about 6,000 acres of plantation where they would do harm. These enclosed areas change, for the Forestry Commission has kept in the Dean the power of rolling enclosure which the crown lost in 1877 in the New Forest. Outside the enclosures, sheep roam and graze freely. Like the New Forest's ponies, they stray about the roads, appear in pub car parks or nibble the front lawns of council houses.

On the western side of the forest a few coppice woods survive. They are now being cut for the first time since large-scale charcoal burning died out 60 or 70 years ago. The Forestry Commission plans a 25-year rotation, and sells the oak cuttings for hardwood pulp. This is the only major market for such wood which contains much tannin and if used for chipboard, for example, stains where it comes in contact with iron. Chestnut, however, makes fencing posts, and sycamore, birch and alder are all in demand for turning. In some forests there is more profit to be made by selling coppice wood and the limb wood of timber trees as firewood, and the Dean sells about 3,000 tons a year for this purpose, but if it offered the remaining 6,000 tons it would flood the market. Firewood is also a seasonal trade, and the Dean's 90 foresters need work which continues throughout the year.

In the Dean the Forestry Commission takes seriously two of its other responsibilities: conservation and recreation. Two areas have been set aside as nature reserves: Ladypark near the Wye and Nagshead south-east of Coleford. This last is managed by the Royal Society for the Protection of Birds, and has the longest history of bird recording in the country. As in other forests, the best areas for birds are not the pure broadleaf plantations, but the interfaces between broadleaf and conifer. Though the Dean's deer were supposed to have been shot out in the late nineteenth century, it now has two herds again, one of about 50 dark fallow deer around the Speech House, the other of 80-100 in High Meadow Woods.

The Dean also has picnic and camping sites and forest walks, each with informative guide. More perhaps than other forests, it should be explored on foot to catch its flavour. Among its rocky outcrops, red earth banks and small clear streams, there is usually more to discover than fauna and flora on even the shortest walk. Old mine workings, quarries —there are records of about 800 quarry leases—overgrown iron works, old railway lines, abandoned piles of millstones —everywhere there is evidence of the ways in which it has been exploited during the last 2,000 years. And though the last commercial iron-ore was produced in 1944, and the last deep mine for coal was abandoned in 1965, there are still eleven coal mines working in the forest.

A small black tip and a short narrow-gauge track are the first signs of these. Then a hole in the hillside appears among the trees, about five foot high, more like the burrow of a large forest animal than a part of the twentieth-century industrial world. Most of these small mines have only two or three miners. Presently they may surface, 'black'd by coals', just as their ancestors were when the Hon. John Byng saw them 200 years ago.

Wyre

The king had a number of other forests in the counties bordering Wales. There are records early in the thirteenth century of the Forest of Hereford, but the name probably meant only the part of the Forest of Dean which extended into that county. In Shropshire, on the other hand, he had the **Forest of Brewood**, till it was disafforested by John, and the **Forest of Morf**, sometimes known as the **Forest of Bridgnorth** which it lay near.

Here in 1209 there was an incident which shows how powerful forest officials were at the time. When a hart strayed into the bailey of Bridgnorth and was taken by the guards into the castle, the verderers of the forest brought the sheriff to justice for the offence, though he was Thomas de Erdinton, a man much favoured by the king, sheriff of both Shropshire and Staffordshire.

An even larger forest which has survived longer was Wyre. It took up a large part of the south of Shropshire, and extended into Worcester, giving that county its name. Wyre-ceaster was a Roman station in the forest.

Later, however, Wyre Forest centred on the small town of Bewdley and became known as Bewdley Forest. It was largely a coppice oak forest and for several hundred years was known for its charcoal-burning and bark-peeling industries. Though both these forest crafts were practised elsewhere, charcoal burning continued in Wyre as long as anywhere in the country, and some bark peeling still continues today. Surprisingly, the two seem never to have been connected, though the stripped wood might in theory have provided the charcoal burners with their raw material.

The bark was used for tanning leather and Bewdley became a centre of tanning, partly because it had such a convenient source of bark, but also because it lay on the Severn, 40 miles higher up than the Dean, which provided it with the ample fresh water which tanning needs. Bark can only be stripped easily when the sap is rising and the leaves expanding from the bud. This period was considered in Wyre to begin on 24 April, the day after Bewdley's annual cattle and cheese fair, and continue for six weeks till 14 June. Men cut the wood and trimmed off the side shoots. Women peeled the bark, placing the poles on X- or Y-shaped supports and working with a special peeling tool. They formed gangs of as many as 40. Each pole is said to have taken 'a few hours' to peel, but this seems hardly credible for the smaller ones.

The bark was then piled, inner side down, to prevent rain leaching the tannic acid. The stripped wood was known as black-poles and was sold for rail and hurdle making.

Like most mediaeval woods, those of Wyre contained a proportion of standard trees, which the crown, shipbuilders and as a consequence foresters came to consider their most important product. Such woods might well have produced timber *and* coppice wood, but in practice there were problems. Andrew Yarranton's description of these in the seventeenth century concerns the conflicts between timber-growing foresters and tanners, but it can stand for similar ones between foresters and charcoal burners or miners. He wrote:

The Tanner's interest is to have as much bark as he can, and the Workman's interest to have it so too . . . now the Tanner and the Workman are in private Combination, and either by night or by day down the Standals are cut, but if there should chance to be any little question made, who fel'd the Standals, there is sufficient Advantage in point of gains betwixt the Workman and the Tanner to stop the Gentlemans Bayliffs mouth, but if it comes to be questioned by the owner of the Coppices, the Tanner excuses himself, and saith he bought the bark of all the wood that was fel'd that year, and he found the Standals cut down, and, hopes bark being for the good of the Common-wealth; it should not be lost, and so he frees himself; then the Workman comes under question, this is his guard, he sayeth he did not cut them down, but rather believes some of the Tanners did cause them to be cut down, or else what would you have a poor man to do, but live by his labour, these hard times, for saith he, all others cut them down in all the Copices in the Country, and why should not I do so as well as the rest?

Charcoal burners, unlike bark peelers, worked all the year. And while bark peelers mainly used oak, charcoal burners in Wyre preferred holly or beech. Oak produced flakier charcoal, and the charcoal of ash, elm, birch and willow was less dense. All these were preferred to charcoal made from conifers.

At the centre of a hearth, fifteen feet in diameter, the charcoal burner set a stake, then leaned his wood in towards this. Eventually the pile would be eight feet high, and entirely covered with turf. He then removed the stake and lit the pit by dropping red-hot charcoal down the flue this had created. The pit burned for up to ten days and was watched day and night. If the fire ever burned through the turf it had to be covered instantly.

The last commercial charcoal was made in Wyre during the Second World War, on a site opposite the Green Dragon, Finger-post, Rock. Bewdley's last tannery closed in 1928, and the small amount of bark which is still peeled goes to a tannery at Grampound in Cornwall.

Though these crafts have virtually died out, Wyre Forest, as a picturesque expanse of woodland, survives, and is managed by the Forestry Commission. The forest walks give fine views of the Clee Hills and of the River Severn. But the Deputy Surveyor, who has it in his charge as well as the Dean, considers it a forestry disaster. Because much of it is pure oak, it suffers even more severely than the Dean from oak leaf roller moth, and its soil it so lacking in phosphate that there are places where even conifers won't grow. Another country craft, he believes, may have been responsible. In Wyre oak twigs, rich in phosphate, were taken for hundreds of years for vinegar making. Even so there are successful stands of Douglas fir, dating from the 1920s.

Cheshire Forests

Cheshire, most northerly English county bordering Wales, had three royal forests. In the east, **Macclesfield Forest** lay on the edge of the Peak District, with which in a geographical sense it had more in common. It was disafforested after the Restoration, but 2,000 acres of broadleaf and conifer plantations in the Goyt Valley today form part of the Peak National Park. To the west and closest to Wales was the **Forest of Wirral**, occupying the long rectangular peninsula which sticks out between the estuaries of the Dee and the Mersey. In the fourteenth century the citizens of Chester successfully petitioned to have it disafforested because it harboured so many outlaws.

Connected to Wirral and reaching east across the county was the **Forest of Mara** or **Delamere**, with Nantwich at its centre. Its land was mainly fertile and continually encroached upon, till it was finally disafforested in 1812. The crown, however, was granted 8,000 sandy acres, 4,000 of which were to be used for timber growing. Oaks, the timber trees of the time, were planted, but when they failed, they were replaced with Scots and Corsican pines. Some of these, now managed by the Forestry Commission, have grown into fine trees.

Red Squirrel

FORESTS
OF WALES

As the ice retreated, trees began to arrive in Wales from about 8300 BC in roughly the same succession that they arrived in England. First came juniper and birch, followed by Scots pine. Somewhat later came hazel, elm, oak and, to suitable moist valleys, alder. Between 5000 and 3000 BC in the warm moist Atlantic period, pine decreased sharply and small-leafed lime *(Tilia cordata)* arrived. By the end of this period oak was already the most important tree of the lowlands. Here it was English, pedunculate oak, mixed now with wych elm, lime, maple, cherry, aspen, holly and yew.

Around 3000 BC neolithic man arrived, and began systematically to clear woodland for crop growing and animal grazing. As in England, much less elm pollen is found from this date onwards, and though elms may have suffered from some pest equivalent to Dutch elm disease, most ecologists believe that they declined because they were regularly cut for fodder. During the next 2,000 years oak also became the most important tree of the country's highland zone. Here it was durmast, sessile oak, mixed with birch. Some highland areas of Wales have almost certainly been wooded with oak from then until today, for example Tycanol Wood on the north of the Preseli range, but this is not to say that man has never interfered with them.

By about 1000 BC pine as a native species had probably died out. A little pollen is still found, but so little that it was probably windborne. Beech reached Wales in this period, but though it now grows in most parts of the country it is only native in the south-eastern counties.

For many centuries this predominantly oak forest, covering almost the whole country, played a central part in Welsh life. It was their retreat when attacked, as the Romans discovered. 'When we used to plunge into the woods and thickets,' Tacitus wrote, 'all the hostile tribesmen charged straight at us.' Caesar described a British village as just a wood surrounded by a wall and ditch into which the tribesmen could retreat. The mediaeval chronicler, Giraldus Cambrensis, wrote that the Welsh 'neither inhabit towns, villages nor castles, but lead a solitary life in the woods, on the borders of which they ... content themselves with small huts made of the boughs of trees twisted together, constructed with little labour and expense, and sufficient to endure throughout the year'. The forest's oak trees and its mistletoe were the central symbols of the Druid religion and used in all its ceremonials.

With typical thoroughness, the Romans set about subjugating the Welsh, first by enticing them out of their forests to fight, then by destroying the symbols of their resistance. In a well-known passage Tacitus describes the Roman attack on Anglesey, to which their infantry crossed in boats and their cavalry by ford.

On the beach they met 'a serried mass of arms and men, with women flitting between the ranks. In the style of furies, in robes of deathly black and with dishevelled hair, they brandished their torches, while a circle of Druids, lifting their hands to heaven and showering imprecations, struck the troops with such an awe at the extraordinary spectacle that, as though their limbs were paralysed, they exposed their bodies to wounds without any attempt at movement'.

The Romans rallied, however, and slaughtered the Druids. 'The next step,' Tacitus continues, 'was to install a garrison among the conquered population, and to demolish the groves consecrated to their savage cult.'

During the following three centuries the Romans affected the trees and forests of Wales in two other ways. They felled quantities of timber for building fortifications; and, as in England, they introduced several exotic species, including fruit trees and the Spanish chestnut.

The Normans found the forests of Wales as much of a military inconvenience as the Romans had. William Rufus fought three unsuccessful campaigns in Wales. In 1094 he was heavily defeated at a wood named Coedysbys (still unidentified). In 1095 he was unable to root the Welsh out of their woods, and two years later he retreated to England 'not daring to invade the woods or wildernesses against the Britons'. In 1157 Henry II was even more severely defeated when he fell into an ambush at a wood named Hawarden (probably between Hawarden and Ewloe).

Eight years later Henry began a policy of systematic felling of forests, especially those blocking border passes, which was continued under different kings for over 100 years. Edward I pursued it on an enormous scale. Hundreds of foresters were employed in the work—1,500 to 1,800, for example, between Flint and Rhuddlan in 1277, when he was advancing from Chester to the river Conwy, and 2,000 in 1287 at Brecon. When passes were opened the way made was of a bowshot's width (200 to 250 yards). As such routes continued for many miles, huge numbers of trees had to be felled.

Once established in Wales, the Normans like the Romans needed timber to build and repair their fortifications. Norman castles at Llangibby, Kenfig, Caenarfon, Beaumaris, Harlech, Carmarthen and many other places all took large amounts. Some was at first imported, but much was taken from native forests.

Meanwhile the English lords on the Welsh borders began to establish hunting reserves inside Wales which were in many ways like the chases or royal forests of England. As part of such forests, or separately, they impaled parks for deer. In the early fourteenth century 100 forests and 21 parks had been mapped in South Wales, including the **Forest of Tintern** which lay just across the river Wye from the Forest of Dean, and the great **Forest of Brecknock**, which spread over 50 square miles of the county, much of it above 800 feet in altitude. Close to the borders of central Wales were such forests as **Radnor** and **Clun**. Forests of the north included the Earl of Chester's near **Soughton** in Flintshire, which was fifteen miles long and four and a half miles wide, and—best known of all—the Forest of Snowdon in the counties of Caernarfonshire and Merioneth.

Snowdon

If most Welsh forests have less-well-recorded histories than English, they have even finer scenery and rarer wild life. For this reason, and because more is known of its development than of others, the Forest of Snowdon must come first. Today, inside the old forest bounds (which have never been definitely established) there are four modern forests.

One of these, the Forest of Beddgelert, consists of a detached group of woods and plantations to the south-west of Snowdon. The other three—Lledr Forest, Machno Forest and Gwydyr Forest—form an almost continuous block of woodland to the south-east of Snowdon around Betwys y

Coed. Each of the four has its splendours—the word is no exaggeration—but Gwydyr is the largest and in some ways the most impressive. It lies in the main to the west of the river Conwy between Betwys y Coed and the village of Llanrwst. Here the land climbs dramatically from the valley bottom to a rolling plateau at 700 to 800 feet, then still higher. Within today's forest there is a peak of 1,312 feet (Mynydd Deulun) and trees have been planted on the slopes of Creigiau Gleision up to 1,600 feet.

In mediaeval times this wild country accumulated as much legend as verifiable history. Snowdonia was the stronghold of Llewelyn the Great during his wars with Edward I, and the well-known story of the death of his dog, Gelert, is set in the forest of Beddgelert. When Llewelyn returned home and found his child's cot overturned and Gelert's jaws red with blood he ran the dog through with his sword, only then looking under the cot and discovering the baby alive beside a dead wolf. Gelert's alleged burial place in the village of Beddgelert is still visited by dog lovers.

At the beginning of the fourteenth century Snowdonia was affected even more severely by Owen Glyndwr's rebellion. Then, according to Sir John Wynn (whose family owned the Gwydyr estate for many centuries) 'all the wholle countrey . . . was but a forrest, rough and spacious as it is still, but then wast of inhabitants, and all overgrowen with woods, for Owen Glyndwrs warres beginninge in Anno 1400, contynewed fifteene yeares w'ch brought such a desolation that greene grasse grewe' in the market place of Llanrwst. Glyndwr's cave can still be found (with difficulty) in the present Forest of Beddgelert, on the slopes of Moel Hebog.

Later that century, during the Wars of the Roses, a successful supporter of the Lancastrian cause, Dafydd ap Sienkin, is said to have operated with his guerrilla band from a cave high above Gwydyr Castle on Carreg y Gwalch. At this time most of the valley sides were densely covered by the kind of mixed but predominantly oak forest that still covered much of Wales. The population was sparse, and after the Black Death, which came to Wales in 1349, and again in 1361, had become even sparser.

By the middle of the sixteenth century, however, travellers were beginning to admire the forest's timber, and John Lleland, who visited Snowdonia between 1536 and 1539, found good woods in the valleys of the Lledr and Llugwy —the rivers which divide the three modern forests in the Betwys y Coed area.

Soon afterwards the same Sir John Wynn inherited the estate of Gwydyr. The family traced its ancestors to David, Prince of Wales, whose elder brother had married Henry II's sister, but Sir John remains its most interesting character, arousing such local anger that his spirit is supposed by the people of Llanrwst to lie under the great Swallow Falls of the river Llugwy, 'there to be punished, purged, spouted upon and purified' of its foul deeds in life. Precisely what these were seems uncertain. As a Member of Parliament he is supposed to have been one of those who were forewarned of the gunpowder plot and to have helped to forestall it. He was also a member of the Council of the Marches, keeping this position at one difficult moment with the help of a £350 bribe. But at Llanwrst he founded a school and a hospital, as well as rebuilding Gwydyr Castle.

His attitude to the trees of his estate is not known, but he took an interest in the minerals of the forest, writing to a friend in London in 1625, the year before he died, 'I have lead-ore on my grounds in great store and other minerals near my house, if it please you to come hither.' He seems to have been asking for technical help. He clearly believed that these rights were his, though at the time the Forest of Snowdon was still under the king's forest law and remained so till 1640.

Forty years later, in the 1680s, there is evidence that the forest's trees were providing timber for a well-organized trade. On the estate there was a saw pit where oak planks were cut for ship building at Liverpool. Timber was floated down the Conwy to its markets. In 1685 Gwydyr was also selling bark for tanning, sometimes ready harvested, sometimes 'on the tree' to be harvested by the buyer.

The eighteenth century, as in many English forests, was a time of heavy felling. Gwydyr was particularly affected during the Seven Years War (1754-60) when £50,000 worth of timber was sold. These were years when Welsh woods, as well as producing timber, were being extensively coppiced for charcoal for iron works. The little town of Furnace close to the Dovey estuary gets its name from an iron-smelting furnace (recently restored) which was supplied with charcoal from the neighbouring oak coppices and with iron-ore by sea.

Towards the end of the century the Forest of Snowdon had apparently recovered, for travellers again began to comment approvingly on its trees. In his *Tours of Wales* (1778) Edward Pennant, squire of Downing in Flintshire, found 'the noblest oaks in all Wales' between Gwydyr Castle and Betws y Coed. Twenty years later, Iolo Morganwy reported that at Carreg Y Gwalch there was 'a very fine grove of many thousands of beech planted within the memory of living' which 'once introduced will propagate themselves'. By this time Scots pine had also been planted and was already provoking hostile comment. R. Fenton, in *Tours of Wales 1804-1813*, described the views at Gwydyr as 'disfigured by a straight belt-planted line of grim fir trees'. There were larch here too, which he considered to suit the soil better, 'outshooting every other species'. Foresters also preferred larch because they thought sheep found it less to their taste.

Planting and harvesting of conifers continued at Gwydyr during the nineteenth century, but on the valley sides above the Conwy these were still mixed with standard oaks, coppice oak, ash, birch and hazel. During the First World War, in the most extensive felling since the mid-eighteenth century, these areas were largely cleared, so that when the Forestry Commission began to take over land in Snowdonia soon after the war ended it found much treeless hillside.

The Commission was faced with two separate tasks: to replant these felled areas which had been traditionally coppiced but more lately planted with conifers; and to plant uplands which for many generations had grown only grass, heather, gorse, blue moor grass, deer grass, bilberry and dog myrtle. Centuries of grazing had reduced such land to a thin acid soil with large areas of bog and peat. Here conifers would grow successfully, but not broadleaf trees.

The great conifer controversy, which has aroused even more passion in Wales than in England or Scotland, thus seems to officers of the Forestry Commission in Wales to be a non-controversy; if they were to grow trees at all on such land, conifers were the only possibility. Sitka spruce, above all other species, suited these moist uplands. Today 90 per cent of Gwydyr Forest is conifer, and wherever the uplands were moist as well as poor sitka spruce has been used.

On dry, thin-soiled ridges, however, Scots pine and later lodgepole pine were found to do better; and lower down at intermediate levels larch has been tried, at first European, later the faster-growing Japanese. On low sheltered ground, Douglas fir and silver fir have both proved successful.

During the last 60 years there have been minor changes in this policy, and several other conifer species have been tried. More broadleaf species are now being planted on valley sides for ornamental reasons. But in general the planting policy has remained the same. Though well-conceived in theory, in practice it suffered serious and unexpected setbacks.

Some of the early plantations were overwhelmed by gorse, which sprang up in huge quantities as soon as grazing animals were excluded. Where sheep continued to get into the plantations, as some did, the young trees were uprooted or topped and stunted. Rabbits and hares did serious damage until myxomatosis reached the forest in 1954. Above all, from 1929 onwards, fires regularly destroyed plantations. Many of these were caused by sparks from passing railway engines, but the great Parc fire of 1938 when 411 acres, mainly of Norway spruce, were destroyed, was started by a tramp. Fires continue and there were large ones in the dry summer of 1976 and the dry spring of 1980.

Today it is easy to visit the forest and be unaware of such problems. Tall and successful plantations grow on every side, varied with picturesque lakes and the stone ruins of abandoned homesteads. Because of its height there are a succession of spectacular views from cliff tops down the green valley of the Conwy or the tree-filled valleys of the Lledr and Llugy. The forest's set pieces are its several spectacular waterfalls, and such mainly broadleaf plantations as 'Artists' Wood', where many not-very-well-remembered Victorian painters used to set up their easels. Regularly, across lake or moorland, down conifer-edged forest rides, Snowdon appears, formidably grey and massive on the skyline in summer, snow-covered in winter.

The failures in the forest which cannot be missed are its mines. In many parts, especially around Lake Geirionydd, they can be seen, either as abandoned furnace chimneys, or as excavations among the trees. Some of these are deep and dangerous, some shallow water-filled pits, which could have been dug by two or three miners in a week before they abandoned hope. Lead and zinc were mined before and after Sir John Wynn's time, and even after Gwydyr had been leased to the Forestry Commission the estate kept the mineral rights.

It would give the miners a 'take note' which allowed them to explore a site for three years before committing themselves to a full 21-year lease. For centuries small parties would

Red Squirrel

speculate with their time and effort in this way, but the two periods of serious mining were 1850 to 1919, and again from 1950 to 1959. It is from these that most of the remains date. Some miners came from Cornwall and Scotland, others from the villages of Llanrwst and Trefriw. The steep wooden Miners' Bridge over the Llugy was the route up into the forest taken by those from Betwys y Coed.

Forest charcoal, called 'black coal' was needed for smelting, but for lead it produced too hot a fire and was mixed with small pieces of wood dried in a kiln and known as 'white coal'. In Tudor times the crown grew anxious about the damage which charcoal burning was doing to Welsh timber, as it did about similar damage in English forests. In the late sixteenth century, for example, Hugh Nanney, a local landowners in the Forest of Snowdon, was heavily fined for taking 30,000 trees. He had been supplying iron works in the valley of Ganllwyd.

In Snowdon's forests there are more and rarer mammals than in any English forests, but strangely there are few deer. Instead wild goats climb about the crags. Goats were once commonly kept by smallholders in this part of Wales, and these are almost certainly their descendants. Feral cats also live in the forest but there are no true wild cats. Rarest—and now found only in England in the north—are pine martens, red-brown tree-climbing creatures which are hard to see and can move so fast that they catch squirrels as prey. Slightly commoner, but extinct in England is the polecat, the wild equivalent of the ferret, which is smaller than the marten and a darker brown with shorter, less bushy tail. In Snowdonia the red squirrel survives, though its numbers have always fluctuated, further proof that it was *not* driven out of

south-east England by the grey squirrel, which only arrived in Snowdonia in 1959.

Snowdon's birds also include species now rarely found in England. On the highest ground, ravens breed, and so do the red-legged, pink-billed chough of the same family. The golden eagle has probably not nested in Snowdonia for 150 years, but buzzard, merlin, kestrel and peregrine are all seen around the peaks.

The birds of the upper grasslands are the skylark and the meadow pippet, and of the moorland the golden plover, red grouse, curlew, snipe and, where there is scrub or bush, the whinchat and stonechat. Around the lakes the common sandpiper is often seen, and on some of them, Lake Elsi for example, huge colonies of gulls have taken up residence, their raucous crying audible through the trees long before the lake appears.

The conifer plantations of the forest are still so comparatively new that it is less easy to be dogmatic about their typical birds. When the trees are young the grasshopper warbler, nightjar, black grouse, short-eared owl, willow warbler, chiffchaff and garden warbler all occur. When mature, coal tits, chaffinches, goldcrests, robins, wrens, wood pigeons and jays are commonest. Snowdon's long list of birds includes many other species, from thrushes and blackbirds to the now rare corncrake which is still sometimes heard in hayfields by the river Conwy.

Coed y Brenin

Twenty miles south of Snowdon, near the small village of Ganllwyd in the county of Merioneth, lies another great forest, its 22,000 acres, like those of the forests of Snowdonia, today largely planted with conifers and producing some 30,000 tons of wood and timber a year. In 1935 it was renamed Coed y Brenin (forest of the king) in honour of King George V on his Diamond Jubilee.

In mediaeval times it was granted to the Cistercian abbey of Cymmer, the order which had abbeys and extensive rights in many English forests, for example at Beaulieu in the New Forest. In Wales various religious orders, but especially the Cistercians, held enormous areas of land and their influence on Welsh forests was important. They assarted forest land for crop growing, and were often ordered to clear forest where it gave shelter to outlaws. Since they were great sheep farmers, coppices they cut for wood were inclined to disappear when grazing prevented regeneration.

Cymmer Abbey, founded in 1189 under a charter from Prince Llewelyn ap Iorwerth, drew its early monks from another Cistercian house at Cwmhir in Radnor. Cymmer Abbey itself was built on the east of the river Mawddach, a short way above the point at which it joins the river Wnion; *cymmer deu ddwfr* means 'the meeting place of waters'.

Little is known for certain about the tree species of the forest at this time but it can be assumed that oak predominated, and details from similar forests suggest that despite the grazing problem the monks managed it carefully, some as high forest, some as coppice with standards, some as pure coppice. Parallel to the forest there grew up in the area a typical Welsh agricultural system of homesteads in the valleys surrounded by enclosed fields, woodland above supplying wood for burning and sheltered pasture, and above that open mountain pasture to which the flocks were driven in summer, with a summer farmhouse known as the hafod.

From the fourteenth century the farms of this part of Wales began to supply England, especially London, with Welsh black cattle for beef; part of the forest had an interesting connection with this trade. On Dolgefeiliau farm, between what it now the forest's visitor centre and its picnic site on the Eden river, the cattle would be assembled and here six smiths would work to shoe them for their journey. Each animal needed eight shoes, two for each cloven hoof; the smiths made and stored these in the winter for the summer droving season. The droves, which could be as large as 400, travelled at 2mph, would reach the London area in two or three weeks, and would then be fattened in Essex or Kent before they were sold at Smithfield market. Droving was at its height in the eighteenth century when 30,000 Welsh cattle a year would be sent to England, but declined when railways reached this part of Wales. There are people alive today who remember the old drovers.

In 1536 the Abbey of Cymmer was dissolved and the land passed to the Nannau family, whose house stood in the green hills above it. As at Gwydyr, conifers came to Nannau long before the Forestry Commission planted them. In 1774 the estate was already noted for 'the large Scots firs which grow here'. In 1775 it passed by marriage to the Vaughan family. In the following years, during interludes in the Napoleonic wars, Sir Robert Vaughan gave work to the unemployed of the district, building cottages, barns and bridges, and his initials or his wife's can still be seen on many of these in and around the forest. It was the Vaughan family who, after the First World War, leased then sold the forest to the Forestry Commission.

Unlike some estates which it acquired, Vaughan Forest, as it was then called, was well wooded. The last two owners had taken an interest in forestry, and fine oaks had always grown in the valley. The King Oak, felled in 1746 during the time of the Nannaus, had a trunk fifteen feet long and 25½ feet round. As the story is told, a merchant bought 60 oaks for £1 each, to be of his own choosing; after a fierce legal battle he managed to get the King Oak included among these, though that was not what the Nannau estate had intended. This great tree alone he sold for £60. The bark weighed six tons, three main limbs made 45-foot mill shafts in different parts of the country and from other timber a table was made for the University of Wales.

The forest still has 600 acres of broadleaf woodland, its trees now including beech, southern beech and red oak, but no trees of this size, and its broadleaf plantations are maintained for ornamental rather than commercial reasons. They grow at a rate of four to five tons per year per hectare, compared to a growth rate of thirteen tons for Douglas fir.

Oaks, as they once covered much of Wales, can be better seen in the National Trust's wood at Dolmelynllyn, near the village of Ganllwyd. This wood borders the Forestry Commission's forest and was part of the original forest. By 1924 when it was given to the Trust it had come into the possession of Campbell Blair. Here, among ancient fern-covered oaks, many of strange shape, on carpets of emerald moss, are the little-known but spectacular Rhaladr Dhu falls on the River Gamlan. Where such woods were once coppiced it is now the National Trust's policy to 'single' stools. If a number of stool shoots are allowed to grow out together, being genetically identical, they grow to similar heights and at a certain age are liable during gales to knock each other to pieces. Singled oaks develop more variously and in the end produce a wood composed of trees of more varied ages.

Above its valleys today's forest of Coed y Brenin has the thin acid soil, low in phosphate, of so many Welsh hill and mountain forests, in which only conifers will grow. Sixty per cent of those here are sitka spruce, but species like lodgepole pine are grown on the most exposed heights, and Douglas fir on the sheltered valley sides. Norway spruce has done better here than in Snowdon's forests, but neither European nor Japanese larch have proved very successful. The faster-growing larch hybrid *Larix decidua x kaempferi* is now being tried. About 85 men work in the forest, 60 as foresters, 25 on haulage.

Like other forests of North Wales, Coed y Brenin has found it impossible to sell in Britain as much softwood for pulping as it can produce, and has actually *exported* some to Scandinavia to be re-imported as paper. It waits hopefully for the promised plant at Shotover.

At Coed y Brenin the Forestry Commission is conscientious about its wider social responsibilities. Eighty thousand to 100,000 people visit it each year and about 260 parties of school children are shown round its small but unusually well-designed information centre. The present head forester, makes his own film strips for showing here. There are 50 miles of forest walks. Stiff climbs lead to peaks, many of them still treeless, with magnificent views over the valleys of the Mawddach and its tributaries. There are two more waterfalls, one of which (Rhaeadr Mawddach) once powered the forest's most exotic industry: gold mining.

Gold is sometimes said to have been found in this part of Wales by the Romans, but if so they left no evidence, as they did elsewhere. The first recorded find in Merioneth was made in 1843 in debris from a coal mine near the forest. A small gold rush followed in which 24 mines were opened and fifteen shafts sunk.

The gold belt is about three miles wide and runs through the forest on the west bank of the Mawddach. The most successful mine, not found till 1888, was in the forest at Gwynfyndd. Its ore was taken about half a mile to the Rhaeadr Mawddach falls where it was treated by the Britten Pan method—a restored Britten Pan machine is displayed at the visitor centre. The mine produced gold for four years but never at a profit.

Forty years later, in 1934, it was restored and was about to be worked again when it was burnt to the ground. Its ruins are now all that remain and the mine level is flooded, but miners of the valley continue to believe that the forest's gold will one day make someone rich.

Dolaucothi

Gold mines are at the centre of another National Trust property: Dolaucothi, near Pumpsaint. This estate lies between the small towns of Lampeter and Llandovery, a few miles west of the Great Forest of Brecknock, but was never part of it, and can claim to be forest only in the sense that it is a survival of the great oak forest which once covered most of Wales. Its ancient contorted oaks, set around the black mouths of mines, are even stranger than those of Dolmelynllyn.

Though gold was probably extracted here either from river deposits or from open cast workings in pre-Roman times these mine workings are Roman, indeed the Romans may have come to Wales for Dolaucothi's gold. The only other sources of gold in the empire at that time were in Spain and Roumania. Here they established what has been described as the most technically advanced industrial works of the period.

They dug the large adits (horizontal mine shafts) which are the most obvious remains to be seen today and created a water supply for washing the gold and 'hushing' (jetting water at the ground to break up the ore) which included aqueducts of four and seven miles length delivering about three million gallons a day. These can be seen best in winter when the undergrowth has died. The mines were probably abandoned in the third or fourth centuries and they have not been worked since then, but a hoard of golden jewellery was ploughed up in a nearby field in the late eighteenth century.

Oaks would certainly have grown on the hillsides around the mines in Roman times and been cut for the timber they needed. They have continued to grow here throughout the succeeding centuries. In mediaeval times they would have been managed as typical coppice-with-standard woods to be cropped for the firewood and building timber essential for villages of the time. Today's oaks seem to have been last coppiced in the 1920s and 1930s. The estate, 2,577 acres in total, included 600 acres of such woodland when it was finally given to the National Trust in 1941-44 by H. T. C. Lloyd-Johnes, whose family had owned it since the reign of Henry VII.

There is another reason for finding Dolaucothi interesting. It is typical of the woodland properties which the Trust is today actively managing with new aims, using new techniques. For 30 years after the last war its way of re-establishing

or reviving broadleaf woodlands, whether plantations or
ancient woods, was to set a group of nine oak or beech, for
example, in a matrix of conifer nurse trees, typically Corsican
pine. The conifers, at first 75 per cent of the plantation
—would eventually be taken out, leaving a pure broadleaf
plantation, but for 20 or 30 years it would seem to be almost
entirely coniferous. One argument for this policy was that it
was in the national interest to grow conifers. But the Trust
now believes that it is not right to alter the look of a

broadleaf wood for such a long period, even if the ultimate result is good. It also admits that growing conifers, even temporarily, 'can have a very damaging effect on the more fragile herbaceous communities typical of ancient broadleaf woods'.

It has developed one simple new method of re-establishing broadleaf woods without using conifer nurse trees. In many parts of the country, where an area of woodland is clear felled or a clearing made in a wood by the fall or cutting of old trees, ash and sycamore seedlings appear in quantity, as well as the oak or beech which are ultimately wanted. Till now such ash and sycamore have been treated as weeds, but it has been found that they can be just as effective nurse trees as conifers. When they are eventually removed the ash make a valuable crop.

Various technical developments are now making it possible to dispense entirely with nurse trees, in particular so-called Tuley tubes. These simple plastic devices, described more fully in the introduction (known to foresters as plastic headstones) are already producing dramatic changes in forestry practice in lowland forests all over England, Wales and southern Scotland.

Regeneration alone may not produce enough of the broadleaf trees which are needed. At Dolaucothi about 4,000 trees are currently being planted by Manpower Service workers, including beech, ash, rowan, cherry and maple. But the ultimate aim is to produce a mature oak wood and, as at Dolmelynllyn, the present coppiced oaks are being singled where appropriate.

Brecknock

South-east from Dolaucothi, the Great Forest of Brecknock measured seven miles from east to west and reached from the river Twrch and the upper Usk as far as the borders of Herefordshire. This vast expanse of hill country was made a forest by Bernard de Newmarch during the years 1090-93, after he had defeated the local Welsh ruler. Though few records of its early mediaeval history survive, it seems to have been managed in the style of English royal forests, with typical forest officers, forest laws and forest courts. But it was *not* a royal forest, and the noble families who ruled it for nearly 400 years behaved much like the absolute princes of small kingdoms.

It had passed into the hands of the Duke of Buckingham by 1483 when the Duke was executed by Richard III and his lands, including the lordship of Brecon, confiscated. After Richard's defeat at Bosworth Field the Buckingham family recovered Brecon but were permanently deprived of it in 1521 and for the next 300 years it was a royal forest.

From its first afforestation the Commoners had exercised their right to graze their animals on the forest, paying a sum of money per animal which was known as *Cyfrif* (meaning 'number' in Welsh). Others who lived in the Lordship of Brecon paid a higher rate for similar rights. The gathering of these payments was more and more often sold to a collector for a fixed sum and this caused much resentment among the Commoners. Because their rates were fixed the collector would do his best to introduce and favour the animals of outsiders, whose rates he was allowed to raise, so depriving Commoners of the grazing they needed.

But the final disafforestation of Brecknock between 1815 and 1819 was a scandal on a larger scale. In compensation the crown received nearly 14,000 acres in the centre of the forest and the Commoners became joint owners of two areas to east and west, amounting in total to 17,000 acres. They lost their grazing not only on the crown land, but on a further 8,000-9,000 acres which were sold to pay the costs of disafforestation. The money raised in fact went on fees to the Commissioners (£4,000), the surveyors (£5,000) and the solicitors (£5,000).

There were at one time a number of well-wooded valleys in the forest, which made it suitable country for a deer reserve, but the greater part consisted of uplands lying between the Brecon Beacons and Carmathen Van, almost all over 800 feet, much of it over 1,250. Here the tree cover was always sparse, and by the time it was disafforested had mostly been reduced to the treeless moorland of today.

Margam

Close to the south coast of Wales, Margam is today one of the Forestry Commission's forests which make industrialized Glamorgan more wooded than any of the wilder, mountainous counties of the north. Its 10,000 acres lie just across a motorway from Port Talbot. Cranes and furnace chimneys rise close beyond the tree-decked lawns of Margam Castle, and the Afan Valley which runs inland to form the forest's north-western boundary is set along its lower slopes with terraces of miners' cottages.

In mediaeval times Margam was another Cistercian property. When the Normans reached this part of Wales the country was still about three-quarters wooded, and it had probably changed little by 1147 when Robert of Gloucester founded the abbey. The Margam watershed would have been lightly covered with oak, ash and birch, the more densely filled valleys would also have grown willow and alder, except where cleared for cultivation. But at Margam, as elsewhere, the Cistercians kept huge flocks of sheep, depasturing them in summer on the uplands, where they consumed seedlings so preventing regeneration and producing first wood pasture, then treeless grass. They also cleared land in the traditional mediaeval way, by burning, and though they would have enclosed some woods and cropped them for firewood and building material, the estate when it finally passed to Sir Rice Mansel in 1537 must to a considerable extent have been deforested.

Margam forest remained in the hands of Mansel descendants till the 1920s, though it passed twice through females and the family name changed first to Talbot then to Fletcher.

Not much is known about it during the first 150 of these years, though the family itself steadily improved its status. In 1611 Thomas Mansel was the third on James I's list when he devised the Order of Baronets, and exactly 100 years later another Thomas Mansel was made a baron by Queen Anne. At this time they still occupied the old abbey buildings, and two paintings of the late seventeenth or early eighteenth century give a good idea of the surrounding landscape. To the west, thick broadleaf forest covers one hill and scattered broadleaf trees, presumably oak, another. On either side of the house are plantations, though it is difficult to say whether these are of forest or fruit trees. The distant hilltops have a few hedgerow trees but are mainly bare. Nowhere is there a sign of a conifer.

Some 30 or 40 years later this had changed. In 1738 the Margam forest was surveyed by three men including Edward Harris, described as house carpenter, though in practice he was also head forester. He estimated that there were some 7½ tons of 'ffirr' tree. This was a tiny amount compared to 12,500 tons of oak and 400 tons of ash, but nevertheless proves that conifers were by then being re-introduced to Wales and suggests that Margam was one of the first estates to plant them. Since none is described as full-grown, they were probably planted during the first ten or 20 years of the eighteenth century. Just what species they were is uncertain but probably Scots pine. A fine ornamental plantation of Scots pine stands today beside the drive to Margam Castle, and though this is more recent it could be on the site of those earlier firs. In the same survey of 1728 the timber of different species is valued; surprisingly 'fir' and walnut are considered most valuable at 30s per ton and chestnut comes next at 25s per ton.

Trees also growing on the estate at this time included oak, lime, ash, elm, poplar, beech, sycamore, lignum vitae, horse chestnut and a single yew. Some of the oaks were 'very large', but a substantial number of them and also of the ash are described as pollards. At this date it seems that large amounts of wood (as opposed to timber) were still needed and that to preserve the woods which produced it in a sheep-farming area pollarding was extensively practised.

Nevertheless the forests of Wales began to be exploited during the eighteenth century for timber for ship building. Only eight years after Edward Harris's survey, Lord Mansel sold to the Navy Commissioners 90,850 cubic feet of timber,

including straight oak timber, elm timber, oak planks and timber described as 'square and raking knees' or 'compass timber' which was needed for particular parts of ships.

Towards the end of the century, Thomas Mansel Talbot, the second Talbot to own Margam, practised forestry more systematically. Between 1780 and his death in 1813 he planted a million trees, more than enough to compensate for 81 large oaks overthrown by a violent storm in November 1810. By this time mining had transformed the part played by forests in the economy of the south of the country.

The monks at Margam had mined a certain amount of coal and iron-ore (in the Cwm Kenfig area they left pillars of coal to support their mine shafts which can still be seen) but large-scale mining only began in the sixteenth century when ironmasters from the Dean and the Weald moved into Glamorgan. Here they found ample wood for making charcoal to smelt and forge the local iron-ore. They also found copper which was smelted in the area from late in the same century.

The industry itself was transformed in the second half of the eighteenth century when ironmasters from the Midlands brought to Glamorgan Abraham Darby's technique for smelting iron with coke. In the south of Wales coal to make coke played the part which forests to make charcoal had previously played and until about 1830 Welsh coal was largely produced for and used by the local iron industry. This by no means broke the connection of the iron industry with forestry. If wood was no longer needed for charcoal, timber was now needed in much larger quantities for mining. Forests like Margam supplied it.

Today there are no mines in the forest although the galleries of a small private pit near Bryn village run below it. But there are remains of many larger mines which operated between 1750 and 1950. A number of their tips have been planted with pine and a discerning visitor can discover them by observing where such dark pine clumps stand out from surrounding larches.

Most interestingly, the whole of the hillside area on the north-west of the forest was mined in 1926 by striking miners during the long strike of that year. These workings have now fallen in, leaving scars on the hillside which follow the seams and run diagonally up the slope.

Margam Castle—the mock-Tudor house built in the 1830s by the third Talbot to own the estate—together with the abbey's ruins, an orangery considered the finest in Britain, and the surrounding park, eventually passed to Sir David Bevan. In 1973 he sold them to Glamorgan County Council, which now runs Margam as a country park. Today it chiefly practises ornamental forestry. Apart from the Scots pines already mentioned and some hillsides of once-coppiced or pollarded oak, the so-called Breast Plantations are most striking. The local story is that Sir David meant these conifer clumps which stand half way up the bare Craig Coch escarpment to spell out the initials of his firm (Vale of Neath Ales) but that Lady Bevan disuaded him.

During the 1920s the rest of the estate was gradually taken over by the Forestry Commission at the time when it was acquiring most of its Welsh forests. Though Margam is in many ways typical of these, it has interesting differences.

Douglas fir, for example, often planted in the valleys further north, does poorly at Margam. Here 85 per cent of the trees are sitka spruce, twelve per cent larch and the remainder *Abies grandes*, Norway spruce and experimental plots of such trees as southern beech. Even where Margam's soil and climate might make it possible to grow broadleaf trees as a commercial crop, grey squirrels make this risky. Poisoning them with Warfarin, the most successful method, is considered unsafe at Margam because of its closeness to Neath and Port Talbot. Margam's position, on the edge of Wales's sprawling coastal towns, causes most of its other problems, one of which is poaching.

There were probably red deer at Margam in prehistoric times, but the first record of a stag hunt dates from a visit of the Duke of Beaufort in 1684. Red deer survived at least till

1788-89 when accounts show a payment for building a red deer pen, but some time after that they died out, and only fallow deer, introduced by the Normans, are found here today. Margam Castle Country Park has about 400 and there are around 1,000 in the forest.

In the 1970s, if Margam's forester heard a shot he would drive his fire truck into the forest with flashing blue light and siren, believing that this—not easily distinguishable from a police car—would send poachers hurrying home. Recently he has found cross-bow bolts in the forest and suspects that poachers are now operating silently. Certainly they cull the deer, something which the Forestry Commission would otherwise have to do themselves but not in the best way. The Forestry Commission's new ideas about deer management and the importance of sanctuaries which they are putting into practice in Sherwood and other forests of the North Midlands have not so far spread to Wales.

Margam's position, near the large towns of the coast, also gives it a fire problem. For years it had the worst fire record of any forest in the country. Though many of the fires were started by carelessness, there was also a tradition in the Afan

Valley of 'burning the mountain' in early spring to encourage the grass. At this time the dead grass of the previous year is highly inflammable and the months of February to May, not the hotter summer months when the grass is green, are the most dangerous.

In 1929 two fires destroyed practically all the forest's first two years of plantation. In 1956 there was another serious fire. Though less destructive, the chief forester's description of this outbreak gives a vivid idea of the speed and destructiveness of such fires:

It was an extremely cold Sunday morning in February, a strong N/E wind was blowing across the hill tops. The time was 11.15 when the fire tower . . . reported a fire on Foel Trausnent, south of the Afan, sweeping towards the plantation.

Two landrover parties were despatched immediately and the fire service was called. The fire with the strong wind behind it travelled at high speed and ignited fragments of grass were carried a long distance. When the fire entered the plantation, there was no shortage of inflammable material—six years of accumulated *Molinia* grass, together with a promising crop of spruce trees soon turned the mountain into an inferno. In the early stages the fire was consuming eight to ten acres per minute. In less than half an hour a fire fighting force of between 180-200 were actively engaged on the western flank of the fire in an attempt (which turned out to be successful) to save a 1,500 acre block of plantation. A small party, which had been cut off in the early stages, remained on the eastern boundary and succeeded in saving 70 acres near Ton Hir car park.

In the meantime the spearhead of the fire was shooting across the plantation and did not stop till it ran out of fuel when it reached the Bryn-Maesteg road. When the last flames had been put out 447 acres of six-to-seven-year-old trees had gone up in flames in about 150 minutes. The fire fighting forces consisted of over 200 forestry personnel, 30 general public volunteers and eleven Glamorgan fire service tenders. In addition a lorry load of 25 men were despatched from the Forestry Commission's Taironen Nursery, but it was all over when they arrived.

In the early 1970s there were still an average of 300 fire incidents a year. In the first six months of 1983, however, there were only three. Margam's Forester believes this is the result of a systematic programme of visits to schools by foresters, who take with them models of wild animals and explain to the children that these are the creatures which fires destroy.

Yet another nuisance in Margam is urban litter on a grand scale. This includes an annual average of 30 stolen, dumped and usually wrecked cars.

Today Margam is a highly productive and professionally managed forest, selling 16,000 tons of wood and timber a year. Its tree species seem less monotonous than the statistics make them sound. Whenever broadleaf trees are found during felling they are left. The conifer plantations are now often not replanted but allowed to regenerate from seedlings which spring up among the felling brash, a practice which not only saves money but results in a natural distribution of trees. There are now magnificent walks through the forest, the most ambitious of them running ten miles from the Afan Valley at Afan Argoed to Margam Castle and forming part of the 27 mile Coed Morganog Way. At the forest's highest point (1,020 feet), reached by a new forest road known as Queen's Way, there are panoramic views over Swansea Bay, Mumbles Head, the Gower Peninsula and on clear days the Devon coast and Lundy Island.

Typically, the Forestry Commission was blamed at Margam in the 1920s and 1930s by the people of these Welsh valleys for covering with monotonous conifers the once open sheep pastures. Today when it 'clear-fells', it is criticized for destroying these same plantations.

SHERWOOD AND THE MIDLANDS

Throughout the Midlands of England there were royal forests. In the west, **Needwood Forest** in Staffordshire was well known for its size, fine timber, beauty and rich grazing. In 1266 it became one of the first estates of the Duchy of Lancaster, when Henry III granted it to his son Edmund, later Earl of Lancaster.

Forest law was administered by typical forest officials in Needwood, and these included woodwards who, as elsewhere, were appointed by landowners in the forest but also had a responsibility to the king for protecting woodland which provided his deer with a suitable habitat. When the monasteries which held land in Needwood were dissolved at the Reformation, the employees of those who acquired their lands seem not to have behaved so responsibly. As early as 1540 so-called keepers of the various wards of the forest were taking timber for themselves at the rate of over 800 loads a year.

Commoners of Needwood claimed one unusual right, known as 'hoar lynt'. This entitled them to the wood or timber of lime trees after the bark had been stripped to make cord or mats.

A description of Needwood in Elizabeth's reign shows that although it was 'lately sore decayed and spoyled', almost 8,000 acres still consisted of classic coppice-with-standard woods 'thinly sett with old oakes and timber trees, well replenished with coverts of underwood and thornes, which might be copiced in divers parts thereof for increase of wood and timber'.

The forest was extensively felled in the Civil War, but by 1684 there were still many trees 'of soe large dimensions and length, that there may be picked out such great quantities of excellent plank and other tymber, fitt for shipping, as is not to be found in any of your majestie's other forests of England'. It also had many deer, and the damage these did to neighbouring farms in the end led to its disafforestation in

1804. Many protested, including Needwood's poet, F. N. C. Mundy, who composed a 45-page poem called 'The Fall of Needwood' in this sort of style:

> Twas Avarice with his harpy claws,
> Great Victim! rent they guardian laws;
> Loos's Uproar with his ruffian bands;
> Bade Havoc show his crimson'd hands;
> Grinn'd a coarse smile, as thy last deer
> Dropp'd in they lap a dying tear . . .

Close by in the same county was **Cannock Chase,** called a chase because it included the Bishop of Lichfield's large chase, but in fact a royal forest. Here, too, deer, both red and fallow, were numerous, and here today, in the part of the chase now managed by the Forestry Commission, the deer are being controlled on the interesting new principles described below at Sherwood.

Also in the west was the so-called **Forest of Arden,** but although it is well-known for the use Shakespeare made of it, Arden was never a royal forest but a once well-wooded piece of Warwickshire, which now lies south of Birmingham.

In the centre of the country, Oxfordshire was particularly well supplied with forests. In the east were **Shotover** and **Stowood**. In the north-east near Bicester was **Bernwood** and in the north-west were the adjacent chase of **Woodstock** and **Forest of Wychwood**. At Woodstock Henry I enclosed a park with a seven-mile stone wall (the first stone-walled park in England) where he kept 'wonders from distant countries' which he begged from foreign kings, including lions, leopards, lynxes, camels and 'a creature called a porcupine'.

Wychwood was still considered a sufficiently important forest to form the main subject of number ten of the reports which the Commissioners of Woods and Forests made on English forests in the late eighteenth century. It, too, was then walled, and its 3,709 acres included eighteen coppiced woods. But of timber trees, the Commissioners' chief interest, they found only 173 fit for naval use.

Many nearby parishes had common rights in Wychwood and it seems unfortunate that although it was not disafforested till 1862, they failed to save these. This was the period when Commoners of Epping, Ashdown, Dean and the New Forest were all more successful. The forest's deer were perhaps the reason. Though red deer were said by the commissioners to have died out in about 1782, they were still reported in 1853, when a woodsman complained that they would break through fences seven feet high and do great damage to young trees. There were also many fallow deer (about 1,000 in 1792) and the clerk of the magistrates considered that as a whole the forest was 'attended with great disadvantages to the morals and inhabitants of the adjacent districts and forest parishes' because it produced habits of poaching and immorality. Though Wychwood is now privately owned, the old forest area is still well-wooded.

To the north-east, the **Forest of Rockingham** was particularly important to mediaeval kings, who regularly came to Rockingham Castle (built by William I) and treated this as an administrative centre for the East Midlands. In 1286 the forest measured 33 miles in length and seven to eight miles across. It lay between Stamford to the north-east and Northampton to the south-west, and was bounded by the river Welland to the north-west and the river Nene to the south-east. The deer were numerous, and often sent for by the king at Christmas or for special feasts, or ordered to be dispatched as gifts. The records of the forest courts for Rockingham describe many poaching cases, some of them in bloody detail. The trees, on the other hand, seem always to have been sparse, and there are comparatively few records of gifts of timber.

Several interesting terms were used in the forest, some peculiar to Rockingham, which give insights into how it was managed. 'Derefal wode' was the loppings of holly and other trees for winter feed for the deer. 'Fox trees' or 'fox stubbes' were trees or coppice stools granted to certain foresters in return for controlling foxes and other vermin. 'Faldage' was a payment made by a township for the right to fold sheep in the forest. 'Houndsilver' was the fee paid, either for having a dog lawed (its front claws cut so that it could not chase game) or for the right to keep a lawed dog in the forest.

Rockingham was disafforested in 1795–96 and extensively felled between 1820 and 1880, then again in the Second World War, but today there are still large wooded private estates in the old forest, one of the largest the property of today's owners of Rockingham Castle.

Bordering Northamptonshire to the east and virtually an extension of Rockingham Forest was the **Forest of Huntingdonshire.** At one time almost the whole of this county was forest. Northamptonshire and Huntingdonshire have a special importance in the history of British forests because David

I was already Earl of Northampton and Huntingdon before he became (in 1124) king of Scotland. It was David who first established royal forests of the Norman (and English) type in Scotland. They were based on his English experience and that of the Norman barons who moved from these counties and others into the lowlands of Scotland.

Sherwood

Of all the forests of the English Midlands, Sherwood in Nottinghamshire has for centuries been best known. Unlike Arden, it *was* a royal forest, afforested by William I soon after the Conquest, and though it no longer exists as a single entity, its woods were preserved in the woodland sense by the aristocrats who, from the mid-sixteenth century to the early nineteenth century, acquired large parts of it. It also survives in name as the Forestry Commission's 15,000-acre Nottinghamshire forest, which mostly stands on land that was once royal forest. And though almost all the original woodland has been replanted, one 450-acre wood—the Hay of Birklands—survives, now managed by the Nottinghamshire County Council as a country park. Here, among magnificent ancient oaks and silver birches, it is still easy to imagine Robin Hood performing his deeds of philanthropic robbery.

Though Robin Hood and the legends of his life explain Sherwood's fame, for the last 200 years historians have not only argued about his identity and period, but doubted whether he ever existed. The *Dictionary of National Biography* gave him an entry but the aim of its editor, Sidney Ley, was to prove him a fiction. Recently J. C. Holt, in his splendidly incisive and thoroughly argued *Robin Hood*, has concluded that he was probably real.

Robin Hood was first given a definite period by two Scottish historians. Anthony de Wyntoun, in 1420, dated him 1283–5, and Walter Bower, in 1440, dated him 1266. One real historical event could support the 1266 date. Robin might have been a supporter of Simon de Montfort who had taken to the woods after Simon's defeat the year before.

At the time these dates were suggested the Robin Hood legend had already been around in rhyme and song for at least 40 years. In 1377 Langland wrote in *Piers Plowman*:

I kan noght parfitly my Paternoster as the preest it syngeth
But I kan rymes of Robyn Hood and Randolph, earl of Chester.

By then the legend may already have been turned into folk drama. Certainly in 1473 Sir John Paston complained in a letter that a keeper had left him, although he had retained him for many years to play the parts of Robin Hood, the Sheriff of Nottingham and St George.

At the end of this century or the beginning of the next Robin Hood rhymes were printed for the first time, in a complete form in England some time between 1492 and 1535 entitled *A Lyttell Geste of Robyn Hode*, and in partial form on the continent between 1510 and 1515, as *A Geste of Robyn Hode*. These collections seem to have put together, without much effort at continuity, the tales current at the time. At about the same date, 1521, a third Scottish historian, John Major, for no apparent reason dated Robin during Richard I's reign in 1193–4.

It was this date which on the whole came to be preferred. Walter Scott, in 'Ivanhoe', makes Robin operate in Richard's reign. And Martin Parker, in 1632, claimed that there was a gravestone at Kirklees which put his death as 1198. Certainly the stone existed, but it commemorated Robert Hude, William Goldburgh and Thomas, and the last two do not occur in the Robin Hood legends. During these centuries most of those who wrote about Robin Hood did so in a wildly unscientific way. Most fantastically, the eighteenth-century antiquary, William Stukeley, took up a suggestion that Robin was a noble by the name of Robin fitz Ooth, Earl of Huntington, and invented a spurious pedigree which connected him to Henry II.

At the same time Robin continued to be a popular folk hero. In the mid-sixteenth century Bishop Latimer complained that he had stopped to preach at a local church on his way to London but found the church shut and been informed by a parishioner, 'Syr, thys is a busy daye with us, we cannot heare you it is Robin Hode's daye. The parish are gone abroad to gather for Robin Hode.'

The first to search for the real Robin Hood with anything like a modern historian's thoroughness was the nineteenth-century Presbyterian, Joseph Hunter. He discovered two Robins, one a yeoman named Robert Hood who lived near Wakefield and was last reported in 1317, the other Robyn or Robert Hood, a porter of the chamber in the king's service from March to November 1324. Hunter guessed that these two might be the same and fitted them around a real piece of history: the Earl of Lancaster's rebellion of 1322. Robin joined the rebels, he suggested, submitted to the king when he came north in November 1323, worked for him for a while and then, finding he preferred an outdoor life, returned to Nottingham where he operated for another 22 years. Unfortunately Hunter failed to decipher a document which shows that Robert Hood was in the king's service in July 1323, *before* the king went north, and ignored the reason given for his finally leaving the king: 'because he can no longer work'.

But Hunter's late date is interesting, and there is some evidence to suggest that the compiler of the *Geste* tried to fit the legends around the real event of the Earl of Lancaster's rebellion.

Hunter's discovery of Robert Hood of Wakefield is also interesting. In fact there was a family of Hoods in this area, which is only ten miles from Barnsdale. At Barnsdale, an area of Yorkshire some 30 miles north of Sherwood and not royal forest, several of the legends are set. The landscape which these describe is far more identifiable than that of any of the Sherwood tales. And in 1936, to make it still more probable that Robin belongs to Yorkshire, the most important clue so far was found. This was contained in a document of 1226 which stated that the Sheriff of Yorkshire owed 32s 6d in the matter of the chattels of Robert Hood, fugitive.

Though nothing more is known of this Robert Hood, Holt concludes that he is the most likely candidate for the real Robin, that this is Robin's most likely date, that Barnsdale is the most likely setting for his deeds (though he could of course also have operated in Sherwood) and that he was either related to the Hoods of Wakefield or they absorbed his reputation into their family traditions.

But Holt admits that the whole affair should be seen alongside other tales of disaffected outlaws of the period, for example 'The Outlaw's Song' of 1305, which is specific about a particular outlaw's grievances and names the justices responsible.

Whether or not Robin Hood was real, his legends were, and their interest lies in what they imply about the people who liked to hear them and about the condition of the country at the time. Robin's role has continued to change to suit audiences, and today his robbing of the rich to give to the poor is often seen as an act of revolution. But Robin as originally portrayed was religious and (apart from living off his deer) loyal to the king. His enemies were the middle men of the administration, the rich landowning clerics and corrupt crown officials.

Though the Sheriff of Nottingham, Robin's special enemy, was one such official, Sherwood Forest, like other forests, was controlled by a warden. True, it had no castle and was for many years administered from Nottingham, but its forest courts were held first at Mansfield, later on the forest itself, to the south-west of this town near Lindhurst Farm. Today a stone marks the place but no building survives.

From Nottingham the forest spread north, in a long ellipse, for some 25 miles as far as Worksop, and at its greatest was nine or ten miles across. The whole area consisted of sandy infertile soil and was a natural one for William I to afforest. Its infertility also accounts for its survival as woodland. When it was finally enclosed, many of its new owners found that their land was better suited to silviculture than agriculture. But large parts of it were originally heath rather than woodland, and in this it must have resembled Ashdown Forest on the Sussex Weald, where the soil is also sandy. As at Ashdown, such trees as it had were oak and birch—the same species which almost exclusively form the Hay of Birklands today. Again like Ashdown, Scots pine was once native, was probably burned out in prehistoric times, but does well wherever reintroduced.

The Village of Blidworth, lying at the centre of the old forest, is the best place to start to make geographical sense of the confusing complex of estates which Sherwood has become today. In 1926 a colliery was opened here and a small town of red-brick houses grew around it, but the old village still stands on the hill above. A cross in Blidworth churchyard demonstrates its long connection with the forest. This once marked the place where a Jacobean forester died; inside the church a marble tablet carries his epitaph:

> Here rests T. Leake, whose virtues were so knowne
> In all these parts, that this engraved stone
> Needs naught relate but his untimely end,
> Which was in single fight, whylst youth did lend
> His ayde to valor, hee w^t ease oerpast
> Many slyght dangers, greater then this last;
> But willfulle fate in these things governs all,
> Hee towld out threescore years before his fall
> Most of w^h tyme hee wasted in this wood
> Much of his wealth, and last of all his blood.
> 1608 Febr 4.

The black marble of the inscription is surrounded by white marble carved with stag, long bow, crossed swords, hunting horns and other hunting symbols. Leake was clearly a well-known forester and though the cause of his death is not recorded it is still believed in Blidworth to have been the result of a duel which (at the age of 60) he fought about a girl. Tablet and cross have had a disturbed history. The tablet was on the church's south wall till this collapsed in the eighteenth century. The cross was brought to the south-east corner of the churchyard, but moved from there when the Needs family, local squires, wanted the site for a family vault.

In the second half of the nineteenth century Blidworth had a more curious connection with the forest, when for 40 years the Rev. R. H. Whitworth was its vicar. The forest fascinated Whitworth and he composed what the forest historian, the Rev J. Charles Cox, described as 'delightful modern ballads . . . saturated with the forest spirit . . . eminently worthy of collective publication'. Together these two clergymen wrote the *Victoria County History*'s chapter on Nottinghamshire forestry, though it has Cox's scholarly, rather than Whitworth's romantic, tone. In particular Whitworth was interested in Robin Hood, and, finding few facts, in their absence invented them. Such landmarks as Friar Tuck's well were not only given their names by Whitworth, but included on Ordnance Survey maps on his advice.

Robin Hood names proliferate to the south-west of Blid-

Newstead Abbey

worth, around what is now known as Newstead Abbey, and at its entrance stands another optimistically named feature: the Pilgrim Oak. Mediaeval pilgrims are supposed to have gathered below it to listen to gospel readings. Though a fine tree, it is clearly not much more than 300 years old.

Newstead was in fact a priory, founded by Henry II in about 1165 and granted lands in several parts of the forest. It was surrendered to Henry VIII at the Reformation in 1539, and the following year came to the Byron family, who held it until Lord Byron, the poet, sold it in 1817. Of the various idiosyncratic Byrons who lived at Newstead the last but one, the fifth or Wicked Lord Byron, the poet's great uncle, was by a long way the most curious.

In 1765, having killed his neighbouring landowner, William Chaworth, in the Star and Garter Tavern, Pall Mall, after an argument about who owned Bulwell Manor and been found guilty of manslaughter by the House of Lords, but let off with no punishment (apart from his fees), he retreated to Newstead and lived as a recluse. His fixed determination for the rest of his life was to ruin the estate, so that his son should inherit something valueless—they had quarrelled about the son's marriage—and to achieve this he had all its deer killed and almost all its timber trees cut down. By the time he died he was living in the only room in the abbey which did not leak. Local rumour credited him with more spectacular eccentricities. He was said to muster and drill the abbey's population of crickets; and to have shot his coachman and forced Lady Byron to drive about with the body sitting beside her.

Byron, the poet, developed an early romantic attachment

223

to Newstead. When he first arrived there at the age of ten he planted an oak (now gone), and he claimed that he would never sell it. He gave at least one notorious party there, at which he and his guests dressed as monks and drank wine from the skull of a friar. A Cambridge friend, Charles Matthews, called him always the abbot. To Newstead he brought a bear, a wolf and Athenian tortoises. But ultimately he was glad to sell it and gain from the sale the sort of income which he needed to travel in gentlemanly style.

Newstead was subsequently owned in the nineteenth and twentieth centuries by various conscientious restorers before coming to the Nottingham City Council. Today it has impressive gardens and woodlands, with a distant view across the upper lake to low hills densely covered by the Forestry Commission's conifer plantations around Clipstone. All make a remarkable contrast with the estate's condition in 1809 when a friend of Byron's wrote that it was 'surrounded by bleak and barren hills, with scarce a tree to be seen for miles, except a solitary clump or two'.

Further away from Blidworth, beyond Newstead Abbey on the boundaries of the old forest lies Annesley, home of the wicked Lord Byron's victim and also of the poet's first love, Mary Anne Chaworth. Now Annesley's lands are largely Forestry Commission plantations. Circling from Annesley in an anticlockwise direction, due south of Blidworth lies Bestwood, one of the two original royal deer parks in the forest, now overrun by Nottingham's suburbs. Closer to Blidworth, however, are plantations known to the Forestry Commission as Blidworth Main Block, which it treats as a recreation area. Because the conifer plantations are of different ages and heights, and because the area is large, its many walks are pleasantly varied, and though close to the city rarely crowded.

Circling clockwise from Newstead, north-west of Blidworth are the most impressive of today's woodlands, both ancient and planted. Here too are remains which genuinely date from mediaeval times: the jumbled earthworks which were once King John's hunting lodge, which stand in a field near Old Clipstone. Clipstone was the second royal deer park of the forest. Nearby but with a more doubtful history is the Parliament Oak. Here Edward I is said to have called a Parliament in 1290. Like the Pilgrim Oak, it is a fine tree, but certainly not 700 years old.

Due north of Blidworth (the farther side from Nottingham)

are the Forestry Commission's earliest and largest holdings in the area, consisting of the adjacent forests of **Clipstone** and **Rufford**. The Commission acquired these on 999-year leases in the early 1920s from the Welbeck (Portland) and Rufford (Savile) estates respectively and has planted them largely with conifer. In its total Sherwood Forest (which includes some woodland beyond the old forest) 75 per cent of the trees are conifers, 80 per cent of the conifers are pine and 80 per cent of the pine are Corsican. In the Clipstone and Rufford forests the proportions of pine and of Corsican pine are even higher.

There are good reasons for this. Though Scots pine grows well here, Corsican matures faster, and has been found to resist air polution better than other conifers. This is important at Sherwood, which lies at the centre of a ring of industrial towns—Worksop, Mansfield, Nottingham, Newark—with total populations of two million.

Though the Forestry Commission's Sherwood Forest now produces 30,000 tons of wood and timber annually, it would be producing more but for the disastrous gale of 2 January 1976. This swept through the Midlands, blowing down hundreds of thousands of trees and destroying in Clipstone and Rufford a fifth of the forest. On the windward edges areas of up to 100 acres were flattened and the same happened to smaller areas inside the plantations. Some trees were uprooted, others snapped off half way up their trunks, creating a scene of destruction which resembled a Western Front battlefield of the First World War. The trees most affected were around 65 feet high, and almost mature, so that during the next two years most were satisfactorily sold, but their loss has produced a shortage of mature trees for felling which will not be made up till about the year 2000.

The Forestry Commission also grows some broadleafed trees in its Sherwood Forest, for example to the west at Whitwell Wood, which is entirely oak, and to the east, where it is now coppicing small-leafed lime in Wellow Park, once part of the Rufford estate. In both these areas different soils and the existing woods have made it economic to retain broadleafed trees. But the Commission now plants some on Sherwood's sandy soil as fire barriers. Throughout Clipstone and Rufford and around their boundaries there are belts of mixed sycamore, Spanish chestnut, beech, oak, American red oak and birch. Birch is especially effective because a grass sward develops below it which prevents the spread of ground fires.

Though there are good economic reasons for these exceptions to the Commission's more usual conifer planting on poor soils, they also encourage birds and animals by providing them with varied habitats, and illustrate the two forms conservation must take: the preserving of special woods, usually primary woodland, which have interesting trees, creatures or history; and the managing of conifer plantations so that they support rather than discourage wild life. This means, for example, planting conifer blocks of different ages alongside each other to produce a woodland of different stories, providing artificial aids like bird and bat boxes, and leaving unplanted the best habitats for such species as reptiles, butterflies, badgers and blackcock. The 1976 gale provided a good chance to replant in this way. Felling and replanting blocks of about 30 acres is also good forestry practice: they are as large as timber merchants want to buy, and smaller fellings may produce frost hollows. It also means saving old broadleaved trees in areas to be planted with conifers, not overplanting natural features like rocky outcrops and marshland, and leaving half a chain (eleven yards) unplanted on both sides of streams to allow natural vegetation to establish itself. The Commission now allows measures of this sort to use five per cent of the total forest.

Of all the conservation activities at Sherwood, the management of its deer is most interesting. These are the particular concern of a senior ranger in charge of conservation, who believes that Forestry Commission deer management at Sherwood is equal to or better than anywhere in the world for integrating wild deer into a modern landscape. Sherwood's deer and their history provide an interesting angle from which to see the history of the forest.

Red deer have lived here since prehistoric times. The ranger believes that Sherwood's herd of exceptionally large deer is one of only three pure indigenous herds in the British Isles. Elsewhere the deer have either been imported from other parts of the country, or have hybridized with the smaller sika, deer from Japan but genetically compatible.

Sherwood's red deer, its infertile soil and its strategic position in the North Midlands made it ideal for the Normans to afforest. But they also brought with them fallow deer—'in their hand luggage', the ranger believes, not, as sometimes suggested, during Henry I's reign. They were the species they hunted in the ducal parks of Normandy, and were particularly suited to living off poor land. To manage them they created the parks at Bestwood and Clipstone. Throughout the Middle Ages red and fallow deer survived, though the forest as a legal entity declined. Some private deer parks were created in these times and others in Tudor times, when the first great aristocratic estates were formed from the forest's confiscated monastic lands.

As in many parts of the country, the deer suffered severely during the Civil War, when all these parks were thrown open, and many were killed. Those which remained suffered a far more serious and almost fatal disaster at the end of the eighteenth and beginning of the nineteenth centuries when the surviving parts of the forest were disafforested and most of its new landowners attempted, in the fashion of the times, to plough and cultivate. Only three deer parks now remained: Wollaton (run by Nottingham City Council), and Thoresby for fallow deer and Welbeck for red deer.

These still existed at the start of the Second World War, when again they were thrown open and the deer spread into the countryside. It was a disaster which might have proved final, but by then the Forestry Commission's forests, started from 1920 onwards, provided them with ideal sanctuaries. Here they have lived ever since.

Throughout the subsequent 40 years all who have been responsible for deer have managed them, in the ranger's opinion, in a way related to the sport of deerstalking rather than to their real needs. This has meant little more than one thing: the culling of old and sick beasts. Sensible as this may seem in theory, in practice it may often be hard for even an expert to tell the age, let alone the condition of a deer he is about to shoot. Above all it is a policy which ignores the most essential need of a herd of deer: a breeding sanctuary. Shooting an out-of-condition beast in a sanctuary may be the very opposite of what is good for the survival of the herd.

It is no use picking any piece of countryside and calling it a sanctuary. It must be away from crops which the deer could damage—a sanctuary is not a park and has no pale. And it must be an area which the deer habitually choose to use, especially when they gather in groups of a male and several females in the rutting season. Above all, this will be an undisturbed area, but it will also provide good food. Here the females and fawns will stay much of the year. The males, on the other hand, will stray as much as 20 miles after the rut, with the aim of putting on condition, and will expose themselves to cars, poachers, dogs and other dangers. A successful sanctuary must provide good enough conditions to tempt a certain number of males to remain there in safety the whole year.

At Sherwood today there are three herds of deer, each with its sanctuary. To name them would be to destroy them. Here the deer will emerge, for example on a summer evening, to graze among young pines and the remains of old broadleaved woodland in large numbers, the fallow in a great variety of colours, some almost black, some fawn, some spotted, some with great white splashes on their hocks, as pretty as ornaments for a park and the more so for being in wild country. Unlike roe or red deer, fallow happily graze, but will also raise their long necks to browse off the lower branches of oak or ash.

There are almost no mediaeval records of roe deer at Sherwood, but these are now approaching from the north. In theory the Forestry Commission will keep them out of areas where they are not indigenous, but in practice this will be almost impossible, and their arrival is awaited with anxiety because of the damage they do to young trees. Muntjak (which also do damage) are already here. These dog-size deer, which originally escaped from the Duke of Bedford's Woburn estate, may now be the commonest in England.

Muntjak

East from Clipstone and Rufford Forests lies Rufford Abbey itself, the second after Newstead of the religious houses which held much land in the old forest and were taken by Henry VIII when he dissolved the monasteries then sold. Though it formed one of the complex of aristocratic estates which gave the eighteenth-century forest its name, 'The Dukeries', it was never owned by a Duke, but from 1537 to 1938 was in the hands of the Talbot family. Through a female line these later became Saviles.

The monks of Rufford were Cistercian, and though they do not seem to have been great keepers of sheep, they farmed actively—during 25 years in the second half of the thirteenth century they cut 7,000 oaks and 1,000 saplings to clear land for cultivation. But typically the order seems in the sixteenth century to have become lax, and the last abbot was accused of breaking his vows of chastity with two married and four single women.

In 1637 about a third of the estate of 9,500 acres was still described as forest, and there was also a large deer park. In the Civil War, which soon followed, the Saviles were keen supporters of the king and were rewarded with the title of Viscount Halifax, but in 1700 this title died out. In 1769 the eighth baronet, Sir George Savile, wrote that the county of Nottingham consisted of four dukes, two lords and three rabbit warrens. By this time the forest had been much exploited but Sir George planted so extensively that Defoe hoped 'Shirewood Forest' might one day again 'be clothed in all the dignity of wood'.

In the 1920s Rufford Forest was leased to the Forestry Commission, and in 1940 much of the remaining woodland, including Sir George's plantations was felled. The army, then the Civil Defence, used the house, but it is now a ruin, in the charge of the Ministry of Works. Meanwhile Nottinghamshire County Council has transformed the grounds and lake into a country park and wild life reserve, and allowed one area to the west of the lake, known since 1725 as the Wilderness, to grow into a dense thicket of coppice shoots.

North-west from Rufford lies the Hay of Birklands, the one area of oak, birch and open heath which retains the vegetation of its mediaeval forest days, even if many of its trees would then have been coppiced and much of its ground cover controlled by grazing. Edwinstone is its village and the road running north from Edwinstone once separated it from a similar area, the Hay of Bilaugh, but within the last few years the National Coal Board has been allowed to tip on this from Thoresby Colliery. Ultimately it will no doubt become the sort of vast half-moon-shaped meadow now common in Nottinghamshire, but even if reforested its original trees, animals, birds and insects can never be recreated.

Birklands at least survives, leased from the Thoresby estate in 1973 by the Nottinghamshire County Council for 65 years, now a well-established country park. Like many such parks, there is a honey-pot area, around the cafés and souvenir shop, of picnic tables and worn paths, but within a few hundred yards the woodland is quiet and little visited. Although its trees are, first and last, what most people will notice, the Birklands was made a SSSI grade II for its insects. Here 218 species of spider have been found and over 1,000 of beetle, some known nowhere else in the world.

Insects depend, above all, on dead or decaying trees, and partly for this reason the 450 acres of the Birklands are left almost unmanaged. Everywhere stand gigantic oaks either reduced to pillars with a few green side shoots or entirely dead. The dead ones stand about the forest less like trees than the phallic symbols of some primitive religion, and give the Birklands a character unlike that of any other woodland in the country, even the Ancient and Ornamental woods of the New Forest. Curiously, there are few stagheaded oaks of the spreading shape so common, for example, at Windsor and this is perhaps because they were neither coppiced nor pollarded but harvested for wood by shredding (cutting off their side branches).

Such huge dead or dying oaks are up to 500 years old—the rings of fallen ones have been counted. Oaks which claim to be older are usually replants. This did not stop some getting Robin Hood names. Robin Hood's Larder, where he was supposed to have hung his poached venison, no longer stands, but was once particularly spectacular. Most remarkable today is the Major Oak, named probably after Major Rooke, who in 1799 published the Sherwood classic, *Sketch of the Ancient and Present State of Sherwood Forest*. Its untypically short trunk (33 feet in circumference) suggests that at one time it may have suffered some accident. Today it is fenced, and as a result stands prettily on grass. Its many visitors were so consolidating the ground around it that it could get no moisture. In other ways it is a much revived veteran. Its branches are held up from below with props, and in winter they can be seen to be supported from the inside by a spider's web of steel hawsers and spars. But in summer these are hidden and, as a result of regular trimming by its own tree surgeon, it is not even stagheaded but looks remarkably healthy. This is even more surprising considering that in 1982 young arsonists lit a fire inside it which burned for 24 hours, the flames rising from its centre to half its height.

The oaks of the Birklands are puzzling in another way. They form several well-defined age groups with long gaps between. The monstrous dead and dying ones will have no immediate successors because the next group, though well grown, are more like normal forest or hedgerow oaks and probably a mere 200 years old. There are two further gaps before the young seedlings which have regenerated or been planted in the last 20 years. Such gaps would be most easily explained if they corresponded with times when the forest was heavily grazed.

Even more curious than Sherwood's monster oaks, there were until lately two or three cuckoo oaks: dead hollow oak trunks from the centre of which tall silver birches grew. The last fell in 1983, but as long as dead hollow oaks survive other birches are likely occasionally to appear from inside them. Birch, largely self-regenerating, is almost though not quite the only other tree of the Birklands.

Some are old for birches—140 years—but most die at about 80 years. Everywhere they stand in ornamental clusters or avenues, as if they have been planted, and a few have been, but other apparently artificial avenues have grown up where the earth was disturbed during the last war beside tank tracks or when foundations were dug for amunition stores.

The northern edge of the Birklands provides two further puzzles. Here there are species other than oak and birch —small-leafed lime, for example—and though there is no record of coppicing here, many consist of outgrown coppice shoots. Perhaps they were cut when needed to repair the boundary pale which ran along this edge of the Birklands.

This boundary is the other puzzle. It was at one time formed by a ditch, which can still be seen, inside a bank on which the pale stood. Such an arrangement would have prevented deer jumping out, but there is no record of a deer park here.

Outside this boundary lies Assart Field, its name showing what it was in mediaeval times. In the last 20 years it has continued to represent in miniature the whole history of

Sherwood Forest. From an assart, it had been allowed to revert to scrubby woodland, no doubt because of its infertile soil, but new farming techniques have now given its owner the confidence to clear and sow it again. Such confidence may be premature. On any dry windy day in old Sherwood Forest the sandy soils of one-time assarts can be seen blowing away in pale-brown dust clouds.

Like Clipstone and Rufford forests, the Birklands was hit by the gale of 1976, which cut three parallel swathes through the woods, each 50 yards wide; the clearing of the paths of fallen timber took twelve months. The Birklands has survived storms of the past. Sherwood was one forest devastated by the great gale of 1222 and the king sent instructions to four separate people or groups at Sherwood—verderers, foresters, keeper's widow and keeper of the hays—about disposing of the timber.

Nottinghamshire's mines are a more serious threat to its future. One of the richest seams in the county runs directly below the Birklands, and this has lowered the water table and dried the many ponds which were essential to it when it was wood pasture. At present its oaks and birches seem unaffected.

North again lies Thoresby, which, unlike Rufford was one of the genuine dukedoms. Parts of this large estate came into the hands of the Pierrepont family in Henry VIII's reign, but it was not till 1628 that Robert Pierrepont was created Earl of Kingston upon Hull, and not till 1715 that Evelyn, the fifth earl, became Duke of Kingston.

At the start of the Civil War, Robert, the first Earl, protested his neutrality, declaring that if he joined either king or Parliament 'let a cannon ball divide me between them'. Subsequently, when he had fought for the king and become a parliamentarian prisoner a royalist cannon ball did precisely this.

One hundred years later the then Duke of Kingston caused one of the great scandals of the eighteenth century when he married Elizabeth Chudleigh, who had already married Augustus John Hervey (later the Earl of Bristol). Though his supposed wife bribed the clerk of Lainston church to let her destroy the record of her marriage, she was later found guilty of bigamy and forced to live abroad for the rest of her life.

The present grandiose, mock-mediaeval house was built in Victorian times by the architect Anthony Salvin. By this time the family were Earls Manvers. As at Rufford much timber was felled during the Second World War, but large areas of the 15,000-acre estate have been replanted, and though the line has died out the Dowager Countess survives.

Beyond Thoresby to the north lies Clumber, the second genuine dukedom, property of the Dukes of Newcastle from 1707 to 1946, though, as a complicated device for handing down the title, the nephew who inherited in 1768 was no longer Duke of Newcastle-upon-Tyne, but the Duke of Newcastle-under-Lyme. It was a cannonball fired by the troops of the first Duke of Newcastle which cut in half the first Earl of Kingston.

The third duke (second creation) obtained from Queen Anne a licence to enclose Clumber from Sherwood Forest in 1707. At this time it was described as 'A black heath full of rabbits, having a narrow river running through it, with a small boggy close or two', and its dramatic transformation did not begin till about 60 years later. Then, at the height of the landscape gardening movement, Stephen Wright, who had been one of William Kent's assistants, built for the second Duke (third creation) a Palladian house and land-scaped the valley of the River Poulter, creating an 85-acre lake. Today the house has gone. It was pulled down in 1938 after a sensational week-long auction of its works of art. But the splendid lake survives with the old stables and a late-Victorian chapel as features near the shore. The National Trust owns the estate, which is the largest and most delightful country park of the Midlands.

West of Clumber lies the Duke of Portland's Welbeck Abbey, the third dukedom of the old forest. (The fourth, Worksop Manor, lay west of Welbeck. It was at one time owned by the Duke of Norfolk, but bought by the fourth Duke of Newcastle in 1851 then resold and is now a comparatively small private estate. The fifth, the Duke of Leeds' estate at Kiveton, lies further north and was never part of Sherwood.)

Welbeck, an abbey of the white canons of the Premon-stratensian order, became Henry VIII's at the dissolution of the monasteries, then was acquired in 1584 by Gilbert Talbot. In 1590 Talbot succeeded to Rufford, but the two estates were separated and Welbeck passed to the Duke of Newcastle. It was his descendants who subsequently enclosed Clumber, and briefly, from 1707 to 1711, the third Duke of Newcastle owned both estates, but when he died Welbeck was again separated, passing to his daughter, Lady Henrietta

Cavendish. It became a dukedom again when *her* daughter married the second Duke of Portland.

The fifth Duke of Portland was an aristocratic recluse on an even grander scale than the fifth Lord Byron, building miles of gas-lit underground passages at Welbeck, including the largest underground unsupported dance hall in Europe, driving about his estate with the blinds of his carriage drawn and instructing his workmen not to recognize him but to 'treat him as if he were a tree'. Nevertheless he gave each of them when they started working for him a donkey and an umbrella. He employed 15,000 labourers on his building works which lasted eighteen years and were never finished. In the huge house he lived in a four-or-five-room suite, communicating with his servants by two letter boxes, in and out. Chickens were always kept roasting in case he fancied one. Shooting parties would arrive and leave Welbeck without ever seeing him. To visit London he went first by coach through a tunnel which ran for a mile and a quarter below the lake. When he died in 1879 a man named Druce claimed in a celebrated law suit to be his legitimate heir by a Baker Street bazaar keeper, whom the duke had secretly married, but the case failed, and Welbeck remains the Portlands'. The vast house was restored, and as a result improved, after a fire in 1902 had destroyed one wing.

The estate was always well afforested, as it remains today. When Defoe visited it in the early 1700s he described it as 'beautify'd with large additions, fine apartments, and good gardens; but particularly the park, well stocked with large timber, and the finest kind, as well as the largest quantity of deer that are any where to be seen; for the late duke's delight being chiefly on horseback and in the chase, it is not to be wondered if he rather made his parks fine than his gardens'.

Welbeck's land extended far to the south, and at one time included most of the western half of the old forest. On a hilltop near Old Clipstone the fourth Duke of Portland built, in 1842–44, one of the forest's principal oddities: Archway House. This large arch, an imitation of the priory gate at Worksop, is decorated with statues of Robin Hood, Little John, Friar Tuck, Allan-a-Dale, Maid Marian and Richard I, and stands at about the centre point of a great ride edged with holly which the Duke hoped one day would stretch from Welbeck to Nottingham. It can still be followed from the point where it crosses the road west of Edwinstowe, though the 50-yard-wide avenue is heavily overgrown with broadleaf

The Greendale Oak, 1775

saplings or planted with young conifers and the hollies have grown into 30-foot trees.

At one time the Welbeck estate included the most celebrated of all Sherwood's trees: the Greendale oak. This had a circumference of 33 feet in John Evelyn's time. By 1724 it was already hollow and that year Lady Henrietta Cavendish's husband, the second earl of Oxford, to win a bet had it so enlarged that a carriage and six with a cocked-hatted coachman on the box drove through it. 'From the wood cut out of the opening for the foolish freak of 1724,' wrote Cox, 'a beautiful inlaid cabinet of considerable size was made, which is considered one of the treasures of Welbeck Abbey.' The tree was (and is) only 'a shattered propped-up wreck'.

235

FORESTS OF THE NORTH

The High Peak

Of all the royal forests of the north of England—there were many—only the forest of the High Peak in Derbyshire survives as a complete entity, and this only because it has been included since 1950 in the Peak National Park. The park is larger than the mediaeval forest, extending from Bollington in the west to the edge of Sheffield in the east, and from Meltham in the north to Ashbourne in the south. The forest was confined to the north-west corner of Derbyshire. Here the river Wye bounded it to the south, the river Goyt to the west, the river Etherow to the north-west, the river Derwent to the north-east and to the south-east a line running from Hathersage back to the river Wye. It measured 40 square miles.

Today the park forms an island of wild upland country surrounded by Manchester, Sheffield and the pottery towns. The forest, on the other hand, is better pictured as the most southerly extension of the Pennines—the Pennine Way, which ends 250 miles further north in the Cheviots, starts at Edale near the old forest's centre—and for this reason it should be considered a forest of the north although only a few miles separated it from Sherwood.

There were special reasons for the disafforestation of each northern forest, but the underlying reason for the king relinquishing them more willingly than those of the south is easy to guess. They eventually became more trouble than they were worth. From the start William I was keen to delegate responsibility for the High Peak, granting it in 1068 to William Peverel, who had other extensive properties in the area including Sherwood Forest. To govern the Peak, Peverel built a castle, probably on the site of an earlier one, at Castleton. Once well described as 'perched on a rock, like the nest of a foul bird of prey', its ruins are still the most formidable surviving evidence of the mediaeval forest. The steep hillside to its north is hard enough to climb in light clothes by today's zigzag path. To have climbed it in armour under attack from above would have been a lot harder. South and west, the ground falls vertically to a deep ravine, making attack impossible.

William Peverel's castle consisted merely of an outer wall, though its defenders would no doubt have had some shelter inside from the weather. Their followers lived in the small town of Castleton which lies below, around which they eventually had their own protective wall. Today this is called the Town Ditch and can still be traced, though much of it has been obscured by ploughing and building. William Peverel is believed to have staged a tournament at Castleton at which the first prize was the hand of his daughter, Millet, and this would certainly have been held on the valley floor, not on the castle's slopes.

The castle and the office of steward of the forest remained with the Peverels till 1155, when another William Peverel was banished, and his estates forfeited, for poisoning Ranulph, Earl of Chester. From then for 220 years the forest was in the hands of the king, who governed it through a succession of non-hereditary stewards, the first of whom was John, Earl of Mortaigne, later to become King John. It was in this period that the High Peak and its castle were most valued by the king as a northern stronghold. Henry II received the submission of Malcolm, King of Scotland here and visited it twice in later years. During his troubles with his barons in 1173 and 1174 he had the walls strengthened and paid for provisioning a garrison of 20 knights and their servants. Though the enclosure measured 220 feet by 160 feet and the accommodation now included a hall, this number of men can hardly have been comfortable. Two years later he paid the large sum of £135 for building the keep.

When his son John became king he had the castle further strengthened during the rising of the barons. Henry III stayed here before the battle of Lewes, and Simon de Montfort's supporters subsequently held it for a while. Edward I used it a number of times on his way to and from his campaigns in Scotland. Thereafter it decayed, becoming at one time a local prison, then a pound for animals found straying on the forest, and finally a stone quarry for local builders. But some of the outer walls survive, and though the keep has lost its battlements, stone facing and wooden floors, it remains a rare and interesting example of a Norman donjon with walls eight feet thick at the base. These are made of a broken limestone and mortar mixture, but the original inside and outside facings were of gritstone ashlar, which must have been brought from some distance for Castleton stands on the northern edge of the limestone Peak, and stone of this sort does not occur in the neighbourhood.

Though Peverel's castle was and is the forest's most impressive landmark, it was never used by forest courts. At first these were held at Peak Forest, where there was a hall which has disappeared, and here the visiting justices came for periodic forest eyres. In 1225 a new hall was built at Bowden, which then became known as Chapel-en-le-Frith (chapel in the forest). After this swainmotes for the different wards were held here as well as at Peak Forest and at Hope, but by 1285 the visiting justices of eyre were coming not to any of these but to Derby.

As with many royal forests, the best picture of them and of the life they supported in mediaeval times is to be found in the records of these courts, particularly those of forest eyres. In most forests, eyres should have been held every three years, but for some reason in the Peak they were only expected every seven. In practice they came far less often, and in the thirteenth century, the time when the English forest system as a whole was at its best-organized, there was a 35-year gap between the eyres of 1216 and 1251, and another of 34 years before the next eyre of 1285.

Their rarity is one thing which makes them interesting. Eyres reviewed all cases tried by swainmotes and passed or confirmed all sentences except very minor ones. At a time when lives were on average shorter, it is hardly surprising that after such long intervals many of the accused were found to be dead. What *is* surprising is that the courts show in their records no sign that they felt they were being expected to do something difficult if not absurd, but performed their functions solemnly and systematically. Sometimes they solved the problem of dead offenders by holding their heirs responsible for crimes.

Many of the cases which these three great eyres considered concerned men of low rank or standing, who had poached the odd deer, assarted small areas of forest or taken small amounts of wood or timber. But in 1251, and again in 1285, there were accusations of venison offences on a dramatic scale, in which numerous deer had been killed by men of high rank.

In 1251 the Earl of Derby was accused along with three

other noblemen of taking 2,000 deer illegally during his six years as bailiff of the forest. The earl had by this time been dead for five years, and his period as bailiff had ended 29 years before, but his three noble accomplices were imprisoned and only released when they had paid heavy fines. Though all this had happened during the first six years of Henry III's reign, when the young king had not yet taken full charge of the country, it adds to the impression that the High Peak was a difficult forest for the king to control.

The case also suggests how numerous the deer were in the forest. Sixty years earlier, the chronicler Giraldus Cambrensis wrote that there were so many in the Peak that men and dogs had been trampled to death when herds stampeded to escape. They were entirely red deer. A roe deer is only once mentioned in any case at this time, and though fallow deer had been introduced to forests in the south for at least 50 years and indeed were the deer of the forest of **Duffield Frith** in the south of Derbyshire, there were none in the High Peak.

In 1285 similar but more specific accusations were made against another Earl of Derby. On three occasions 21 years before in the summer of 1264, he was said to have hunted with a total of 38 others in the Campana Ward of the forest, killing a total of 130 deer and driving a further 150 out of the forest. Again many of the accused were gentry, including eight knights and one clergyman. Again the earl was by this time dead. Many of those named seem to have come from other counties—Warwickshire, Yorkshire, Leicestershire, Lancashire and Cambridgeshire—suggesting that the English aristocracy of the time were well aware that the Peak's remoteness made it a good place for illegal hunting. These three escapades had occurred in the months immediately

following the Battle of Lewes, where Simon de Montfort had defeated the king's forces, before the king re-established control of the country. The noble huntsmen were presumably taking this especially good chance for sport, and the king in having them brought to justice was no doubt emphasizing that times had changed.

Just how wild and remote the High Peak was at this time is shown by the frequent mention of wolves in its records. Two foresters-of-fee, one appropriately called John le Wolfehunte, held their positions in return for the service of wolf trapping. These were their duties, as described in 1251:

Each year, in March and September, they ought to go through the midst of the forest to set traps to take the wolves in the places where they had been found by the hounds; and if the scent was not good because of the upturned earth, then they should go at other times in the summer (as on St Barnabas's day, 11 June), when the wolves had whelps, to take and destroy them, but at no other times; and they might take with them a sworn servant to carry the traps; they were to carry a bill-hook and spear, and hunting knife at their belt, but neither bows nor arrows; and they were to have with them an unlawed mastiff trained to the work. All this they were to do at their own charges, but they had no other duties to discharge in the forest.

Foresters-of-fee in fact had the general duty of preserving the forest's deer and woods, and, together with the verderers, they presented accused persons to the courts. In the High Peak there were special names for some of the circumstances in which they could make an arrest: 'Stable-stand', when the offender was found with his bow drawn or his dogs in a leash; 'Dog-draw', when he had wounded a deer and his dog was following it by scent; 'Back-bear', when he was carrying a dead deer on his shoulders; and 'Bloody-hand', when his hands were covered with deer's blood.

The High Peak's thirteenth-century eyres are interesting for other reasons: they show clearly that although assarting—the turning of woodland into crop-growing land—was an offence against forest law, the payments which the courts ordered were more in the nature of rents than of fines. By 1251 they had become fairly standardized at a fine of one or two shillings per acre on making an assart, and a subsequent annual rent of 4d per acre. When a tenant died his heir paid 8d per acre for the first year, the church was entitled to his best beast and the king took his second best. All this suggests that, especially in the north, the king was as interested in raising money from his forests as in preserving them for his hunting or as sources of venison. Certainly poaching offenders were punished, but so many of them were aristocrats that it seems unlikely that they felt much guilt at what they had done.

The court records also show that from the thirteenth century onwards there were numerous horsebreeding studs on the forest. This is surprising, since Peak ponies, unlike those of Exmoor, Dartmoor or the New Forest, have not survived as a native breed. The abbots of Welbeck, Merivale and Basingwerk each had about 20 mares, and other landowners had smaller studs. In 1285 the Queen consort had a stud in the Campana part of the forest of 115 mares and foals. Nineteen foresters were taking advantage of her stud to run their own horses on the forest, pretending that they were the queen's. Horses in this quantity were considered a nuisance (just as they are today in forests) but whereas now it is for the damage they do to paths, then it was because they took the deer's feed.

As impressive as Peverel's castle, though in an entirely different way, is another of the forest's surviving landmarks: the Edale Cross. This stands above the hamlet of Barber Booth, above the steep ascent known as Jacob's Ladder, an hour's walk up the alternative first stage of the Pennine Way. Here sheep graze among rocky tores and deep brown-black peat ditches. Far to the west, the smoking chimneys of Manchester can be seen in the haze of the horizon. A number of crosses marked the forest's internal divisions, most now reduced to stumps, but the Edale Cross is almost intact, missing only a small part of one arm. It marks the point where the forest's three wards met. To the north lay Longdendale, to the east Hopedale and to the south-west Campana (or Champion as it was sometimes called). The Edale Cross is also called the Champion Cross, supposedly after a crusader who took up residence here as a hermit to expiate some crime, but more probably got this other name from Campana or Champion Ward. The ward's name is itself interesting, derived as it is from Champagne, meaning 'open country', and suggesting that even in Norman times this part of the forest had lost most of its trees.

The same certainly did not yet apply to the whole forest. Throughout the Middle Ages villages, institutions and individuals were regularly brought to court for illegally felling trees. In 1285, for example, Hope, Tideswell, Wormhill, Castleton and Bradwell were all accused and fined. At Castleton and Bradwell, wood was no doubt needed for smelting lead from their mines. Bradwell was also fined for taking wood from Pin Dale, a narrow and today totally treeless valley leading into the limestone plateau south of the Vale of Hope. In Longdendale Ward in the north, successive abbots of Basingwerk had damaged the King's Wood, though this wood, which measured fifteen miles in length and one mile across, was still said to be full of beautiful oaks and underwood. Even in Campana Ward the villagers of Bowden (Chapel-en-le-Frith) had taken 100 oaks. This year (1285) a special report on the woodlands of the forest was made to the eyre at Derby.

Apart from the forest's smelters, its farms would have regularly taken wood and timber for fuel and repairs. And many new houses were being built on the forest—131 between 1216 and 1251. Though these would have been of stone and not timber-framed, as they were in counties which had no stone, timber would have been needed for roofs, door and window frames and in due course floors.

Felling does not in itself destroy woods but only when followed by grazing. As in so many forests, sheep were the most destructive grazing animals, and here, too, monasteries kept sheep. Surprisingly, there were no great religious houses actually on the forest, but much forest land was held by those of nearby counties of which Welbeck in Sherwood Forest and Basingwerk in Flintshire were typical. To manage their lands in the Peak they established granges.

In the High Peak, however, the monasteries were by no means the only keepers of sheep, for large numbers belonged to tenants of the king's land. These tenants would drive their animals to the uplands in summer and build temporary sheds there, known as booths, for their herdsmen. All over the forest, but especially in Edale, the word 'booth' still forms part of place names. Throughout the Middle Ages sheep were not only kept for wool and meat, but milked for cheesemaking; ten ewes gave as much milk as one cow. It was only in the last years before Henry VIII's dissolution of the monasteries that there began to be serious complaints about the damage sheep were doing.

At first these were mostly concerned with the way in which sheep were taking the deer's feed, and scarcely ever with the damage they did to the forest's woodland. In 1526 Henry

VIII ordered an inquiry into the overstocking of the forest, which was leaving no grass 'for our game of dere'. Certainly by this time a stone wall had been built round part of the Campana Ward which would allow the deer to jump out and feed in the rest of the forest, but would not allow farm animals to jump in. Soon afterwards four foresters-of-fee, who were afraid that they would be blamed for the decline in the forest's deer, asked that all hunting should cease for six years, so that the deer could increase again from 30 to their previous 360.

By Elizabeth's reign the Campana's wall seems to have become ineffective, and tenants and foresters were ranged on opposite sides. In 1561 on Easter Monday nineteen foresters drove 800 wethers and ewes from Campana (now described as 'a very barren country of wood or tynsell') and impounded them in the castle, where they were said to have failed to feed or water them so that many died. In their defence they claimed to have released them after half an hour on the usual payment of a penny per score.

Gradually, and more typically, the tenants of the forest began to complain about the damage done by the deer, rather than the foresters complain about the grazing of farm animals. Finally in 1635 Charles I agreed to have the forest surveyed and divided appropriately, a part going to the king to compensate him for his loss of hunting, part to the tenants, Commoners and freeholders to compensate them for their common rights. Arrangements were completed by 1640 and at once Charles had all the deer destroyed. They have never returned. But the Civil War followed almost immediately and the High Peak was not finally disafforested till 1674.

Though the great period of Derbyshire lead and zinc mining came after this, in the eighteenth and nineteenth centuries, lead had been mined in the Peak since Roman times. Twenty-seven lead pigs with Roman inscriptions have been found in different parts of the country. Mining continued on a smaller scale in Saxon times and, from 874, when the Danes destroyed Repton Abbey and took the Manor of Wirksworth with its important mines, most of the mines of the Peak have formed part of what is known as the King's Field.

The mineral veins occur only in the limestone or southern part of the Peak (though in later centuries they were pursued north where the limestone continued below shales and gritstone). Only the southern part of the forest lay on limestone.

The Roman mining centre was further south, either at Wirksworth or near Matlock, and it was in these parts that the richest veins were found. But there *were* valuable ore deposits on the forest which were eventually exploited by the Odin mine at Castleton and by the mines around Bradwell. The steward of the forest, as well as the king, made profits from these. In 1251 the various stewards who had held the forest for the king during the previous 35 years were reported to have received between £5 and £40 from the Tideswell mines, and between £4 and £12 from the Wardlow mines.

Miners in the Peak had similar rights to those of the miners of Dean or Dartmoor, but there were many differences in detail and in the terms used. Though their rights had probably been customary since Saxon times, they were not defined till an inquisition of 1288 and not finally embodied in Acts of Parliament till 1851 and 1852.

A miner might look for ore anywhere except in a churchyard, garden, highway or orchard—landowners sometimes protected their land by planting it with fruit trees. If he found a vein he had to apply to the Barmaster, an official of the Barmote Court, which controlled all mining matters, to have it 'freed', and to pay him one 'freeing dish' of ore. For this the miner got the right to two 'meers' of the vein. A meer was a 32-yard length (in the High Peak), but could be of any width or depth. A third meer was the lord's, who might be the king or the person to whom the king had leased the mineral rights. The miner could either work through this third meer, the ore remaining the lord's, or buy it outright from the lord.

Beyond this he could acquire further meers, and demonstrate that they were his and he was working them by erecting a windlass over the mine for raising the ore. This was known as the 'stowes'. If the miner failed to keep his mine working it could be claimed or 'nicked' by another miner. The barmaster then cut a nick in the stowes. After the third nick he handed it over to the rival claimant.

Mining had a considerable effect on the forest where it went on, producing strung-out villages of farmer/miners, of which Bradwell was once typical. In their search for ore the miners worked over the land many times. In crushing it they often allowed finely powdered lead ore to spread across land and poison it. This land and any animals who were poisoned were said to have been 'bellanded'. Lead also got into the streams when the ore was washed. Even more significant for the future of the forest, they took wood for smelting the ore.

They may have taken some timber too for the mines, though less than in such forests as the Dean because the limestone was more stable.

At first smelting was carried out in 'boles'. These were merely small stone circles, with openings facing towards the prevailing west wind, in which alternate layers of wood and ore were piled. The molten lead ran out by a small channel and was collected in a basin. The slag from boles still contained much lead, and was often reprocessed using a mixture of wood and charcoal, but 'whitecoal' (kiln-dried wood) was not apparently used as it was in Welsh lead mines.

For the convenience of miners, who were often illiterate, Edward Manlove, steward of the Wirksworth Barmote in the mid-seventeenth century, put into verse the many curious laws and customs of mining in the Peak. The punishment for stealing ore was severe.

> For stealing oar twice from the minery,
> The Thief that's taken fined twice shall be,
> But the third time, that he commits such theft
> Shall have a knife stuck through his hand to th' Haft
> Into the Stow, and there till death shall stand,
> Or loose himself by cutting loose his hand;

Blast furnaces for lead smelting had by then been invented for 100 years, but it was only in the eighteenth century when large underground drainage 'soughs' were dug and later when steam engines were introduced for pumping that the mines were able to deal satisfactorily with flooding, their most serious problem, and to expand. They prospered till the mid-nineteenth century, producing large quantities of ore and in 1861 were still employing 2,333 men. Forty years later this had fallen to 285. One large mine continued to work till the Second World War, but from 1900 onwards fluorspar, a mineral discarded by the early miners, became more valuable than lead and the mines at Eyam and Longstone Edge (both close to the edge of the old forest) now make the Peak district one of the largest fluorspar producers in the world.

Of the surviving royal forests of England, the High Peak today competes with Dartmoor and Exmoor for being least forest-like in the woodland sense. Even the valleys are mostly treeless. The upper Edale is typical. Occasional ash and sycamore stand by the river but on the slopes above there are only isolated stunted thorns. A very few ancient woods survive, but the real exceptions to all this are the water board's and the Forestry Commission's plantations around the reservoirs of the Derwent and Ashop valleys.

These reservoirs in themselves have transformed parts of the forest landscape more completely than even its dis-afforestation. They are not new. Between 1848 and 1877 the river Etherow was dammed in four places to provide water for Manchester, flooding the valley where the King's Wood once stood as well as several mills, creating what was at the time the largest expanse of artificial water in the world, and causing much local anger and alarm. In 1852, when the dams were partly built, there was continuous rain for a week and 'the whole valley was thronged by persons, many of whom came from a distance, notwithstanding the heavy, continuous and beating rain to see the reservoirs, examine their state and speculate as to the possibility of some of the embankment giving way'. By the time the four were finished they had better reason for alarm. In 1864 Dale Dike Reservoir to the east of the forest had failed, flooding the valley below and drowning 24 people. Soon afterwards Bilberry Reservoir near Holme also failed, drowning 80.

The Derwent reservoirs have proved more reliable. The upper two (Howden and Derwent) were built between 1901 and 1916. During the Second World War the Dambuster squadron of the RAF practised here for their attack on the Ruhr dams. Between 1935 and 1945 the far larger Lady-bower reservoir was built, collecting its water from the Ashop as well as the Derwent and flooding the small villages of Derwent and Ashopton. The lower slopes of both these valleys are now extensively forested with conifers. The waterboard's plantations came first, the Forestry Commission's not till the 1960s. Scots pine, lodgepole pine, Corsican pine, sitka spruce and hybrid larch have all been used. At the water's edge, beside the roads which bring large numbers of tourists from Sheffield, beech, rowan, birch and other broadleaf trees have been used in a worthy attempt to make these plantations look less alien, but the fact remains that the Alpine landscape they have produced seems even more out of keeping with its setting than Dartmoor's conifer plantations do with theirs.

Worthy, too, are the National Park's attempts to preserve and plant broadleaf trees in and around the old forest, though at present they are on a small scale. At their best they can be seen in a wood like Hathersage Booths, where natural regeneration is being encouraged and beech, hazel, lime and alder have been planted. Today's National Park Forestry Officer has found over the last 20 years that farmers on the limestone Peak have begun to take much more interest in their woods, and been more willing to provide land for tree planting. Even half-acre plots he considers worthwhile in a landscape still so bare.

If the king had difficulty in controlling the Forest of the High Peak, he had even greater problems with those forests which lay further north. In **Pickering**, one of six Yorkshire forests, which measured sixteen miles by four miles and lay in the fertile Vale of Pickering, there was a 54-year gap before the eyre of 1334. This eyre tried to deal not only with offences of vert and venison committed during that interval but with assarts made up to 117 years before. Just the same, early kings took a particular interest in Pickering, which had a reputation for its wild boar. John hunted them here himself and in 1214 twice sent his huntsman to kill them, with instructions carefully to salt the meat and soak the heads in wine. Henry III had his father's taste for wild boar and on one occasion sent for 30.

Men of good family apparently treated Pickering, like the High Peak, as a safe forest for illegal sport. In March 1334 over 40 took part in a particularly defiant hunt probably on Blakey Moor in which they killed 43 red deer and left the heads of nine stuck on stakes in the forest. At first none of them troubled to attend the eyre held later that year, but eventually some were imprisoned until they paid fines.

Much of the higher, eastern part of Lancashire was at one time royal forest and here too there was much poaching and long intervals between eyres. But in this county Henry III seems to have accepted the sort of disafforestation which he (in the Forest Charter of 1217) and John (in Magna Carta) had both agreed to, and in 1228 all but seven areas were disafforested. These remained forest, however, till as late as 1697, when William III ordered the 'master foresters, bow-bearers or keepers of the forests, chases and parks of Lancashire' to send precise accounts of the remaining deer.

Today much of the old forest of Lancashire has been built on, but the magnificent barren uplands of **Bowland** (where the Forestry Commission has now planted 5,000 acres of oak and spruce around Stocks Reservoir) are an exception.

One of the Lancashire forests, **Lonsdale**, extended into Westmorland. In this county, too, Henry III took his promises seriously and confirmed in 1225 that even the land of the royal demesne was no longer subject to forest law. In Cumberland, on the other hand, the great forest of **Inglewood** extended from Penrith in the south to Carlisle and contained many fallow as well as red deer. So did most of the northern forests; their absence in the High Peak was an exception.

Though Inglewood became smaller, it survived longer than any other forest in the north. In 1823 in the parish of Hesket on Wrangmire Moss the last tree of Inglewood is said to have fallen 'from sheer old age'. Seventeen years later, however, an annual open air swainmote was still being held in the same parish beside the road to Carlisle. The place was marked by a

stone set in front of a thorn tree which was known as Court Thorn, and here the lord of the forest collected dues.

East from Cumberland, the large and wild county of Northumberland had a number of royal forests around the small towns of Rothbury and Alnwick. Here, as in Lancashire and Westmorland, there was early disafforestation, and after 1281 forest law did not apply in the county. Most of this central area, except for the valley of the Croquet, was never forested in the woodland sense. The same became increasingly true of the north of the county, where it includes the southern Cheviots and borders Scotland. It was here, on bleak and treeless moorland, much of it over 1,000 feet above sea level, that the Forestry Commission began in the early 1920s the greatest of all British forestation schemes.

Kielder

Today Kielder forest is certainly the largest in the country and often said to be the largest man-made forest in Europe. It can be called Kielder for convenience, though in fact it is divided into six forests, two of them in Scotland, each of which has its own name. Already it produces 100,000 tons of wood and timber a year, and this will rise to 300,000 tons, which it will be able to maintain indefinitely.

Kielder was not always moorland. As the ice retreated and trees spread north it was covered with the same forest, largely broadleaf, but including Scots pine, which covered the rest of Britain. For a short period in the Bronze Age it was partly cleared for agriculture, but the forest had returned by Roman times. The Romans were the first to make substantial permanent clearings. They may have done this by burning or grazing, but accounts of the way in which their legions spent their time suggests that they probably felled large areas with the axe. Whatever method they used, it was logical that they should want to clear the forest from these hills which lay immediately north of Hadrian's Wall, and during the 285 years they were here they cleared very large areas.

In early mediaeval times felling continued. The valleys were probably cleared of trees for farming, and any which remained formed isolated woods on the moors. During the centuries of border wars, however, the area became lawless and a good deal of secondary woodland spread back both on the moors and in the valleys. It was only when systematic sheep farming returned in the sixteenth century that this new woodland and almost all that had survived from earlier times was finally destroyed. A few estates planted trees. In the nineteenth century 12,000 acres of plantation were established in the North Tyne (Kielder) district, mostly Scots pine and Norway spruce, but on the whole estate owners were happy that their land should be moor and provide them with the grouse and blackcock shooting they enjoyed. The Duke of Northumberland, whose estate was sold in 1932 to the Forestry Commission to become the core of Kielder Forest, had transformed his farms into a sporting estate in the eighteenth century. Here, in 1771, he built the shooting box known as Kielder Castle which still stands at the centre of the forest. The only planting of trees which such estates did was for shelter in the valleys or for ornament around shooting boxes. Old limes and horse chestnuts still stand around Kielder Castle.

Meanwhile the moors had developed for the most part a vegetation which was not even useful for sheep. This consisted partly of heather growing on peat bogs—it was the heather which gave cover to the grouse—but around Kielder of far larger areas of *Molinia* or purple moor grass. This is known locally as flying bent because its leaves break off in autumn and are blown about the moors. So when the sheep need it, it has gone, while during summer they prefer the better grasses of the occasional limestone outcrops.

The soil which supported the *Molinia* was a layer of acid humus, no more than a foot thick, known as 'peaty gleys'. The heather grew on an equally thin and poor but sandier soil known as 'peaty podzols'. On the Cheviots, where 35-55 inches of rain fall a year, both types existed in a permanent state of semi-saturation, and seemed highly unsuitable for tree planting.

Certainly it can hardly have been the soil or climate which recommended Kielder to the young Australian, Roy L. Robinson, who in 1910 suggested to the Board of Agriculture that the North Tyne around Kielder was a possible area for afforestation. Kielder is above all the creation of Robinson, who lived long enough to watch its first trees being harvested in 1946. But for nine years nothing was done. Only after the First World War was the Forestry Commission formed with the object of creating a strategic reserve of timber. Robinson was a member of its board, and later became its chairman.

The first trees were planted in 1920 at New Castleton in

the west part of the present forest. The results were poor. Four years later the Commission bought land 20 miles further east near Falstone. Again Norway spruce was planted directly into the wet soil and again they failed. On rocky outcrops Scots pine did better but were badly damaged by blackcock. It was another four or five years before the most basic problem of the soil was solved.

The technique followed had been developed in Belgium and consisted of cutting a shallow turf, reversing it vegetation downwards on to a nearby piece of ground and planting the young tree through the reversed turf, so that its roots fed on the sandwich of vegetation. This had the double effect of providing nourishment, and of raising the young tree above the sodden ground. The turfs were cut in lines, so making shallow channels which formed a drainage system.

At first Norway spruce were still mainly used, but sitka were later substituted. For ten years virtually all the digging and planting was done by hand. Forest workmen were recruited from the unemployed of Newcastle—from the start it was one of the aims of the Commission to provide rural employment—and a forest village was built at Kielder, but many found the work too hard and returned to the city.

From 1940, however, tractors were used. These, sometimes in double harness, reversed a line of turf on one side of a furrow, and this now formed the raised sandwich of vegetation into which the young trees could root. By now the Commission had made its large purchase of 25,000 acres from the Duke of Northumberland. It continued to buy land till the early 1960s, and the 20 years from 1940 to 1960 were the great planting decades at Kielder which largely created the forest as it exists today. Quite often each of its individual forests would plant 1,250 acres a year.

Since then Kielder's problems can be divided into those of looking after the newly-planted forest, those of replanting when felling eventually began, and those of adapting itself since the early 1960s to different purposes from those for which it was created: recreation and the conservation of wild life.

Thinning and brashing—cutting off side branches—were two established forestry methods of producing well-grown conifers with good diameter trunks. In its early days both were used at Kielder. In the 1950s Kielder had a women's brashing squad, recruited from wives and dependants of foresters, who would operate, in the words of the Principal

District Officer of the time, 'in a line, all within hailing distance of each other, keeping up a continuous chorus of gossip'. This was excellent for the community, but brashing became less and less economically justifiable as wages increased. Thinning was also costly when done by hand, and when done mechanically the avenues which a tractor cut through the young trees let in the wind. As long as Kielder's close-planted trees stood undisturbed their branches interlocked and they gave each other support, all swaying together in a gale, but once they lost this support they were far less stable—hardly surprising since trees which would ultimately be 60 feet high were growing on less than one foot of soil. Today in the high, more exposed plantations thinning and brashing have both been abandoned, and the trees are left to grow together in a thick mass. As a result they remain thin and a high percentage must be sold as pulpwood, but the total tonnage produced is almost the same.

Replanting began at Kielder as soon as the first trees had been felled and the lop and top had rotted. Again there were dismaying failures. Year after year areas had to be bashed up or entirely planted a second or third time. Partly this was because they were destroyed by roe deer which had now arrived in the forest in large numbers. They are Kielder's only deer, and though deer counts are notoriously unreliable it seems probable that today there are about 4,500. Partly it was that the successes of 40 or 50 years ago suggested all would be simple a second time and the importance of good planting and care had been forgotten. Now a slightly different technique was developed, but the principle was the same: to raise the roots of the young trees above the wet soil. Each was planted alongside the stump of a felled tree, where they would have the needed extra height as well as a little shelter.

During the last 20 years Kielder would anyway have come under pressure to become less a timber factory and more a country park, and might to some extent have adapted itself. But the huge reservoir which was built at its centre between 1974 and 1980 gave it the chance for a far more dramatic transformation. Like Kielder Forest, Kielder Water claims to be the largest man-made one of its kind in Europe. Purists will say that it has no more place in the Cheviots than a conifer forest, but once accepted, it is of considerable beauty and staggering size. The first view from the lower dam seems to be of an expanse of land and water the size of a county.

Unlike many reservoirs, its catchment area is flat rather than deep. Beyond the far shores the forest stretches away to the horizon in bank after bank of hills which in fact reach 1,900 feet but look easily climbable.

The 3,000-acre reservoir took comparatively little forest. What it did, sadly, take was the best land of the valley where small farms had been left. It also took the road to Kielder and meant the making of a new one higher up the valley side. This had to be cut through Kielder's dense, unthinned sitka plantations. The newly exposed edges were, the District Officer says, 'filthy, grey, whiskery stuff'. Landscape architects were consulted—the aim round the lake was now to make an area which, though still commercial forest, would look good as a recreation area—and suggested what he describes as a chastity belt of broadleaf planting. At much less expense and, he believes, more effectively, he reverted to thinning, brashing and high pruning. Small amounts of broadleaf have also been planted but the principal effect has been to edge the new road with elegant plantations of tall conifer trunks which it is easy to see into and walk among, and which thoroughly justify the policy.

None of this touched the great bulk of the forest, which forms the more distant background to the reservoir. Here the land had been blanketed with trees, without respect for its natural features. The first proposal was to fell in smaller coups and when replanting to creating neighbouring plantations of different ages. But this made no dramatic change and also produced a much larger number of exposed edges where windblow is most likely. To avoid edges it was decided to fell, not in arbitrary coups but up to the natural breaks in the forest: its roads, rocky outcrops and above all its streams. These will in future form the permanent structure of the forest and streams and roadsides will be planted with oak, alder, willow and other broadleaf trees. Such trees will never be commercial, but will be chosen to suit the conditions and to grow as healthy vegetables. They will use between five and a half and three per cent of the forest.

They will also encourage wild life, since in the jargon of today, many more plant and animal species flourish where there is a change of eco-tone, or to put it more simply, on edges. Edges are what roads, rocks and streams provide.

Certainly roe deer are the forest's most picturesque animals—they prefer the younger part of the forest, where they are least wanted—but they are nocturnal and not easily seen except in midsummer months when dawn is early and dusk late. They drop their young, often twins, in May or June and gather for the rut in July or August. The bucks cast their antlers in October, grow new ones during the winter and rub the velvet from them between March and May. From May onwards they shed their dark winter coats and grow chestnut summer ones.

Kielder's wild (feral) goats are even more unusual than its roe deer. About 50 live in the forest, mostly in the north-west part on Kielderhead Moor. Kielder also has brown and mountain hares, and, to the foresters' regret, more rabbits again since they are beginning to be immune to myxomatosis. The commonest of all its mammals is the field vole, which provides food for foxes, weasels, stoats, kestrels, short-eared owls and barn owls.

Of the many bird species which have survived or have now returned, the meadow pipit is the commonest. It makes prey for merlins and provides nests for cuckoos. In the less dense plantations all the common woodland birds from tits to wrens can be seen in summer, though most winter in the lowlands. On the moors red grouse survive, and so do black grouse on the plantation edges. In spring the blackcock provides Kielder's most curious ornithological sight, when they gather at established sites to display to each other and give challenging calls while the grey hens wait to be served by the dominant males.

Though some of Kielder's wild life could be found on the moors before the forest came and some the forest destroyed, on balance it has produced a great increase both in numbers and in species. In short, Kielder is a far more varied and interesting forest than critics of the Forestry Commission often suggest. High up in its southern plantations stands a monument to its creator, Lord Robinson of Kielder and Adelaide. When he died in 1952 his ashes were scattered in the forest.

Red Grouse

Scots Pine

FORESTS
OF SCOTLAND

The history of forests in Scotland begins, as in England and Wales, with the retreat of the last ice age, about 8300 BC. Juniper and birch followed the retreating ice; next came Scots pine. By about 5000 BC a group of broadleafed trees—hazel, elm, oak, alder, ash, lime, holly and cherry—covered most of the country. None of this forest has survived untouched by man, though some areas have always remained wooded.

The first to interfere were mesolithic and neolithic men, and though they probably numbered only 4,000 and 20,000 respectively in the whole of Britain, over many hundreds of years they gradually cleared considerable areas by burning or ring-barking trees then grubbing out the stumps. During the Bronze and Iron Ages—in Scotland from about 1900 BC onwards—this process continued, but it was the Romans who set about forest clearing in a typically thorough and far more extensive way.

Mark Louden Anderson, historian of Scottish forestry, has done an interesting calculation about Roman tree cutting, based on written evidence that Roman troops and their followers made it one of their main tasks. If half the members of a legion, helped by as many followers (5,000 in total) worked at tree felling 100 days a year, and each cut ten trees a day (as they might have done in the birch forests of the southern uplands) for 100 years out of the 235 during which they occupied this area *a single legion* would have cleared a million acres. Though he admits that the rate would have been slower in other kinds of forest, his estimate suggests that the effect in the southern part of the country was dramatic.

During the six or seven centuries which followed the withdrawal of the Roman troops from Britain an important change gradually occurred in the attitude of the people of Scotland to their forest land. For centuries they had used it as a source of wood and timber for burning and building—there are vivid accounts from the seventh century of the floating of large timber trees from the mainland the 50 miles to Iona,

257

where presumably there were only unsuitable birch and willow. Now they also began to realize that it provided important feed for pigs and shelter and grazing for deer. At the same time the waste areas of the clans came to be considered as the property of the king, who might reserve them to himself for hunting or grant them to nobles as private forests.

From the early twelfth century the Scottish kings established royal forests in almost every Scottish county. They were valuable not only for the hunting which they provided but also, as in England, for their venison which the king ate when he and his court stayed there, or ordered to be delivered to him.

Early Scottish forests differed in several interesting ways from English. Although there was a Scottish forest law similar to the forest law of England, its punishments were on the whole less severe. And in the twelfth and thirteenth centuries when the king made grants of land in royal forests he usually gave the hunting rights. Such forest holdings became the equivalent of English chases.

But from the reign of Robert Bruce onwards (1306–1329) the kings usually kept for themselves their hunting rights. And in another way Scotland now began to follow closely the English pattern: separate justiciars were appointed, probably first by Robert Bruce, to visit and hold courts in the forests north and south of the Forth.

During the rest of the fourteenth century royal forests declined in area in Scotland, as they had in England under Edward I and Edward III. But in this and the next century all the Scottish kings hunted, some of them obsessively. As young men both James II and James III were abducted while out hunting. And from 1405 James I began systematically to expand royal land, and as a result royal forests, by confiscating estates in many parts of the country.

From the twelfth century the king had granted forest land to religious houses as well as noblemen. These kept sheep and as a result destroyed much woodland. But the sheep which now began to arrive in huge numbers in the lowlands of Scotland and dramatically changed the landscape were brought by the king to pasture on his own holdings in his forests.

For another three centuries the north of the country remained wild, though some forest land was cleared to destroy the retreats of robber bands. Around 1600 in the

Lochewe district of Inverness-shire 'so grievous became the assaults of such outlaws upon persons and purses of lieges, and upon the preserved game of the forests as well, that only by the destruction of their haunts could the land be rid of them'. At the same time in this part of the country there were still 'fair and tall woods as any in all the west of Scotland', consisting of holly, tall 'fyrrs' and 'excellent great oakes'.

As in England, forests had nominally been created for the king's personal hunting, but in Scotland, because of the size of forests, and because red deer, which were the main quarry, had been driven from the valleys on to the mountains, by the sixteenth century a hunt usually took the form of a campaign rather than a battle. It could last many days, cost an enormous sum and need many hundreds of beaters. These were known as Tinchels—the hunt itself was also called a Tinchel.

The most magnificent of all Tinchels was staged in 1528 by the Earl of Atholl in honour of James V. The king's mother and a papal ambassador also attended. But the best-described Tinchel took place in the Brae of Mar in 1618 and was joined by the English travel writer John Taylor—who once described himself as 'a sailor, a waterman, a poet, a composer—on the shortest possible notice and on the most reasonable terms—of nipping satires, epigrams, anagrams, odes, elegies and sonnets . . .'

The expedition lasted twelve days. After passing the castle of Kindrochet, Taylor saw neither house nor local inhabitant for the whole of that time but only deer, wild horses and wolves. The party stayed in 'lanchards', which may have been standard stopping places in remote forests, where there was continuous feasting on venison, beef, mutton, goats, kid, hares, salmon, pigeons, hens, capons, chickens, partridge, moor-coots, heath-cocks, capercailzies, termagants, good ale, sack, claret, Alicante and 'most powerful Aquavite'.

The complete party numbered 1,400 to 1,500 beaters and horses. Five to six hundred beaters would rise early in the morning and spread out into the countryside for up to ten miles to bring in the deer to some chosen valley in which the huntsmen waited.

Then, after we had stayed there three hours or thereabouts, we might perceive the deer appear on the hills round about us (their heads making a show like a wood) which being followed close by the Tinchel, are chased down into the valley where we lay, then all the valley on each side being waylaid with a hundred couple of strong Irish greyhounds, they are let loose as the occasion serves upon the herd of deer, so that with dogs, guns, arrows, dirks and daggers, in the space of two hours four score fat deer were slain . . .

Being come to our lodgings, there was such baking, boiling, roasting and stewing, as if Cook Ruffian had been there to have scalded the devil in his feathers.

Soon after this, from about the death of King James VI in 1625, almost all the remaining royal forests were sold to private owners and though some hunts continued for a time, the new owners found it increasingly difficult to protect their deer, or indeed to establish their right to do so. From this time onwards the woodlands in the old Scottish forests were widely devastated. But at the same time some were protected, some wisely managed and some replanted.

On the one hand timber was felled, as it had always been, by farmers and builders. Felling of this sort does not necessarily destroy woods provided trees are allowed to regenerate if they are conifers, or to coppice, sucker and regenerate if they are broadleaf and in Scotland tenants often held their land by agreements which should have compelled them to protect or plant trees, but in practice they did not keep these agreements, particularly after the 1715 and 1745 rebellions when the owners were absent from the forfeited estates. Tenants resented trees, which harboured birds and made land unproductive with their roots and shade. In many parts of the country there was a well-established farming pattern in which each valley farm had a mountain shieling where they had grazing rights. In the Highlands in the forest of Mamlorn a witness in 1733 stated that 'the woods on the lands of our shielings are now wore out' and that he now took what could be found from his master's woods.

Besides taking wood from their shielings, farmers used them for pasturing goats—the most destructive of domestic animals—sheep and beef cattle in small numbers. When the price of beef rose after 1760 they kept more beef cattle for export to England. But it was when the whole system of land tenure changed, as it did from about 1750 onwards, and the mountains were turned into vast sheep walks, that the greatest disafforestation occurred. Some observers of the time saw clearly what was happening, and in 1791 one wrote, 'the whole country being turned into pasture land . . . has prevented the wood from getting up, which it would do naturally, if it were only protected ... as clearly appears from several spots about Fassifern's house, where the cattle are not suffered to go, being covered with very fine oak and beech'.

Forests were cleared for other reasons. The occupying English troops in 1746 felled some to build roads. They also sometimes behaved like vandals. Near Blair Castle 'some of the officers of the garrison were in the habit of lopping off the tops of His Grace's newly planted larch trees, with their swords, no doubt imagining during their temporary exhilaration, that they were lopping off the heads of their Jacobite opponents'. But after sheep, the other serious devastator of Scottish woodland was the iron industry. In England, especially in the forests of the Weald, it can be convincingly argued that the charcoal burners used wood rather than timber, were anxious to preserve their sources and were an influence for preserving rather than destroying woods. In Scotland this seems to have been less true. From 1715, when the country was thrown open to southern enterprise, English businesses cut timber as well as wood, making little attempt to coppice or manage their woods. The York Building Company which operated in Abernethy from 1729 was typically wasteful. It made so much charcoal that it exported quantities and at one time brassworks in Edinburgh were importing Scottish charcoal from Holland. The company went broke after ten years owing £7,000. Sixty years later the Old Statistical Account of Scotland described the owners as 'the most profuse and profligate set that were ever heard of in this country. Their extravagances of every kind ruined themselves and corrupted others. Their beginning was very great indeed, with 120 working horses, sawmills, iron-mills, and every kind of implement and apparatus of the best and most expensive sorts. They ... went off in debt to the proprietors and the country'.

On the other hand the large tanbark industry which grew up in Scotland at about the same time seems to have treated the sources of its bark (mainly oak coppices) with care. They were felled in rotations which varied from fifteen to as much as 60 years.

And at the same time the practice of planting trees for timber rather than for ornament or shelter had begun in Scotland earlier than in England. The oaks whose ancient remains can still be seen near Cranbourne Lodge in Windsor Great Park, planted in 1580, are generally thought the earliest English plantation. In Scotland there were plantations of oak near Selkirk in 1510, and there is evidence of another (1539) in the memoirs of Sir John Clerk.

On the 13 of this month of January 1739 a very memorable Hurricane happened in a stream of wind from the South-West which spread about ten or twelve miles in breadth from sea to sea ... It is certain that nothing like it happened in Scotland for 200 years past, for as I had a plantation of that Age about the House of Brunstone, they had all stood in their rows since their first plantation till this unhappy day.

From the reign of James VI (1567–1625) Scottish kings when granting rights of free forest often made planting a condition. And towards the end of the same century the crown, barons and church all began to sell forest land, and for this purpose to split it into small portions. Those who bought it, and became the lesser gentry of Scotland, commonly built mansions on their new land and planted trees. 1590 to 1645 was a happy period for tree planting in Scotland, and if these gentry never planted on a large scale, there were enough of them to create a considerable area of new plantation.

Early in the next century (1721) the second edition of Reid's *Scots Gard'ner* contained instructions for the planting of an acre of coppice with standards which would give returns in nine, seventeen and 25 years. In 1756 the sixth Earl of Haddington published *A Short Treatise on Forest Trees*. In practice, too, there was extensive planting all over Scotland during the eighteenth century. By 1845 in Inverness-shire there were about 87,000 acres of plantation, in Aberdeenshire 85,000 and in Perthshire 64,000. It is not surprising that experienced Scottish foresters were often brought south in the eighteenth and nineteenth centuries to manage English and Welsh woodlands.

Meanwhile there had been an entirely new development which, although it did not have so great an effect on Scottish forests as sheepfarming, transformed the meaning of the word forest. This was the creation of Scottish deer-stalking forests. The last recorded hunt in the old grand style occurred at Atholl in 1800. About 40 years later what has been described as the English invasion began. For 100 years the English aristocracy came north to rent deer forests all over the Highlands of Scotland, where, with the help of local gillies, they made individual expeditions to stalk and shoot deer. In his definitive book on the subject G. Kenneth

Whitehead lists some 550 Scottish deer-stalking grounds. The English also came to shoot grouse. Neither type of sportsman was much interested in the trees of the Scottish forests they rented.

These were transformed yet again from the 1920s onwards by the Forestry Commission. For 50 years this bought or leased large areas of Scotland, often in the old royal or baronial forests, and planted them, mostly with conifers. By 1982 it managed two million acres, of which 1,300,000 had been planted.

As in England and Wales, the Commission has been criticized for introducing alien species, planting without consideration for the landscape and creating huge monotonous forests in which little wild life can live. Here too it can defend itself by claiming that it merely did what it had been established to do: create a strategic reserve of timber. And that since the 1960s it has shown much concern about the look of its forests and about their wild life. It can also claim that even if a plantation of sitka spruce is not much like a wood of old Caledonian pines, conifers of some kind have been growing in Scotland for 10,000 years.

Affric

Four forests—two in the north, one in the south and one in the south-west—must stand for the many which existed in Scotland in the Middle Ages. The furthest north of these, the Forest of Affric, (once spelt Affaric) lies some fifteen miles north-west of Loch Ness around Loch Affric and Loch Benevian. It is not only one of the most spectacular in Britain, but one in which a particularly interesting conservation project has been under way for the last 20 years.

Otherwise its history is typical of Scottish Highland forests. Because it was remote it was not an early forest in the legal sense. Its remoteness also saved its trees. These were of mixed species—willow, alder and mountain ash in the valley, birch, oak and pine on the mountain sides. Its pine are the trees which today give it special interest. They have a long history. A few years ago the Forestry Commission when making a forest road discovered an ancient tree buried below four or five feet of peat. It was eighteen feet long, fifteen inches in diameter at its thickest, and identified as Scots pine. Since peat accumulates in these parts at the rate of 40mm every 100 years, it must have fallen about 1900 BC. Today's forester at Affric has in his office a piece of two-by-three-inch timber sawn from this tree, which was a seedling in neolithic times. It is pale-brown and light compared to freshly felled pine because it has lost its resin, but in a timber merchant's yard it would be hard to distinguish.

Until the eighteenth century these northern parts of Scotland were ruled under the clan system, though perhaps the early Christian church, returning from Ireland to England via Scotland, was also an influence. Certainly the Chisholm family which was granted the forest of Affric in 1513 was Roman Catholic, as many of the families of the glen are today. The Chisholms had control of a huge area of this part of Scotland, including Affric, Benula, Erchless, Fasnakyle and Glen Cannich, reaching almost from east coast to west coast. In 1596 the head of the clan was known as 'Ye Chessholm'. As Catholics they supported the Stuarts in the 1715 rising, and when this failed their lands were forfeited, but soon afterwards repurchased by friends who returned them, taking no profit.

In 1745 the family was divided, father and youngest son fighting for Prince Charles, the two older sons holding commissions in Cumberland's army. But after Prince Charles's defeat it was in the glens of the Chisholm forests that he took refuge, and though a £30,000 reward was offered for information about him he was not betrayed. For three days he lived in a cave above Badger Falls in Glen Affric, before travelling over the mountains to Glen Moriston then to Moidart and France.

Once more the Chisholms temporarily lost their land, but again there was much hostility to the Commissioners of Forfeited Estates. When these came on one occasion to collect rents, escorted by a company of the North British Fusiliers, they were engaged by locals and forced to retreat to Beauly.

Meanwhile the woodlands of Glen Affric had remained largely intact. When Cromwell built his citadel at Inverness he took pine from Affric, floating it down the river to the Beauly Firth, but this was an exception. It was only in the early nineteenth century that they began to suffer seriously.

Then Affric, like so many parts of the Highlands, was caught up in the great sheepwalk development, which caused the depopulation of so many areas and still arouses so much Scottish indignation. The Chisholms resisted for a time. When Gillespie, who had established vast sheepwalks in

Sutherland, first came to the glen, 1,000 men gathered to protest and he retired. But in 1801 and again in 1810 large numbers of tenants were expelled. Many went to Canada, often giving Highland names to the settlements they founded. The sheep spread across the valley sides and mountains—by 1858 only six tenants remained but there were 30,000 sheep—preventing the regeneration of young trees. Other woodland was destroyed by fires, often started deliberately to improve the grazing. While in eastern Scotland burning was carefully controlled to produce heather of various heights which would give the grouse the different habitats they needed, here in the north it was often haphazard. Twelve square miles are said to have been burned on one occasion.

During the nineteenth century sheep gradually became less profitable—though plenty are still kept—and Affric Forest, like so many, became a deer-stalking forest. Its great lodge was at Guisachan, just over the hills to the south. Here the English aristocracy came to stalk deer by day and hold lavish house parties in the evening. The sport was on a grand scale with six shooting parties out each day and sixteen gillies employed. For a time Lord Tweedsmouth owned this lodge; Gladstone and the Duke of York visited it in the nineteenth century, and Churchill in the twentieth—though he is said to have taken more interest in bridge building on the estate than shooting. Guisachan's last tenant, in the 1930s, was the Women's League of Health and Beauty. Today it is a roofless ruin, surrounded by rampant mauve rhododendrons, but its park-like setting of ancient oak, yew, beech and lime remains delightful; it seems to belong in some sheltered Yorkshire valley rather than in the Highlands.

Millais was another visitor, and so was Landseer, who painted murals on the dining-room walls of the smaller Affric Lodge. This lodge survives intact. Set between the two lochs of Affric and Benevian, below tall peaks which can still be patchy with snow at midsummer, it is a complete contrast and truly Highland.

Though the Chisholms held some land till the twentieth century, they gradually sold their great estates and through various owners it came to the Forestry Commission. In 1934 the Commission bought part of the Guisachan estate and in 1951 much larger parts of Affric Forest. Today it owns about 70,000 acres of these two forests, about 50,000 acres of which are mountain. These are let as deer forest, often to the previous owners. The remaining 20,000 acres are wooded. It is some of these which make Affric of special interest today, for although most are planted with standard Forestry Commission sitka spruce, lodgepole pine and larch, about 5,000 support old Caledonian pine. They are some of the few such areas which survive.

When these woods were examined by Professor H. M. Steven in the 1950s he not only recognized their interest but saw that they would almost certainly soon disappear. Intensive grazing by deer and sheep meant that there were virtually no trees among them less than 100 years old. This was the situation which the Forestry Commission in the 1960s set out to correct.

The problem was a simple one: to get young pines of the old genetic stock to grow again in these woods, either by letting them regenerate naturally or by re-introducing seedlings raised in a nursery. The early results were a failure. Some seedlings died of exposure. And although the 5,000 acres had been enclosed, deer got in. So did Blackcock, which debudded the young trees and capercailzie which uprooted and even ate them.

In 1967 the whole area was divided into three smaller blocks which were each more thoroughly fenced, and at the same time a new policy started of ruthless deer control. Now

Red Deer stags

every deer of any age, sex or condition seen inside the new enclosures was shot. The District Officer of Affric Forest attributes the success of this policy to the skill and devotion to their task of his two rangers. They were helped by good luck. In the late 1960s deer stalking as a sport became popular again, particularly with foreigners, and the deer began to be controlled on the mountains as well as inside the enclosures. The problem remains a serious one. All over these fenced areas young Scots pines of true genetic stock now stand as high as 20 feet among their ancient ancestors. So, too, do young birch, alder and rowan, as they would have done 400 or so years ago before man became the red deer's only predator. But at any time in winter an avalanche can crush a length of fence and let deer in.

Affric today is a place of sensational beauty, to which the two reservoirs, built in 1947, have done surprisingly little damage. Strangely, the first impression is of birch, rather than pine. Groves of these, many 70 feet high, with silver trunks and pale-green drooping branches rise up the steep banks on either side of the Affric River. The pines come later.

Huge ancient specimens stand everywhere about the glen, but are most numerous in the fenced areas on Loch Benevian's southern shore. Inside these woods, where every tree or group is picturesque but which are nowhere dense, it is possible to get an idea of what Affric Forest may have looked like 7,000 years ago.

Rannoch

South of Affric, beyond Loch Ness, there was at one time a district of old Caledonian pine forest which stretched from Loch Laggan and the Spey in the north to Glen Lyon in the south, and from Glencoe in the west to Braemar in the east, amounting in all to 2,100 square miles. Close to the centre of this vast expanse, in an area 'long considered the acme of desolations in the Highlands of Scotland', lies Loch Rannoch, with the forest of Rannoch around it and, on its southern shores, the Black Wood of Rannoch. By the time the *New Statistical Account of Scotland* was published in 1838, this was all that remained of the old forest.

The history of the Forest of Rannoch, and in particular of the Black Wood, is similar but not identical to that of Affric. For centuries it was the property of the Robertsons of Struan, who first owned land in the area in 1398, and were granted their forest estate by James II in 1439 for helping in the arrest of his father's murderers. Like many clan chiefs, they, and the Menzies who held the land north of the loch, remained supporters of the Stuarts. Menzies of Culdares fought in the 1715 rising but was pardoned and felt bound not to join the '45, so he sent Prince Charles a valuable horse. When this was captured the Highlander in charge of it refused to name Menzies and was executed. After the 1745 rising the Robertson property was taken over by the Commissioners for Forfeited Estates, who managed it for 35 years before returning it to the family.

Until this time Rannoch had certainly been an uncivilized place, 'noted for barbarity, thieving and rebellion'. Like several other areas of Scotland, it claims that the last wolf in the country was killed here. But it was less remote than Affric, and its timber had been exploited since the early sixteenth century. Between 1507 and 1516 ash and oak were cut for a bridge 30 miles to the east at Dunkeld, and for the church at Tullelum. Twenty-five carriages were sent to take timber on one occasion, and in 1514 spars were cut for ship building at Dunkeld. Nearly 200 years later the Robertsons operated a sawmill in the forest, and in 1733 Rannoch supplied timber for General Wade's bridge over the Tay at Aberfeldy.

It was the Commissioners for Forfeited estates who first attempted to protect Rannoch's pine woods. In 1759 a dyke was being built, and in 1763 thirty men were employed building a 'pealing' around the wood. Two years later a young girl was rewarded with a crown for discovering a fire and running some miles to raise the alarm. The fire burned for 24 hours and 100 trees were lost, but 'some hundred thousand' would otherwise have been burned. In the same year a visitor reported on 'the fine appearance of young firs in lately enclosed grounds in Black Wood'. A few of the magnificent Scots pines which survive in the Black Wood today date from before the 1760s but the majority must have been seedlings during the Commissioners' enclosure.

The enclosure caused problems. The crofters at the west end of the loch who had had the right to use the Black Wood for grazing their cattle, were now excluded. Some kind of compromise seems to have been reached, because in an area at this end of the wood which is now chiefly pasture with scattered birch, there are still a few ancient pines. Inside the enclosures the same crofters were now no doubt forbidden to 'cut red firr out of the roots of the standing firrs, which makes them soon fall down', as had apparently been their habit. But organized felling continued. In 1784, for example, a merchant of Perth was given the right to cut 2,000 trees a year for three years.

This felling reached a climax in the early nineteenth century when a public company from England started to operate in the Black Wood on a large scale. To extract the timber it constructed three levels of canals, each with gathering points, and floated the huge pine trunks down these, finally discharging them into the loch. Here they are said to have arrived so violently that many lodged at the bottom and could still be seen there 100 years later. The company made such losses that it abandoned the wood, but the canal system, which started some 300 feet above the loch, is still easy to find, though its leats and gathering points are dry and heather covered.

Those were the years in which Rannoch passed through the two metamorphoses common to many Highland forests:

from forest to sheepwalk, then from sheepwalk to deer-stalking forest. When the sheep came many of the valley's inhabitants emigrated and the remaining farms became larger. North of the loch the Menzies retained their land—it was a member of this family who is said, in 1737, to have given two larches to the Duke of Atholl from which all Scottish larches are descended. In 1895 Sir Robert Menzies was 'one of the most hardy and skillful deer stalkers of the north', who had 'never yet . . . availed himself of a seat on pony back to get to or return from the forest'.

South of the loch the Robertsons sold their estate in 1857 to the Wentworths, who held it till the Forestry Commission bought it in 1948. Here deer stalking began in 1895 and the Black Wood was enclosed to keep *in* the deer rather than exclude them. Regeneration, of which there had been little since the Commissioners' enclosure collapsed, now entirely ceased, but felling did not. Over 1,000 trees were supplied to build the stretch of the West Highland Railway which passed west of the forest by Rannoch Station.

Enough of the Black Wood remained, however, for it to be scheduled for felling in 1918. The First World War ended in time to save it, and it survived till the Second, when it was less lucky. Then the Canadian Forestry Corps established a mill at Dall near the loch shore and felled just about every good timber tree in the wood. Today, 40 years later, a vast area of barren sawdust survives as a memorial to the once tall and upright Scots pines of Rannoch.

This, however, was not the end of the Black Wood. Many trees survived, almost all of them heavily branched and beech-like in form, which the Canadians had considered unfit for timber. And in other ways the war had benefited the wood. The troops who manoeuvred in it, firing live ammunition, drove the deer south into Glen Lyon. In 1949 the forester, A. Whayman, reported some young trees six to eight years old—though no others less than 100.

The Forestry Commission now began, at first in a somewhat haphazard way, to enclose and protect the Black Wood. Not all the results are easy to understand. At the western end one small enclosure has become a dense thicket of rowan. Beside it, below the remaining ancient Caledonian pines, the hillside grows only heather and bilberry, showing clearly the damage the remaining deer still do when they are not excluded.

But elsewhere, especially where the earth has been disturbed alongside forest roads, there has been a certain amount of pine regeneration. Most surprising is an area dug by forest workmen during the last war to plant potatoes. Here on the potato ridges 40-year-old pines grow in a dense thicket. There is no obvious explanation for the contrast between this and the rowans of the other enclosure.

In 1975 the Forestry Commission set about reviving the Black Wood more systematically. The whole wood—now estimated at about 2,100 acres, was divided into three areas, one never to be touched, one to be minimally disturbed, one to be in various ways managed. Though today's forester at Rannoch considers that deer are his most serious difficulty, the fact that a certain amount of natural regeneration is occurring in all three areas suggests that they are somewhat less of a problem than at Affric.

The Black Wood at Rannoch gets its name from its sombre appearance when seen from the north side of the loch. In contrast the sitka spruce, lodgepole pine and larch of the Commission's plantations are a lighter green. The whole effect is as picturesque (though the valley is less dramatically deep) as the forest of Glen Affric. When the sun shines the vast blue reservoir which the loch has been since 1947, with ancient pines along its rocky shore, suggests an unspoiled piece of Mediterranean coast rather than the Highlands. From the inside, the Black Wood itself is a place quite unlike a conifer plantation and at least the equal of Affric's woods. Huge branched pines stand on every side, those which predate the 1760s enclosure as much as 300 years old, and the wind is never quiet in their branches. Here on a dense carpet of heather and bilberry, rare wood anemones can be found. Here, too, are the young pines which with luck will become the future Black Wood of Rannoch. Rannoch is a forest where the Forestry Commission is justifying its new reputation for conservation to set alongside its usual one as a ruthless producer of commercial timber and pulpwood.

Ettrick

In central southern Scotland to the south-west of Selkirk, some 25 miles from today's border with England, the Forest of Ettrick is considered—perhaps because most is known about it—to be the most important of all mediaeval Scottish forests. This large area, 26 miles long and sixteen broad, which included the valleys of the Ettrick, the Yarrow and the Tweed, all three of which run parallel in a north-easterly direction towards Selkirk, consists mainly of rolling moorland on which thousands of sheep graze beside unfenced roads, crossed by fast-running burns, with the recently dammed and enlarged St Mary's Loch at its centre. There are remnants of ancient woods, a fair amount of broadleaf plantations or secondary woodland in the valleys, but, far more prominent today, great conifer plantations which blanket hills or stand in odd geometric shapes on their slopes. A few of these are old plantations which were established by landowners in the nineteenth and early twentieth centuries, but most are managed by the Forestry Commission or by private forestry companies.

Nine hundred years ago the forest would have looked very different, and been almost entirely wooded. On today's moors the trees would have been relatively sparse and consisted of birch, hazel, thorn and mountain ash. In the valleys they would have been dense and included most of the other broadleaf trees of Scotland: ash, lime, cherry, elm, oak and, in the damper places, willow and alder. There were also probably native Scots pine. James Hogg, himself a shepherd in this part of the country in the late eighteenth century and known when he became a writer as the Ettrick Shepherd, suggested that the ancient tracks of the area were evidence of this pattern of woodland. All run along ridges and avoid valleys, which would have been too densely wooded for travel, or where there would have been danger of ambush.

Certainly Ettrick was important enough to be sometimes simply called 'The Forest'. It seems to have been the first Scottish forest established on the model of a Norman forest, but this did not happen till 70 years after the Norman conquest of England, when William I had formalized his English forests. Then David I (1124–53), probably in 1136, afforested Ettrick. He was influenced by his own English experiences as Earl of Northampton and Huntingdon and by the Norman barons who had come north with him and settled in this part of Scotland. They brought with them feudal ideas in general, but it is a fair guess that they were responsible for the important difference between early Scottish and English forests, that grants of forest land by the king included hunting rights. Such barons did not wish to be subjected to the restrictions which English forest law had imposed on them in England.

In other ways Ettrick was a forest organized on English lines. There were similar forest officers (though no precise equivalents to verderers or regarders) and forest courts operating a similar legal system. This may in part have come about because of Ettrick's situation, near the border. Between 1296, when the whole country was surrendered by John Balliol to Edward I, and Robert Bruce's rising of 1306, Edward appointed forest officials there, and came to stay at Traquir, the king's residence in the northern part of the forest. This magnificent fortified mansion claims today to be the oldest inhabited house in Scotland. But he seems to have had only partial control of the forest and local guardians in 1299 appointed a rival keeper.

In 1334 Edward III again took control of Ettrick and throughout the rest of the century the English claimed it. But at the same time those great border baronial families, the Percies and the Douglases, also both tried to gain control of it. Gradually the Douglases won, and held it till 1455. This was when James II finally crushed them, after a series of betrayals and bloody murders unusual even in Scottish history. The last occurred in 1452 when James invited William Douglas to dine with him, under safe conduct, at Stirling Castle but personally killed him with 26 sword wounds. The Scottish Parliament recorded that the Earl had been 'guilty of his own death by resisting the king's gentle persuasion'. Three years of warfare followed before the Douglases were defeated at Arkinholm and their possessions including the Forest of Ettrick confiscated.

The Scottish kings who visited Ettrick during these early centuries hunted its red deer, sometimes in English style, pursuing them with hounds on horseback, more often in the Scottish style of a massed round-up and slaughter. But it was the farming activities of James I (1406–37) in Ettrick Forest rather than his or his predecessors' hunting which had more influence on its future. From the middle of his reign at latest he introduced sheep on to his own parts (stedes) of the forest, with the usual results: a treeless moorland with a peaty soil which increasingly supported grasses and heather that were of little use even to the sheep. By 1502 James IV had direct control of 20 of the forest's stedes and on these there were probably 15,000 sheep. He also kept a horse breeding stud on one stede. As there were probably 5,000 sheep on the other 65 stedes, it is not surprising that the mediaeval forest became the moor it mostly remained until the 1920s.

During the last 20 years of the sixteenth century the Forest of Ettrick was transformed into a collection of large estates, often rented from the crown but no longer under forest law. At Ettrick, however, as elsewhere, the king sometimes imposed the condition on the new owners that they would preserve its woods, suggesting that he realized how the forests trees were disappearing. It was a difficult condition to enforce. By 1832 James Hogg could write: 'The upper parts of the country are, indeed, quite bare of natural wood, it being wholly a pastoral country, and nothing else. About the borders of St Mary's Loch, indeed, a few straggling old trees and ancient thorns remain to mark where a forest has once been; lower down, however, on the banks of the Ettrick and Yarrow, as well as at Yair and Elibank, considerable remnants of the ancient woods remain.'

Some of the families of the previous forest's 'currours' acquired large portions of the forest, in particular the Dukes of Buccleuch. They remain the largest private landowners in the old forest, and their property includes some of the ancient woods which still survive. The most interesting of these, known as the Light Oak Wood, lies in the Ettrick valley itself, on a hillside near Fauldshope farm. When the moors above are hidden in mist—as they often are—this strange neglected wood of sessile oak has a stillness and mystery which well suggests its known age—350 to 400 years.

Planting in the forest of Ettrick is not entirely a mid-twentieth century enterprise. For about 70 years from 1800 onwards its landowners established shelter belts in which they mixed pine, larch and spruce with broadleaf trees, or planted small areas for game cover which included yew. And lower down the Ettrick at Howebottom the Duke of Buccleuch in 1829 began an early and interesting experiment in conservation. This whole 300-acre area he 'hained' (enclosed) to keep out sheep and cattle. One reason was 'to improve the picturesque effect', the Duke wrote 45 years later. Another was 'to allow the growth of whatever might prove to be the indigenous trees of the forest'. He had hoped to see 'young oak spring up, but in that have been disappointed'. In 1878, however, the Rev. James Farquharson reported that the whole area now had a delightful boskiness, and that it was carpeted with bright green bracken and large beds of purple heather 'surely never blooming more splendidly than this year'. Its most numerous trees were ash, birch and hawthorn; there were also mountain ash, Scots pine, sallow and a solitary plane, but not a single oak, beech, elm or holly. Today parts of Howebottom have been planted with spruce, fir and pine but some are still untouched and in autumn, when their colours are particularly fine, form an essential part of this Border landscape.

Modern forestry began at Ettrick around 1900 when the same landowners started to plant conifers for timber rather than for ornament, game or shelter, but only on a large scale in the early 1920s when the Forestry Commission bought land in the Tweed Valley. Further south they bought and planted Craik Forest from 1948 onwards, and in the 1960s private companies like Tilhill Forestry, the Economic Forestry Group and Fountains Forestry began to operate around Ettrick. They mostly manage rather than own woodland, planting much the same spruce mixed with pine and larch, and owe their success to persuading its owners (usually pension funds) that the present tax system makes forests a good investment.

Ettrick has similar problems to those of the Border forest of Kielder. The trees have only a heavy shallow soil, known as peaty gleys, to root in. But compared to many Scottish forests it is sheltered, and plantations have been successfully established at 1,800 feet. As everywhere, conifer forests which are harvested like corn are thought by some an unnatural intrusion on the landscape, but they are the only trees which can be grown economically on such soil, and are no more unnatural to Ettrick than the treeless moors which they are replacing.

Buchan

In the south-west of Scotland—a part of the country which, from the arrival of the Gaels in about 500 BC, had had different traditions—a huge area of mountain, glen and loch today forms the Forestry Commission's Galloway Forest Park. At its centre is the old Forest of Buchan, first mentioned in 1294. This was in the reign of John Balliol, shortly before his surrender of his throne to Edward I. It was also when Robert Bruce was Earl of Carrick in Ayreshire, a forest which forms the northern part of today's park. The early history of Galloway is closely connected with Bruce's struggle to drive the English from Scotland.

Interestingly, however, during the next ten years Bruce was granted forests in quite different parts of the country, two near Inverness and one near Aberdeen. This was before his plans for rebellion were fully developed. But in 1306 he had himself crowned at Scone and returned to the south-west.

Here Edward now had garrisons at Wigtown, Cruggleton and Buittle, and Bruce was forced to escape abroad, but in 1307 he returned to Galloway and began to operate with a guerrilla band of a few hundred in the mountains around Loch Trool. From Glen Trool he moved one night that March to attack and rout an English force on Raploch Moss near Clatteringshaws Loch. Loch Trool is at the centre of today's park, and Clatteringshaws is one of its forests.

Soon afterwards Aymer de Valence, the English supporter to whom Edward had granted Ettrick Forest, led a force of 2,000 to attack Bruce in his Glen Trool hideout and was heavily defeated at what is known as the Battle o' the Steps o' Trool. As Valence's troops passed above Loch Trool, below Lamachan Hill, the Scots ambushed them, rolling granite boulders down on to them, and put them to flight. High above the loch on the opposite side a stone now commemorates this victory.

Bruce next went to the north-east of the country where he had more support, and where, seven years later, he triumphed at Bannockburn. Meanwhile his brother Edward continued to operate in Galloway where he defeated local

English supporters at Kirroughtree (another of the forests of today's park) and in several more skirmishes. It is easy to guess why the Bruces were so successful here in Galloway. The remote mountainous country is ideal for guerrilla warfare. Then it was probably heavily wooded, as the lower parts are again now, though today's plantations of sitka spruce and lodgepole pine would have been the old indigenous woodland of birch, hazel, alder, ash, Scots pine and, above all, sessile oak.

Bruce rewarded his local supporters with land, in particular the Douglas family, who were lairds of Galloway (as well as much of the Border country) for the next 140 years. But throughout the Middle Ages it was the various religious houses holding forest land which, as elsewhere, did most to clear the country of its native woods. When they were dissolved at the Reformation in 1560 their lands passed to such noblemen as the Kennedys of Castle Kennedy near Stranraer.

This part of Scotland then became strongly Protestant, and when James I and Charles II appointed bishops in the Presbyterian church, rebellion again began in Galloway. The first skirmish of the so-called Pentland Rising occurred at Daltry near Bennan Forest. But this time the rebels were not successful, the rising was put down and the Covenanters became a persecuted sect. Near the forest's campsite of Caldrons to the north of Glen Trool a memorial stone marks the place where seven were found holding a prayer meeting and murdered.

Though Galloway was less involved than the Highlands in the 1715 rebellion, a force under a local nobleman, Viscount Kenmure, marched south and captured Preston. But Kenmure was executed when the rising failed and there was no rising in the south west for Prince Charles in 1745. The lairds of Galloway, like those of the Highlands, did however begin in the eighteenth century to farm their lands more profitably, at first by enclosing parks. In 1723 local 'levellers' destroyed many miles of walls and banks, but eventually the lowlands of the country were enclosed as large farms and in the second half of the century the hills became sheepwalks. Here a few shepherds managed large herds of blackface sheep, and many families who had previously used such areas for grazing their Galloway cattle were forced to abandon their crofts.

Though the sheep here too reduced the woodlands by preventing regeneration, a few woods were preserved and managed, not for sentimental reasons but because they supported local industry. Today such woods contain the most interesting trees in the forest. One group, the woods of Caldrons, Buchan and Glenhead, lie around Loch Trool and consist principally of sessile oak. Though many of these seem to be standards, they are chiefly grown-out coppice shoots, which used to be cut for tan bark at the unusually long intervals of 60 years. All three are not only designated Sites of Special Scientific Interest but delightful to walk in. Glenhead and Buchan lie low down near the loch, contain many birch and are crossed by burns flowing in narrow channels of rock. Caldrons, high above the loch, is parklike around its campsite but rises to a boggy hillside undergrown with moss and bracken. The Forestry Commission here is encouraging regeneration by planting seedlings grown from original seed and protecting them from browsing deer and goats with Tuley tubes or small wire enclosures.

Cree Wood, which lies lower down to the south-west beside the Cree River, was also coppiced till this century, but is correctly a plantation rather than an ancient wood. It consists mostly of English (pedunculate) oak. It, too, supplied bark to a leather tannery in Newton Stuart which continued to operate till the Second World War.

By any standards today's Forest Park is large. The total area of its seven forests is 155,000 acres, of which nearly two-thirds have been or will be planted—the rest is loch or mountain. Planting began in 1922, but the great majority has been done since the last war, so that although its present production is small for so large a forest, this will eventually rise to 430,000 tons a year. But forestry at Galloway has many problems.

First of these is the quality of the land which the farmers were willing to sell to the Commission. 'We've had dancing in the office the night the contract's been signed,' says the present district officer in charge of several of the forests. Trees were found to grow slowly and unevenly. Now they are sprayed with fertilizer from the air and provided this is done before their growth has been checked they do dramatically better.

Less easy to remedy is the forest's exposed position, which brings it many gales, causing much damage. The Forest Park has been divided according to the danger of windblow into zones of six kinds. Most of Glen Trool, the park's largest individual forest, is classified as five and some as six, the two most hazardous zones. Here (as at Kielder in Northumberland) trees must be left unthinned to give each other support, and felled after little more than 35 years. At this age their timber is worth about £14 per cubic metre, while at maturity it would be almost twice as valuable.

The deer are another problem. Galloway has a few fallow deer and many roe deer, which do damage by browsing on young trees, but its red deer damage trees of all ages. They are not descended from the original red deer of Galloway, but were re-introduced, and like red deer all over the country, are smaller than Scottish deer once were, probably because they have been forced to live on the mountains where food is poor. They have made the growing of species with tender bark like Norway spruce and lodgepole pine uneconomical. Fortunately they damage only about one per cent of sitka spruce, but Scots pine is the only species which, after a certain age, seems entirely safe. Today there is a 3,000-acre deer reserve near Clatteringshaws Loch, but some of the park's 3,000 deer prefer not to be reserved. Close by is a reserve for the park's feral goats.

Here, on comparatively low ground, the forest is pretty enough, and the Queen's Way, through plantation after identical plantation of sitka spruce, is impressive in scale. But Glen Trool is more dramatic and memorable for its ancient oak woods and for its grey rocky mountains. Deeper into this vast forest, beyond and higher than Glen Trool, are half a dozen smaller lochs which cars fortunately cannot reach and which are as remote and beautiful as any in the Highlands.

GLOSSARY

Adit (n) Horizontal mine shaft.

Afforest (v) To include a piece of countryside in a royal forest. In later centuries also used to mean to plant an area with trees.

Agist (v) To let out land for grazing.

Agister (n) One who manages the grazing in a forest.

Assart (v) To turn woodland into farmland. (n) A piece of land transferred in this way.

Bailiff (n) See lieutenant.

Bailiwick (n) A subdivision of a forest.

Bash up (v) To replant parts of plantations which have failed.

Beasts of the forest (n) Red, fallow, and roe deer, and wild pig.

Beechmast (n) Beechnuts, commonly used as pig feed. See pannage.

Bell-pit (n) Early type of mine, so called for its shape.

Bercelet (n) Small dog which hunted by scent.

Bloomery (n) Small primitive furnace for smelting iron ore.

Branche (n) Large dog which hunted by scent.

Brash (n) Side-trimmings of trees. (v) To side-trim trees.

Chase (n) A private forest, but also sometimes used about a royal forest.

Cheminage (n) Payment for the right to transport goods through a forest.

Coppice (n) A wood in which trees are cropped regularly by cutting at ground level. A tree treated in this way. (v) To crop a tree in this way.

Coppice-with-standards (n) A managed wood in which some trees are coppiced for wood, some left as standards for timber.

Commoner (n) Someone with a shared right over land which they do not own.

Conifer (n) A cone-bearing tree.

Coup (n) An area of woodland for felling.

Deforest (v) To exclude a piece of land from a royal forest.

Estovers (n) The right to take wood, usually for burning, house or hedge repairs, from a forest.

Evesfold (n) Pannage of beech nuts.

Eyre (n) The highest Court for the administration of forest law, visiting each forest periodically.

Fench month (n) The month around mid summer when deer calve and forests were closed to grazing.

Firebote (n) The right to cut wood for burning.

Forest (n) An area of land, not necessarily wooded, in which forest law applied. Also called the Royal Forest. Later used to mean any large area of woodland.

Forest law (n) Law which applied in the Royal Forest.

Forester (n) A working forester.

Forester-of-fee (n) A man of rank, with some of a working forester's less menial responsibilities.

Free-warren (n) The right to hunt animals other than 'beasts of the forest'.

Hammer pond (n) Artificial pond used to power a hammer for forging iron.

Housebote (n) The right to cut wood for house repairing.

Law (v) To cut off the claws of the forefeet of a dog to prevent it chasing game.

Lieutenant (n) The second in charge of a royal forest, also called the bailiff.

Lymer (n) Small hunting dog, controlled by a cord of lime fibre.

Marl (n) Baked clay, used for lightening soil.

Native trees (n) The 70 or so species which arrived naturally in Britain after the end of the last ice age.

Naturalised trees (n) All trees growing and reproducing in Britain which are not native, including native trees which died out but have been re-introduced (eg, Scots pine in England).

Nurse tree (n) A fast growing tree, usually a conifer, used to protect slower growing trees when young.

Pale (n) The fence which surrounded a park, to contain its deer.

Pannage (n) Acorns and beechnuts. The right to feed pigs on these by turning them into woodland during certain autumn weeks.

Park (n) An area for keeping deer, usually inside a forest or chase.

Parker (n) One who manages a park.

Perambulation (n) A written definition of a piece of land in the form of a walk around it which describes its boundaries and their features.

Pightle (n) Small enclosed piece of land, usually belonging to a particular dwelling.

Plantation (n) An area of trees created by planting (but not an orchard).

Pollard (n) A tree cropped for wood at intervals of four or more years by cutting its branches at six to fifteen feet from the ground. (v) To crop a tree in this way.
Purlieu (n) Land which lay near to, and once formed part of, a forest.
Purpresture (n) The offence of building in a forest without permission.

Ranger (n) A forest official with duties similar to those of a forester, usually mounted, usually responsible for a forest's purlieus.
Regard (n) Periodic report on the whole condition of a royal forest.
Regarder (n) One of those (usually 12, usually well bred) who made the periodic report on a forest known as the regard.
Ring-bark (v) To kill a tree or limb by cutting (or eating) a circle of its bark.
Royal Forest (n) The complete area of the country which came under forest law. A particular part of this area was one royal forest.

Secondary woodland (n) Woodland which has re-occurred naturally (not as a result of planting) on land which was once cleared for ploughing or by grazing.
Shingle (n) A wooden roof tile.
Shred (v) To crop a tree for wood by cutting off its side shoots.
Single (v) To reduce the shoots of a coppice stool to one.
Slade (n) A woodland glade.
Spring (n) A coppice. A coppice shoot.
Stag-headed (a) An old tree, commonly an oak, with dead outer branches resembling antlers.
Standard (n) A large, single-stemmed tree, intended for timber.
Stool (n) The stump of a tree which will shoot again.
Sucker (v) To put up shoots from a root system. (n) A shoot of this kind.
Swainmote (n) The middle of three courts for administering forest law, with the right to try cases and award provisional sentences.

Tanbark (n) The bark of trees, commonly oak, used for tanning leather.
Timber (n) Trunks, or large branches, of trees.
Tinchel (n) A Scottish deer hunt, or a beater in such a hunt.
Toils (n) Nets for trapping deer.
Tuley tube (n) Plastic cylinder for protecting young trees.
Turbary (n) The right to cut peat in a forest.

Verderer (n) Forest official, ranking next below the warden and the lieutenant, who presided at swainmotes.
Verderer's court (n) Another name for a forest swainmote.
Vert (n) The vegetation of a forest including its trees.
Venison (n) The 'beasts of the forest': red deer, fallow deer, roe deer and wild pig. Their flesh.

Walk (n) A subdivision of a forest.

Warden (n) The senior official of a royal forest, also called the keeper or steward.

Warfarin (n) Poison, commonly used to kill grey squirrels.

Warren (n) A piece of land specially set aside for the breeding of rabbits. Also, the right to hunt animals other than 'beasts of the forest'.

Wildwood (n) Term used by Oliver Rackham (and in this book) to mean woodland which has never been disturbed by man.

Wood (n) Branches and small trunks of less than a certain girth, usually 2 feet. An area of trees which has grown up naturally and not been planted, also called an ancient wood.

Wood pasture (n) Tree-growing land on which domestic animals or deer are regularly grazed.

Woodland (n) Used in this book to describe a tree-growing area, whether ancient wood or plantation.

Woodmote (n) The lowest forest court, commonly meeting every two months, at which those accused were presented but not tried.

Woodward (n) A minor forest official, usually privately employed but in part responsible to the king.

INDEX

Acknowledgments

The author and publishers wish to thank the members of the Forestry Commission and the National Trust, and the officers of the National Parks for their assistance.

For permission to reproduce extracts from published works, we thank the following authors and publishers.

Cyril Hart, *Royal Forest*, Clarendon Press 1966: quote appearing on page 81.

Oliver Rackham, *Trees and Woodland in the British Landscape*, Dent, 1976: quotes appearing on pages 145, 148, illustration on pages 10, 11.

The Marquess of Ailesbury, *History of Savernake Forest*, 1962: quote appearing on page 97.

Illustrations

Thomas Bewick, pages 18, 23, 29, 37, 46, 62, 67, 88, 94, 108, 125, 129, 170, 177, 185, 190, 194, 199, 203, 214, 218, 255, 279

Trees and Woodland in the British Landscape, Oliver Rackham, Dent, 1976, page 10.

English Forests and Forest Trees, London 1853, pages 68, 82, 130, 139, 151, 160, 223, 249, 275

The Noble Art of Venerie or Hunting, G. Turbeville, Bodleian Library, Dowe T. 247, page 25

Sylvia, John Evelyn, 1776, Title page and pages 40, 41, 235, 256

The New Forest, Percival Lewis, 1811, page 74

Microcosm, W. H. Pyne, 1824 (*Rustic Vignettes*, Dover Publications 1977) pages 14, 52, 53, 57, 187, 210, 212, 247

Book of Trades, Hans Sachs, 1568, pages 16, 17

Luttrell Psalter (Institute of Agricultural History and Museum of Rural Life, University of Reading), pages 20, 21, 55

Explore the New Forest, Forestry Commission Guide, HMSO, page 74

Epping Forest, Alfred Quist, Corporation of London, page 143

Cambrian Forests, Forestry Commission Guide, drawing by Colin Gibson, HMSO, page 205

Animals, edited by Jim Harter, Dover Publications 1979, pages 65, 85, 105, 115, 148, 155, 166, 198, 208, 228, 240, 261, 266